Colonial Williamsburg

Colonial Williamsburg

By Philip Kopper

Original Photography
by Langdon Clay

Harry N. Abrams, Inc.,
Publishers, New York
In association with The Colonial
Williamsburg Foundation

*Like a certain marble stone in
hallowed Bruton Parish Church
this book is dedicated to
"a gentleman of the most amiable
disposition, generous, just and
mild and possessed in an eminent
degree of all the social virtues,"
to wit, my esteemed and beloved
brother W. Bruce Kopper, Esq.*

*Project Director: Sheila Franklin Lieber
Designer: Samuel N. Antupit*

*Library of Congress Cataloging-in-Publication Data
Kopper, Philip.
Colonial Williamsburg.
Includes index.
1. Williamsburg (Va.)—History. I. Clay, Langdon,
1949-   . II. Title.
F234.W7K67 1986 975.5' 4252   86-1252
ISBN 0-8109-0787-9*

*Published in 1986 by Harry N.
Abrams, Incorporated, New York*

Times Mirror Books

Printed and bound in Japan

*Endpapers: The British royal
coat of arms, with England's lion
and Scotland's unicorn, adorns
a pediment of the Governor's
Palace.
Title page: A "soldier's" coat
hangs over his tent at the
Colonial Fair.
This page: Weathered walls of
outbuildings frame the wellhead
behind Wetherburn's Tavern.*

Table of Contents

Foreword

The restoration of Williamsburg...offered an opportunity to restore a complete area and free it entirely from alien and inharmonious surroundings, as well as to preserve the beauty and charm of the old buildings and gardens of the city and its historic significance. Thus, it made a unique and irresistible appeal. As the work has progressed, I have come to feel that perhaps an even greater value is the lesson that it teaches of the patriotism, high purpose, and unselfish devotion of our forefathers to the common good.

—John D. Rockefeller Jr.

That basic statement of purpose, although expanded upon by latter-day Colonial Williamsburg Foundation officialdom, still stands. Yet any such statement is a wholly inadequate way to express what Colonial Williamsburg actually means to the American people. It is in their eyes and minds that Williamsburg achieves reality.

Monk and religious writer Thomas Merton spoke of the juncture between myth and reality: "For myths are realities, and they themselves open with deeper realms." Williamsburg today is both myth that has become real and reality that has become myth. These myths and realities need not—and may not always—be distinguished in order to serve, in Williamsburg's most important function, as touchstones for what historian Henry Steele Commager has called America's "search for a usable past."

Colonial Williamsburg is many things to many people, the starting point for a multitude of searches. Visitors come from all over the country—and the world—to walk in the steps of the first American patriots: Thomas Jefferson, George Washington, Patrick Henry, George Mason, Peyton Randolph, George Wythe. Or they come to visit the places their queen or emperor visited when in Williamsburg and to retrace the exact route taken by their country's royalty. Or they come to relive the memories of when they, as children, came to Williamsburg with their parents. Forty percent of those who visit Williamsburg have been here at least once before. Some people have visited fifty times, some even a hundred, and still they come back.

They also come to pursue the fine points of a craft or hobby with an expert Colonial Williamsburg craftsman; gather home-decorating ideas; buy furniture, fabrics, or silver; commission binding of a rare book; study gardens or folk art; revel in the eighteenth-century decorative arts (this called the "golden age" of design); eat; play tennis or golf; renew love and friendship; in sum, to do all those things we do when time and money permit and the spirit moves us.

But most people come, I believe, because they are Americans, and Williamsburg is a uniquely American place. It seems, and in many ways is, like an English village. Yet perhaps more than any other colonial place, it was a point of confluence in the revolution that many Americans believe to be the most important in the history of the world.

To quote Commager again: "The chapter of history that Adams and Jefferson wrote was assuredly the most creative in the history of politics. How sobering to recall that every major political institution we now possess was invented before the year 1800 and that not one has been created since. Making a nation was new (none had been deliberately created before); popular self-government was new; successful federalism, separation of powers, judicial independence and political review were new; the 'exact subordination' of the military to the civil power was new; and so too that most revolutionary of all experiments—the separation of church and state."

Identifying and reflecting on the major myths and realities of our history is a challenge to any American. (One myth, for instance, is that the great patriots were uniformly self-sacrificing; one reality is that a new nation based on an ideal of personal freedom for all—except slaves!—*was* created.) The effort to measure myth against reality is essential if one is to gauge the implications of contemporary history; to test personal beliefs, convictions and behaviors; and to assess the present-day efficacy of institutional forms invented more than two hundred years ago.

It is easy to dismiss Williamsburg as a purveyor of patriotism. And in part it is that, but as long as there are nations, the stimulus provided by patriotic feeling will be a vital tonic to the body politic. It is easy, but inaccurate, to dismiss Williamsburg as an outmoded icon of "cold war" reductionist historiography. But, in fact, to most Americans, freedom is a reality and something toward which much of the world strives in vain.

The notion that Williamsburg is fixed in time—whether in 1776, 1926, 1956 or today—is part myth and part reality. The reality is that Williamsburg, partially because of America's need for myth, has itself become mythologized—an icon of our revolution, of entrepreneurial spirit (in the form of W. A. R. Goodwin), of philanthropic largess (in the person of John D. Rockefeller Jr.) and a host of virtues: creativity, determination, self-sacrifice, courage.

Of course, to the historian Williamsburg is constantly changing, as it stands its iconographic ground. The discovery and evaluation of new evidence, new ways of thinking about history, the recasting of old ideas—all are vital to a research institution's well-being (and its researchers' self-respect). And as the myths and realities respond to intellect and intellectual fashion, the reunderstanding of our past, the re-creation of our usable past, continues.

Colonial Williamsburg is gathering evidence, at an accelerated pace, of eighteenth-century (as well as seventeenth- and nineteenth-century) life. The types of evidence include books and papers of all sorts, decorative as well as strictly functional objects, artifacts, photographs, measured drawings and all manner of ideas, theories, syntheses and hypotheses gleaned from primary and secondary sources. That at one time it was thought that Colonial Williamsburg would be "finished" rather than an ongoing enterprise of great vigor and complexity seems naive today. But, I suppose, it also seemed naive, or at least highly unlikely to many, that the dream of a new nation would ever be realized. So, out of our dreams we find reality and in myth our dreams are forged.

Charles R. Longsworth, *President, The Colonial Williamsburg Foundation*

Prologue: What Year Is This?

Colonial Williamsburg: a place of past and present, a capital reborn and restored, a village revived from vestiges of yore. Thomas Jefferson called the city "the finest school of manners and morals in America" and here Virginians first came to see themselves as Americans, citizens of a new and independent nation. Once Britain's "Seat of Empire," now this life-size stage welcomes visitors to join the drama of historical discovery by the simple act of being here. Come walk these streets and stroll a path beside the lea where a shepherdess tends her flock (opposite). Seek the Governor's Palace formal gardens (left) and harken to the rustling sounds of a remembered past.

Once again—and still—black-smiths hammer bar iron into useful tools like those on the Deane Forge bench. One of more than four hundred "reconstructed" structures in the antique town, this shop was rebuilt on its eighteenth-century site. Eighty-eight "restored" buildings, erected two hundred years ago and since refurbished, also grace Williamsburg today.

A misty sun rises behind the Capitol as first it did nearly three hundred summers past, and the colony's seal proclaims *En Dat Virginia Quintam*—"Virginia makes the fifth [realm of Britain's growing empire]." Royal coronet and monogram grace the weathervane; Queen Anne's Great Union banner hangs limp above the cupola, the only place this flag flies today. At the Magazine militiamen salute newer colors—the Grand Union, first banner to bear America's stripes. On a morning such as this, the windless air furls every flag around its staff. It is as if time itself was hung and waits upon the breeze.

∽

An ox stands still in the lea beyond the Gaol. A ewe still sleeps beneath a wagon on a meadow lot in town. The birds awake: cardinals flaming from bush to bush, white pigeons floating from George Wythe's cote across the garden to quiet stones beyond the churchyard wall, a great blue heron waving its heavy way toward the marsh at College Landing. Mark Catesby, a friend of John Custis whose son's widow married one George Washington, painted these. They fly through time and back again.

∽

At the Governor's Palace a gardener weeds terraced beds in the acres Alexander Spotswood planned. This garden grew vegetables and herbs to season the hundred dishes he served to honor the coronation of King George I. By noon the plot's too hot to work as brick walls soak up sun's heat and throw it back with interest. When the governor designed his house, he did not keep slaves' comfort close to heart. In a few hours, young Alexander Spotswood Clark, his blond hair tied back in a queue, will study the old King's English before starting his day's work in the Palace his ancestor raised.

∽

Behind Raleigh Tavern now an apprentice stokes the fires, fueling the brick oven for the daily bread. Stable grooms harness a pair of bays for the blue phaeton and its gracious work around the town. Across the meadowed hill, James Sampson talks his slow brace of oxen toward the cart for the ten thousandth time or more. A maid with a cloth tied round her head hitches an old mare to the dray; it's time to think about collecting eggs.

∽

A few folk pursue their errands through the dawn, rippling the calm with talk along Duke of Gloucester Street. You can tell it's morning by the noise: the caws and calls and voices. At half past eight a shepherd girl drives her flock along the street from the sheepfold by Prentis Store to pasture near the Capitol. Her skirt swirls around her ankles as she runs behind the ewes and lambs, wielding a crook half again her height. Listen close for the gentle tack of lambs' feet on the cobbled verge. Then come sounds that carry far: fifes shrill enough to pierce the rattle of musket fire, and the rolling drums which reach beneath the boom of cannon. The marchers, whether just two boys with another carrying the colors or a corps of two score behind their major, come up the street that bears Lord Botetourt's name. They wheel westward toward the Magazine to the tunes of "British Grenadiers" and "Yankee Doodle." Some lads look proud, some sleepy as they pace off ninety-six steps a minute. All sweat, none smile. In winter they'll shiver stonefaced and walk the frozen street again at ninety-six steps a minute to mark the miles.

Overleaf: Barking muskets cloud the air with black-powder smoke behind the Courthouse of 1770 as militiamen muster in ragtag mufti and answer their officer's command, "Present... Give fire!"

The dressing table seemingly awaits a fashionable gentleman in the oak-paneled bedchamber of the home of Peyton Randolph, president of the First Continental Congress in 1774.

Spring rains so soak the earth that every gale fells trees, like the big and ancient oak in the ravine near the Gaol where Blackbeard's crew were penned, its roots tearing up china shards and black bottles from the soft-soaked earth. Perhaps its acorn fell when Patrick Henry rent the air with fighting words.

Then shadblow trees burst out in clouds of white throughout the town to mark the time that river fish come up to spawn. The fruit trees bloom: cherries sour and sweet, plums, peaches, lady apples, green apples, cider apples. Men ply the fields with wooden tools, planting corn, cotton and tobacco. Flax ripens in a field glowing periwinkle blue at dawn then fading before noon as the tiny flowers close. By full summer crepe myrtles blaze in every shade of red the rainbow knows and promise to last the season. One day a new flowered shrub appears in a garden where Sir John Randolph walked—tiny purple petals with a crimson hue born upon a bush of dark and shiny boxwood green. A second look reveals just boxwood leaves with myrtle blooms dropped from the tree above by brief rain that blew through here an hour since. This beauty cannot last a day.

In the General Court, a wizened justice doffs the black cap and sends the scullion to hang for stealing a silver spoon from her tavern-keeper master. In the Apollo Room, a stately couple steps the minuet to begin an evening's gaiety. The House of Burgesses, sitting as a jury, weighs the fate of an English firebrand. A company of players presents *Hob in the Well* and Congreve comedies *again* before a mob that drinks and cheers. But these are only actors after all.

The housewright lays wooden sills, hews posts by hand and raises beams at Anderson Forge, which again will see blacksmiths smite glowing iron rods into cold nails for clenching oaken boards on roofs and walls. Painters renew the white and red colors St. George Tucker ordered for his walls and roof in 1798. Just down Nicholson Street, named by and for a governor, Andrew Edwards systematically digs in Peyton Randolph's yard to unearth whatever lies therein: bits of broken china, a button, a buckle. At Greenhill an unmarked grave turns out to have been twice occupied, the first skeleton rewrapped and reinterred above the second burial. At noon the diggers stop to seek the shade.

Soldiers smudge the air on Courthouse Green with the smoke of cooking fires, and the market rings with cries of farmers and tradesmen gathered for the autumn fair. The bell peals for evensong in Bruton Parish, the Church where young Tom Jefferson knelt to pray beside the house where he studied law.

The miller's girl flails her master's wheat. Springtime's flax, now broken and carded into tow, is spun into thread which weavers shuttle into linen cloth. The wind that winnows chaff away also turns the windmill's sails, grinding grain to flour for the flaxen sacks. The wool shorn from last spring's bleating sheep comes out again—as capes of crimson and forest green worn by the workers of this town. Reflecting off the Capitol's curved crown-glass windows (complex as insect eyes) the sun sets lower in the west.

Overleaf: *Furniture in a gabled bedchamber of the Brush-Everard House dates from the third quarter of the eighteenth century, when sometime mayor Thomas Everard lived here. He enlarged the house built in 1717 by John Brush, gunsmith, armorer and first keeper of the Magazine on Market Square.*

15

*The ageless face of time:
a clock wrought by James Craig,
proprietor of the Golden Ball
silversmith shop, who
came to Williamsburg from
London in 1765.*

The sun rises on frosted roofs, and suddenly every fig tree has dropped every leaf. The maple by the Courthouse turned flame red last night. Cooks in George Wythe's warm kitchen set their iron pots on coals and heap more embers on the lids to bake meat pies. They scrub and salt new pork, pack it in wooden tubs to cure, then smoke the hams and bacon sides in the fume of slow oak fires. So they cured the meat for George Washington's breakfast the day he marched on Yorktown.

The crops are in, the shops are shuttered. When folks pass an evening at gambols in Chowning's Tavern they play the ancient games of goose and Nine-Man Morris, drinking toddies now or mulled wine against the chill. The catalpa trees along Palace Green have shed their leaves, their seedpods shake like rattles in the wind. The streets incline toward emptiness until the throngs return for December's Grand Illumination.

Water freezes in the troughs at Market Square and Sampson must break it for his beasts. But there is mirth at Christmas all about, a Yule log in the Inn, and bowls of punch, and Handel plucked upon the harpsichord in the blue-walled Palace ballroom. In Mistress Powell's parlor the young tutor who so pleasingly plays the viola da gamba chides guests for failing to return the favor of his music with their song.

The year winds down. What unnumbered year was this, then? A year like any other in this resurrected place. What men and maids are these? Living, breathing folk of course, except the dead you know: Washington and Patrick Henry; young Jefferson and good George Wythe who taught him law; the sojourning naturalist Mark Catesby, whose name adorns a marble Bruton slab. Ambitious Annabella Powell, whose husband raised the steeple, and great Governor Alexander Spotswood are dead of course. But aging William Penny opens the Golden Ball each dawn even as my toddling son sleeps in a house called the Unicorn's Horn next door. James Sampson has driven oxen around this town for thirty years or more, while the young man who digs in Peyton Randolph's yard plies a profession barely known a century ago, archaeology. Alexander Spotswood Clark, known as Alex and wearing Botetourt's livery, welcomes guests to the halls his ancestor designed. James Geddy wrought silver in his shop two hundred years before James Curtis began to ply the sterling trade nearby. William Parks printed the first newspaper in Virginia; Willie Parker sets the type today and beats the wooden chase of hand-set type with inking balls. Think on this: The town was planned in 1699 and two young oxen now learning to pull together should haul the cart till 1999 at least. The town was paled in the seventeenth century; the fiddle players and hearthside cooks not born until the twentieth was on the wane.

What year is this? Does it matter? Since this place was resurrected, it seems a time returning.

The manner of their fishing.

Preamble: This Historical Watershed

"Heaven & earth never agreed better to frame a place for man's habitation" than the Chesapeake Bay region. So wrote Captain John Smith, thus bolstering the idyllic image presented in John White's 1585–87 painting of Indians fishing rich tidal waters in dugout canoes (opposite). Lured by such claims and images, in 1607 a hundred English adventurers set forth in three small ships to found Jamestown. Now different vehicles bring honored guests to nearby Williamsburg (left), the city that became colonial Virginia's second and most splendid capital.

The colony's godfather, Sir Walter Raleigh, launched the first English attempt to settle America for his patron Queen Elizabeth I. The band he sent to Roanoke Island in 1585 vanished and Raleigh fell out with Elizabeth's successor, who locked him in the Tower of London before sending ships to Jamestown. Still Raleigh championed the cause of New World settlement, an idea that soon swept England, and Virginia owes its birth to the knight who named it in honor of his virgin queen. His portrait, painted by an unknown artist (who spelled Sir Walter's name in the antique manner), hangs in Colonial Williamsburg's study collection.

*B*etween two ancient rivers an eddy gyres in the stream of time. It deepens as it swirls, a slowly drifting whirlpool. It widens, almost vanishing, only to deepen again and alter the course of all within its invisible reach.

This eddy recalls a conundrum as old as any human epic: In every river the same water flows today as yesterday; yet different water must be that river now. So be it here. This eddy remains the same yet ever changing as time, its river, flows on toward an unseen abyssal sea. It is constant yet constantly new, a locus in time's current, a vortex in the course of human events.

The eddy is Williamsburg.

∽

From the beginning this was a realm of water, a land shaped by rains, tides, the ebb and flow of oceans as sea level fluctuated hundreds of vertical feet. When the first human inhabitants found this country, they were sustained by the abundance that rivers, bays, inlets and marshes held for their taking. When alien newcomers arrived millennia later, they gained access via the vast estuary, at once a treasure trove and branching avenue for their transport and commerce—indeed for vital provisions shipped from home an ocean away. They came in search of gold but the land itself between the water and westward mountains barely yielded even useful iron let alone any precious metal. Still these colonists grew rich from the earth which contained the metallic elements that in minuscule amounts nourish a most demanding plant and its golden leaf. The evolution of these people's society and "tobacco culture," the pattern of their towns and settlements, were all dictated by the lay of the land in extended peninsulas; and the lay of the land was defined by the lay of water, the great bay once called "mother of waters," or *Chesapoek,* in the tongue heard here a civilization before our own. In time the area would be known as the Tidewater and ambiguously "tidewater country" to this day. What it would become in human terms was determined by its bounding water.

The first people to find this place—once an ancient river drowned by a rising ocean—fished the broadening bay's tributaries. They settled on its peninsulas, the remains of much older hills which divided the arms of tidal inlets and still-widening rivers. These people foraged the ravines, gathering a wild bounty of roots, nuts and herbs. They planted beans, maize, gourds and tobacco. They waded the warm water to gather clams and snare innumerable fish with wicker weirs. In spring they gathered shoals of horseshoe crabs for food and fashioned the straight, sharp tails into ready spearheads. In winter they tracked the canny deer where mastodons lately ranged, and hunted shaggy bison that would outlive their own culture hereabouts. They collected oysters with each falling tide and struck down waterfowl from flocks so dense they blotted out the sun.

Departing from the wandering ways of their ancestors—who walked all the way from China, after all—the Indians built long-lived towns around the Chesapeake. Here they forged a confederation of tribes, numbering twelve thousand strong, making war with neighbors and love among themselves. They practiced complex diplomacy and commerce, trading their sea's shells for native copper from beyond the Great Lakes. Led by priestly castes, they worshiped a vengeful god and buried their dead with ritual ceremony. Then the strangers of an alien race came from across the even broader water beyond the "mother of waters." Spanish missionaries, meaning to possess the inland sea they called Bahía de Santa María, camped beside a river (later named York) in 1570 and were all slain within the year.

A decade later another light-skinned tribe of seafarers began to probe the coast, soon to leave settlers on Roanoke Island to the south in 1584. The first who stayed simply vanished from the realm they'd named Virginia for their virgin queen, Elizabeth I, who died herself before this place was truly England's. Then came three ships: the *Godspeed, Susan Constant* and *Discovery*. The little fleet sailed up the river named James for the new king whose subjects staked out an armed camp, a "permanent" settlement. It became a city of sorts and the first rude capital of a colony presumed to stretch as far west as the next ocean. Thus the English found a footing in North America and founded Jamestown on May 26, 1607.

The company of five score men and boys nearly met the fate of their vanished predecessors at Roanoke. Having thrown up the fort, they repulsed an Indian attack twelve days after landing. But the fort stood near a swamp alive with mosquitoes that carried killing malaria. During their first years as many as four out of five settlers died—of hunger, disease and battle. Warring was inevitable because, in the wry words of an English archaeologist who'd excavate this region centuries later, the first adventurers did not announce "the rather provocative idea that the Indians' land no longer belonged to them." Ivor Noël Hume observed that "In the manner of most colonial enterprises, the tiresome details needed only to be understood by the new management."

But before the old tenants fully realized the drift of things to come, they'd made brief peace with the immigrants. Powhatan, chief of the native confederation that bore his name, sought new allies against his old adversaries to the north—though the alliance cost him dearly in James River lands. He welcomed the blandishments of one English captain in particular and adopted him as a member of his tribe. The winning diplomat, John Smith, also provided sound leadership for his own people. Where other bands of New World adventurers had wasted energies on ill-aimed treasure hunts and petty conquests, he demanded productive discipline. "He that will not work, shall not eate," Smith declared, though notably the settlers' toil was not for bread alone.

John Rolfe, who married Powhatan's newly Christian daughter Pocahontas, set a few acres in tobacco as early as 1612. Avoiding the strong-smoking native species that gave Indians dizzy delight, he imported a milder, kindred Caribbean plant. It thrived in Virginia and by 1615 Rolfe reaped enough to fill two hogsheads for the voyage home in one of the ships that brought new settlers and vital provisions. By 1618 Virginia exported fifty thousand pounds of leaf and England became a land of smokers though the king had long since called their habit a "custome lothsome to the eye, hatefull to the Nose, harmefull to the braine, dangerous to the Lungs, and in the blacke stinking fume thereof, neerest resembling the horrible Stigian smoke of the pit that is bottomelesse."* King James proposed to ban the addicting weed from his realm, but customs duties on it lined his purse, and the stock company

---

*The Gentle Reader of this modern text may be addled by odd capitalizations and spellings in old quotations. The Author has the honor to remind You that Pecksniffian orthography and rules of spelling came into fashion only in the nineteenth century. He has endeavored to preserve eighteenth-century words as they were written, save only in two respects. First, the "long s" (as in *Princefs*) was never read as an "f" but simply as another shape of "s." Second, the letter "y" was used like a more ancient character, the thorn, to represent "th." These letters will be transcribed according to current usage while eccentric spellings will remain as they appear in the original quotations. Ergo, "Ye Olde Tea Houfe" becomes "The Olde Tea House."

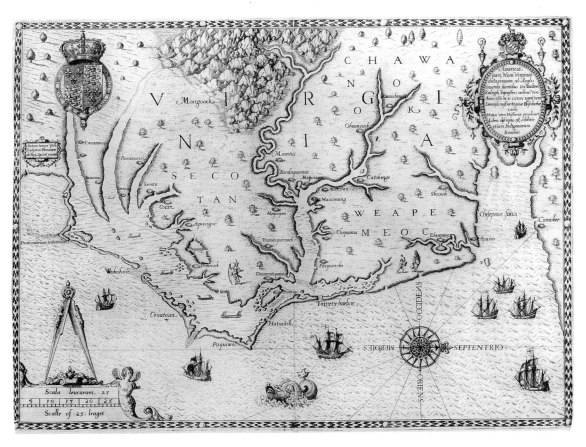

Maloaks als Rebecka daughter to the mighty Prince
Powhatan Emperour of Attanoughkomouck als Virginia
converted and baptized in the Christian faith, and
Wife to the wor.ll Mr Tho: Rolff.

This 1585 map of Virginia's coast (above)—north is right— was the best to be had for decades. Artist and then governor John White drew it two years before his granddaughter Virginia Dare was born and three years before the Spanish Armada's defeat gave England freedom of the seas. James I (below right) gained the throne before the first successful colony was planted and named for him. Its best ambassador was Pocahontas (below left), the fabled Indian princess who captivated the royal court when she went to London in 1616 as tobacco planter John Rolfe's bride.

25

that sponsored settlement needed something to sell back home. The king held his royal tongue (and nose perhaps), the Privy Council insisted that all Virginia tobacco go to England, and the colony's economic future seemed assured. But other problems remained.

There was the simple matter of survival. When promised goods didn't arrive in 1609, most colonists perished during the winter called "starving time." Those few that saw spring come rigged a ship as best they could and meant to flee for home. But before they left, Sir Thomas Gates sailed up the James with new supplies; he'd been delayed, accidentally discovering Bermuda where he was shipwrecked in a storm. There was also the matter of population. At Eastertide, 1619, for example, one thousand English settlers were living here, but one would die almost every other day throughout the year. The next twelve months saw ten ships arrive with more than another thousand new immigrants, yet by the next Easter only 843 remained, the rest having perished or sailed back to England in ships carrying tobacco.

Powhatan, Pocahontas's father, adorns the cartouche of a contemporary map. Chief of a confederacy of Indian tribes, he won English allies by befriending colonists and trading land for support against native rivals.

That new colonists kept coming by the boatload was at least in part due to Smith, who proved as able a huckster as he'd been ambassador and autocrat. Back home he published memoirs—biased advertisements for the Virginia Company in which he held stock. Of the Chesapeake region in particular, he enthused, "Heaven & earth never agreed better to frame a place for man's habitation." If he overlooked the ravages of malaria, dysentery, hunger and fatal friction with the neighbors, there were in fact some splendid things to sing about. For one, the land was fertile; for another, he had promised in England: "No man will go from hence to have lesse freedome there than here" and thus transplanted the seed of British legal custom. His company's de facto government formally established "the rule of law—the common law of England...and orderly process to change the law," as historian Samuel Eliot Morison summarized it. "A legislative Assembly, the very first in America," convened at Jamestown in 1619.

In short order that body solemnized a principle of remarkable ramifications: "That the Governor shall not lay any Taxes or Impositions upon the Colony,...[through any means other] than by the Authority of the General Assembly, to be levyed and ymployed as the said Assembly shall appoint." Thus the matter of local taxes in principle became the prerogative of the colonists' elected representatives, a nicety that gained astonishing political importance a century and a half later.

The colonists imported not only their native law but private enterprise as well, which other proprietary colonies had not enjoyed. The immigrants were mostly men who owed seven years' service to those who had paid their passage. When substantial numbers of these indentures were fulfilled, the decision was made to let individuals work tracts of land as their own property. This brought about a manifold increase in garden crops. The community had depended for its bare subsistence on provisions from home (and on food bartered from Indians or sometimes robbed from Indian graves). Now it developed a market economy boasting surpluses, especially in edibles. Furthermore, women had been encouraged to emigrate in England; while Virginia bachelors were required to live in common barracks, couples could live apart in dwellings of their own. In private terms these habitations, however humble, offered unenumerated delights; in practical terms they contributed to the spread of farmsteads and the colony's territorial growth. In Morison's expert opinion, Virginia gained a firmer footing thanks to the unusual triad of democracy, capitalism and sex.

Each piecemeal step that strengthened the English presence undermined the Indians' dominion. When Powhatan died in 1618, his lands and influence reduced, he was succeeded by a relative of the Pamunkey tribe. Opechancanough secretly strengthened the confederation, promising his allies to rid the land of intruders who now ranged far along the James. With blitzkrieg effect the Indians arose on Good Friday, 1622, to attack every settlement, farmstead and outpost, killing 347 settlers by Smith's later account or nearly one-third of the 1,240 colonists counted in the latest "muster rowle." Only Jamestown itself, a little hamlet that had begun to spread beyond its wooden walls, escaped torch and tomahawk thanks to a friendly native's warning.

News of this disaster reached London, where it prompted new debate about the wisdom of a proprietary settlement, and the king revoked the Virginia Company's charter. Established by entrepreneurs and stockholders, the place became a royal colony ruled by a governor and Council with the Assembly's advice. Wary of new Indian attacks, the colonists secured the peninsula with palisades extending from the James to the York. They divided the unmarked ground into units imported from home: hundreds, plantations, counties and parishes. Thanks to their now growing numbers and always superior weapons, they continued to expand their territory despite persistent unpleasantness with the neighbors.

In its 1632–33 session the General Assembly passed "an Act for the Seatinge of the Middle Plantation," a place whose name remains subject to speculation though its significance is undeniable. The bill stipulated "that every fortyeth Man...be imployed in buildinge of Houses, and secureing that Tract of Land" between Queen's Creek and Archer's Hope (later College) Creek. "And Yf any free Men shall...voluntarilie goe and seate upon the sayd Place of the *Middle Plantation,* they shall have fifty Acres of Land Inheritance, and be free from all Taxes and publique Chardges...."

"Staked out and paled in" in 1633, the place was already inhabited by one Dr. John Potts, whose fortunes waxed and waned like those of the city that would rise here. Once physician general of the colony, he was a respected healer whose skills varied with the supply of "his good Liquor." Governor in 1629, he was a convicted cattle thief by 1630, then five years later a member of the Council that helped unseat another governor. While Potts's name does not exactly echo down through history, those of his neighbors would be heard for generations. Among others there was a Taylor whose line begat a president and a Ludwell whose family home won fame both here and in Samuel Johnson's London.

As a later scholar (Rutherfoord Goodwin) would surmise in the eighteenth-century manner, "The Reader,...should not be misled to picture *Middle Plantation* in his mind, as some have done, as a Town to be compared with the Towns of this present Day, nor even as a Town in the Sense that *Jamestown* was a Town in that early Day. More Truth will be found in looking upon it as a wide-scattered Settlement in which no Man had Need to be disturbed by the Wailing of his Neighbor's Offspring; yet which, with the Years converged upon a middle Point until, of a Sudden, it became a City."

Before that occurred, however, the mother country was rocked by civil war in 1649. James I's successor, Charles I, neglected the colony, then for unrelated reasons lost both his throne and head. Parliament seized power and Oliver Cromwell rose as lord protector of the Commonwealth, but Virginia Governor Sir William Berkeley and the Assembly remained loyal to the crown. Faced with a show of force in ships from England, Berkeley negotiated a bloodless truce: Royalists retained their property in the colony; the established church remained intact (less references to royalty in the Book of Common Prayer) and the Assembly increased its power. The governor had less luck dealing with the local challenge of Bacon's

An English man-at-arms lost this "closed helmet" when Powhatan's heirs attacked every British settlement and massacred hundreds of colonists in 1622. In 1977 it was unearthed by Colonial Williamsburg archaeologists along with another like it, the only examples of such armor ever found in English America. They lay buried at the place called Carter's Grove, a plantation built in the 1750s on the site of the lost hamlet of Wolstenholme Towne overlooking the James River.

Rebellion, the first armed uprising against royal authority—albeit in pursuit of Indian genocide, not English liberty.

Through a series of church mergers, Bruton Parish was established at Middle Plantation in 1674 and named for the English town on the river Brue in Somerset, whence the Ludwell and Berkeley families came to Virginia. The high ground of the peninsula's spine, soon boasting a plain brick church, became a likely site for a college founded (in part) to convert heathen natives to the faith of Protestant England. This college, successor to one planned in more remote Henrico County before the 1622 massacre, was championed by the Reverend James Blair, a Scottish cleric named by the bishop of London as his Virginia representative. Blair was commissary, the agent of the distant diocese of which the colony was an ecclesiastical part. He sailed home and won a royal charter in 1693 for the College of William and Mary, named for Britain's newly crowned monarchs. The second college in English America, it was the first one founded under sovereign patronage.

The College was also the catalyst for relocating the colony's capital. Again quoting one Rutherfoord Goodwin, the modern antiquary who sublimed in archaic style:

A wharf scene brightens the cartouche on a 1775 edition of a map first made in 1751 by one Joshua Fry and Peter Jefferson, Thomas's father. This nice bit of propaganda implies the geographic merit of the Tidewater, where planters could grow tobacco beside their own docks. A reproduction of the map now hangs in the Great Room at Wetherburn's Tavern.

> While the College was yet building at *Middle Plantation* in the year 1698, a final Calamity fell upon *Jamestown* in the Burning of the new State House at that Place. And, now, the Desire to establish the Seat of Government in a more central and healthful Spot having gained great Strength and the Plan having the strong Support of the Governor, the Hon. *Francis Nicholson*, Esq., *Middle Plantation* was brought forward in this Wise: "and forasmuch as the Place commonly called and known by the Name of the *Middleplantation* hath been found by const[an]t experience to be healthy and agreeable to the Constitutions of the Inhabitants of the His Majestyes Colony and Dominion haveing the naturall Advantage of a serene and temperate Aire [,] dry and champaign Land and plentifully stored with wholesome Springs and the Conveniency of two navigable and pleas[an]t Creeks that run out of *James* and *York* Rivers necessary for the Supplying of the Place...." The Thought of rebuilding the State House at *Jamestown* could not stand in the face of so handsome a Reputation; and in the Year 1699 the Assembly was prevailed upon to pass an Act entitled *An Acte directing the Building of the Capitoll and the City of Williamsburgh*, which among other Things in its great Length, directed that the city..."in Honour of our most gracious & glorious King *William*, shall be ever hereafter called and known by the Name of the City of *Williamsburgh*."

The legislature thus moved its seat to the hamlet on the high ground which by mid-century boasted nearly two thousand inhabitants. During its first few decades, the city's population would treble twice a year during "Publick Times" when the elected House of Burgesses met and the appointed Council sat as the General Court. For reasons involving tobacco culture and peninsular geography, the city did not grow large in physical size or permanent population. Since tobacco plantations had their own wharfs, Virginia did not greatly need a shipping center here.

The colony's ruling class—its gentlemen planters who also served as vestrymen, judges and legislators—frequented Williamsburg seasonally. Building town houses or lodging in the taverns, they flocked to this epicenter of Virginia, the crown's most populous and prosperous colony. They built an ideal community, at least one planned according to new ideals imported from the mother country. As Daniel J. Boorstin explained in *The Americans: The Colonial Experience*, "If other colonies sought escape from English vices, Virginians

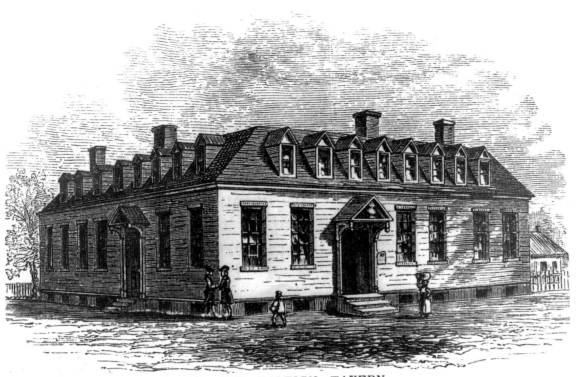

THE OLD RALEIGH TAVERN.

Like a phoenix, Raleigh Tavern has gone and come again. Built about 1717, for six decades it served as a hub of colonial life and politics: Jefferson danced and Washington dined here; Virginia leaders defied the crown by meeting without royal permission in its Apollo Room and took a giant step toward Independence, resolving that "an attack made on one of our sister Colonies, to compel arbitrary taxes, is an attack made on all British America." In 1859 the building burned and a century after the tavern's heyday Scribner's Monthly published this woodcut (above). Rebuilt (below), in 1932 the Raleigh opened again in the town dubbed the "birthplace of the Republic."

29

wished to fulfill English virtues.... If Virginia was to be in any way better than England, it was not because Virginians pursued ideas which Englishmen did not have [at first]; rather that here were novel opportunities to realize the English ideals."

When courts and Assembly met, Williamsburg seemed a crowded and sophisticated metropolis as befitted the seat of a government that claimed dominion as far west as the Mississippi, nay the Pacific—on parchment if not in practical fact. In 1716 the governor himself tested the frontier, leading an expedition across the Blue Ridge Mountains. With a company of scouts and a dozen gentlemen, Alexander Spotswood crossed the head of the Rapidan River (mistaking it for the James), then found a pass to the Shenandoah ("River of Stars"), which his troop dubbed the Euphrates before celebrating. A diarist recorded "We drank the King's health in champagne, and fired a volley; the Princess's health in burgundy, and fired a volley; and all the rest of the Royal Family in claret, and a volley. We drank the Governor's health and fired another volley...." They sported for four weeks, living off the land and covering four hundred miles before reaching Williamsburg again. There the convivial leader gave each companion a little gold horseshoe as a souvenir and dubbed them all Knights of the Golden Horseshoe. This expedition notwithstanding, for the next few decades one governor after another vainly tried to bar land-hungry settlers from crossing the mountains.

The Indians were less tractable there, and France had claimed the territory. Yet because land meant wealth there was no stopping the westward movement by both penniless loners and well-connected colonists who took absentee titles to tracts larger than some European principalities. Defense of this growing realm—and the spreading empire elsewhere—cost England dearly during the first half of the century. The crown sought repayment from its far-flung subjects for successfully waging a series of wars in the Old World and the New, wars that in the end served the interests of both king and colony alike, though colonists would soon object to having to help pay their costs.

The transplanted Englishmen of Virginia still pledged their loyalty to the crown, which had passed from William to Anne, then to the first of the Georges by 1714. During the reign of George II, the colonists had grown accustomed to questioning royal authority over many things—from who had the power of appointing clergy to matters of trade. When George III's minions imposed new taxes from distant London to pay old war debts, still-loyal colonists argued that their traditionally English toes were being trod upon. The transatlantic argument grew hotter, and when the burgesses voiced notions that verged on treason, the royal governor dissolved the House around their ears. But no English fiat could erase this colonial community nor mute its band of leaders. Though disenfranchised, Virginia's burgesses resumed deliberations in Williamsburg's Raleigh Tavern, empowering themselves to speak for Virginia's people without royal permission! Then they joined emissaries of twelve kindred colonies in Philadelphia. Virginians became part of the inner circle of the Continental Congress, which was thus led by men who'd cut their governmental teeth in Williamsburg as burgesses. (Did they then represent the perfect democracy? Not by later lights. To qualify to vote, a person had first to be male, then free and possessed of land. Further, most leaders rose to local prominence as parish vestrymen and justices of the peace, virtually hereditary positions that devolved through ownership of vast plantations.)

In short order an elder son of the Old Dominion, George Mason, would draft the Virginia Declaration of Rights; a younger son, Thomas Jefferson, who'd read law in Williams-

Bruton Parish's "new" church, built in 1715, inspired this 1836 watercolor (above) by Thomas Millington, son of a William and Mary professor. A century later, when restorers were returning the town to its present antique mien (below), documents such as this proved invaluable.

burg, would write the Declaration of Independence; an erstwhile surveyor, George Washington, who'd charted the hinterlands and led militia bands, would become commander in chief of the Continental Army. From Williamsburg, Washington planned the siege of a royal army encamped at Yorktown a half-day's march away, and there fought the battle that won the war called Revolution. But a year earlier the seat of Virginia's government had moved again. In part this was because the upriver site of Richmond was thought safer from attack (though Redcoats and Yankees in turn would prove otherwise). In part the capital was moved because no less a light than Jefferson, the second elected governor, disliked the Tidewater town and perhaps believed the new Commonwealth deserved a capital whose design would more truly reflect the new political order.

Williamsburg might have gone back to woods scarped by eroding ravines and sunk with little swamps except that it boasted the provincial College and the first public insane asylum in America. Grander cities than this have given up their ghosts when History's course flowed elsewhere. Yet this hamlet, once capital of the British Empire's premiere possession, would cling to shreds and shards of its past. In one particular it was nearly unique: Other colonial capitals became seats of states or hubs of industry and commerce in nineteenth-century America. Boston, Providence, New Haven, New York, Trenton, Philadelphia would all be transformed by new forms of manufacture and busyness while the Civil War would see Richmond burned, its edifices razed and precious records turned to ash. But this former colonial capital eluded the cataracts of modern history; Williamsburg escaped because it was a backwater.

Then in 1902 a young minister came to Bruton Parish and the cruciform brick church raised in 1715 according to the design of King George I's governor, Alexander Spotswood. Bruton Church, said to be America's oldest Episcopal church in continuous use, had changed over the centuries, notably when its Victorian stewards—with the best of intentions, no doubt—transformed the interior bric by brac. A visionary of boundless energy, the new rector was inspired by plans to celebrate vanished Jamestown's tercentennial in 1907 and he persuaded his congregation to restore the sanctuary in time to rededicate it during the gala celebration that drew people of every station to the region.

But then the minister left Williamsburg for a spell, and the town lapsed into its old malaise. Suffering a relapse of parsimony, the city fathers decided that the annual appropriation of $50 was too much to pay the man who wound the clock in Bruton's tower. So they canceled his contract, the clock stopped and Williamsburg became known as the place where time stood still. Another year, the sleepy authorities simply forgot to print ballots and open the polls on Election Day, so a nearby newspaper dubbed the backwater "Lotusland" and its denizens "Lotusburgers."

In 1923 the minister returned to teach at the College while building its endowment fund, and ultimately to fill Bruton's elevated pulpit again. He resumed his earlier work of returning the building to its grander simplicity, removing partitions from the interior and a coal bin from the tower and reconstructing high-backed pews like those where Washington and Jefferson had prayed. It was not enough. The Reverend William Archer Rutherfoord Goodwin could no longer confine his vision within the round-crowned churchyard wall. After adapting as his parish house the home where Jefferson read law, he set his sights on the entire town, the nexus between Jamestown and Yorktown, the "cradle of liberty." Through Phi Beta Kappa, which had been founded at William and Mary just before the Revolution, he met one of the honor society's most famous members, one whose stature transcended scholarship per se.

John D. Rockefeller Jr., one of the world's richest men, was also a quiet revolutionary of sorts. Scion of a fortune earned in the industrial century that had passed this city by, he brought into full flower a new estate among men: the business of philanthropy. Rockefeller believed that great wealth—even his father's and thus his own—must be used for the benefit of great numbers of people. He was a pioneer in the causes of charity, a crusader in the force of alms.

A conservationist in the broadest sense, he had already given fortunes to preserve Europe's war-torn churches, created a sanctuary for medieval art in upper Manhattan and dedicated Maine's Acadia National Park to public enjoyment. He had endowed universities, social service agencies and medical institutions around the world. Guided through Williamsburg by Dr. Goodwin, he glimpsed the village parson's patriotic vision and gently seized it as his own. The Williamsburg "Restoration," as it would soon be familiarly called, became his personal cause, hobby and benevolent mania. The colonial capital also became another home, a retreat from his New York headquarters and rambling Hudson River estate.

Applying pure wealth to the re-creation of the place that Williamsburg had been, he bought brick, mortar and talent in fabled amounts. At the outset he wrote to the trusted associate who would handle the details: *"The purpose of this undertaking is to restore Williamsburg, so far as it may be possible, to what it was in the old colonial days and to make it a great center for historical study and inspiration"* (italics added). His successors have never coined a more elegantly succinct expression of the Restoration's goals, though they would benignly give the lie to Rockefeller's next sentence: "The purpose of this letter is to authorize my office to finance this entire program whether it costs three or four, or even five millions of dollars." By the time of his death, he alone had spent more than $68 million here and his heirs would continue to give millions more.

At first the aim was physical: to restore and replicate antique buildings, to frame a town so that modern folk could visit its halls and walk the streets of history. Generations of Rockefeller agents would expand the dream and modify the work; in the process they would pursue the donor's original goal more closely than he had. Not content with rebuilding in brick and clapboard alone, they would probe both earth and history to understand what life had been like in eighteenth-century Virginia. Cultural historians, political scientists, archaeologists would join the army of architects, decorators and laborers. Artisans would come to practice forgotten crafts, rediscovering ancient ways to make beautiful and useful things. Sociologists and the grandchildren of slaves would surmise the forgotten particulars of Afro-American beginnings, for blacks had been nearly half the colonial town's population (a fact the first restorers overlooked). Music teachers, students and performers would rehearse the minuets which the Founding Fathers danced and sing the songs with which they wooed the Founding Brides.

In all their efforts, these researchers discovered an awful fact of historical life and then learned to live with it as they coped with the essential nature of history. Williamsburg's scholars, antiquaries, architectural restorers, archaeologists, antique craftsmen et al. would learn perhaps better than any other community of students in their diverse disciplines that historical examination is the study of the incomplete. It is the reconstruction of lost worlds, of puzzles that inevitably lack more pieces than those at hand. These diverse historians (for

Called the "Cradle of Liberty" by the minister who conceived its restoration, Colonial Williamsburg again echoes the sounds of yore: Modern carpenters rebuild an armorer's forge (opposite), *using antique tools and techniques; a husky nag, no better or lesser bred than a colonial carter's horse, stands outside Wetherburn's Tavern* (above), *where an interpreter in colonial dress awaits visitors; fifers clad in rifleshirts* (below) *march past the Courthouse of 1770, piping airs that raised militant spirits during the War for Independence.*

lack of a better general term) learned of these frustrations because this place offered singular shortcomings along with its unique opportunities.

To seek truth about the past the investigator in any one of these disciplines must of course contend with his own bias and a vast body of accepted but unproved suppositions. Even more frustrating is the inevitable fact of voids in data and proof that will never be filled. Consider:

✻ The account books of a tradesman like blacksmith James Anderson survive, enabling an economic historian to reconstruct his ways of doing business. But only two objects proven to be made by Anderson, two hinges, have ever been found for the modern smith to examine in his effort to rediscover lost techniques.

✻ A practical eighteenth-century jack-of-all-trades like Peter Pelham, jailer *and* Bruton Parish's first organist, was reputedly a musical genius. His life, personality and musicology invite the scholar as enticingly as the Sirens. But a summary of actual information about him barely fills a single file card. There is simply nothing to study—unless some cache may one day come to light like a diary, sheaf of letters or catalogue of his music. (Such things do happen. Ann Blaws Barraud, a colonial physician's wife, played the harpsichord, a fact of little modern import until Bruton's organist and choirmaster James S. Darling discovered a folder of her musical scores in the archives at William and Mary. Recording some of the music on an eighteenth-century instrument, Darling advanced precise knowledge of colonial Williamsburg by finding this accomplished gentlewoman's sheet music.)

✻ The legislative act that established the city survives in an English archives, along with the original survey map of the town's boundaries. Yet despite fifty years of searching no trace can be found of the first town plan. Thus it must be surmised from the scraps of evidence recompiled from later maps, land records, chance details gleaned from diaries and published histories.

✻ This unique city itself escaped the ravages of progress through historical accident: Its reason for being—the government establishment—was removed to Richmond. But half the city lay within the original boundaries of James City County, which sent its land and court records to the capital "for safekeeping" during the Civil War. Thus half of Williamsburg's records were destroyed when Richmond burned. In sum, more of the "fabric" of a colonial city remains here for practical study than for many other eighteenth-century cities of comparable importance. But fully half the documents are missing, while the papers of some other cities remain more complete though the cities themselves are transformed beyond recognition.

Scholarship aside, this place raised a manifold institution eventually attracting a million visitors a year. (As it changed, so did its overseeing corporations, first organized as Colonial Williamsburg, Inc., and the Williamsburg Holding Company, which in 1934 was renamed Williamsburg Restoration, Inc. In 1970 Williamsburg Restoration, Inc., and Colonial Williamsburg, Inc., were merged into the nonprofit Colonial Williamsburg Foundation, which in turn adapted to changing tax codes and spawned a wholly owned subsidiary to run its hotels and restaurants for profit in 1984. Corporate identities notwithstanding, the protean institution has been known among friends first as "the Restoration" then as "CW.") In its commercial guise it became a hamlet of hotels—the flagship Williamsburg Inn, the Lodge and Motor House—and a village of antique guesthouses along with taverns that offer colonial-style food and drink. It also licensed the manufacture of everything from soap to furniture, offering what is arguably America's widest array of home furnishings bearing a single trademark. (Mr. Rockefeller insisted on the trademark to protect Colonial Williamsburg's reputation when vendors started plastering similar names on their vulgar wares.) Purveying copies and adaptations of colonial fabrics, furniture, potpourris, porcelains and more, the Restoration inspired the national interest in period reproductions and changed American tastes—in balance for the better.

Williamsburg became a destination for families in search of interesting relaxation, flocks of children instructed to see history, corporations seeking amiable conference surroundings. It became an academy of sorts as scholars came to study its collections of antique porcelain, furniture and folk art, to gather in seminars, to publish learned works bearing the institution's colophon. It became a diplomatic way station as foreign heads of state used its finest accommodations to recover from jet lag on their globe-girdling flights to Washington, a chopper-hop to the north. Coming the other way, President Franklin D. Roosevelt and seven successors visited on official business or private pleasure. Most spectacularly, in 1983 Ronald Reagan hosted the Economic Summit of Industrialized Nations here, a meeting of eight heads of state attended by three thousand members of the world's press. The Tidewater had hardly seen the likes since Washington marched on Yorktown 202 years earlier.

In the years since Dr. Goodwin and Mr. Rockefeller first shared their dream, much has been done to discover what this place was—from the time Dr. John Potts set his stakes here until Jefferson removed the seat of government. More has been done to restore it to that home of slave and gentleman, silversmith and silver-tongued orator; a city of practical crafts, complex economy and cunning preindustrial technology, at once a hamlet and seat of empire. Williamsburg has become both antique resort and historical laboratory. As its work continues, more accurate images of two centuries ago appear—images that often add to the picture of the past and sometimes contradict our previous understanding of colonial life.

It is doubtful whether Williamsburg will ever again exert the extraordinary—nay revolutionary!—impact that it exercised on the eve of America's War for Independence. In terms of culture, economics and politics, this city led the land in a way that it never can again. Yet the town that was home to two thousand souls lives again as a museum, theater and time capsule in one to preserve the physical evidence of the past that both instructs and inspires—a restoration that restores its visitors in many ways. Looking back over the centuries, colonial and Colonial Williamsburg have several sorts of histories. Their combined story starts as one of exploration, planning and creation; then becomes one of destruction, deterioration and loss; and finally emerges as one of reconstruction, discovery and recall. This place was founded, planned, built and abandoned, then rediscovered, recovered, restored and examined. Volumes of formal "history" have been written about the historic eighteenth-century town, while its twentieth-century resurrection is the keystone of a new historical force, the restoration movement. This book will try to sketch the city in both centuries.

In 1632, the Assembly convened and, among its other business, addressed the matter of having Middle Plantation—the future Williamsburg—"staked out and paled in"; 147 years later, in 1779, the tide turned away from the erstwhile capital, apparently for good. Yet 147 years later, in 1926, a venture began on the basis of a handshake and a dream. It was a partnership between two men certainly, but more important it joined vague visions and hard dollars in an uncommon cause. Who can say what the next 147 years will bring?

The stream of time flows on.

PART ONE

The Colonial Period: Jewel in the Crown of Empire
Francis Nicholson and His Grand Plan

The city that arose from Governor Nicholson's plan seemed grand for its time but it never erased every trace of Virginia's verdant wilderness. Ravines and unkempt pastures would remain, like this glen behind the Robert Carter House (opposite). Duke of Gloucester Street (left) would stretch westward from the Capitol past Bruton Church's spire to the mile-distant College—an avenue uniquely bounded at each end by monumental buildings. Though the boulevard was arrow straight, a carriage running its length would vanish twice from view, so deep were the ravines.

A prime mover, the Reverend James Blair founded the College of William and Mary around which Williamsburg grew. First, the minister persuaded England's monarchs to grant a charter; then to build the school, he took gifts from pirates, from scientist Robert Boyle's estate and from royal coffers with equal speed. Named president of the College for life, Blair also served on the Governor's Council and probably sat for his portrait, attributed to Charles Bridges, after 1735.

Soon after his Accession to the Government, he caused the Assembly, and Courts of Judicature, to be remov'd from *James-Town,* where there were good Accommodations for People, to *Middle-Plantation,* where there were none. There he flatter'd himself with the fond Imagination, of being the Founder of a new City. . . . There he procur'd a stately Fabrick to be erected, which he placed opposite to the College, and graced it with the magnificent name of the *Capitol.*

—Robert Beverley: *The History and Present State of Virginia* (1705)

*W*illiamsburg would become a jewel in the crown of British empire. Yet its founding resulted from failure—from accident, pestilence and other misfortunes that assailed Jamestown which was, in a word, a disaster. Virginia's first government had been seated in entirely the wrong sort of place.

From the beginning Jamestown's pestilential swamp beset the settlers with "Fluxes and Agues" despite the imposition of English America's first sanitary code in 1610. Within the compound Governor Sir Thomas Gates prohibited not only the "unmanly, slothfull and loathesome...necessities of nature" but laundry and pot washing as well. Yet contagions continued, spread no doubt by bad water from the shallow wells and by the marsh's mosquitoes. Settlements established south of the James and upriver near the falls fared better: "There did not so much as one man miscarry, and but very few or none fall sicke," a chronicle recorded. The writing was on the stockade wall.

Jamestown remained the capital because the colony had more pressing problems to address than relocating: security, relations with home, trade, agriculture (especially of the cash crop tobacco, which was planted in the very streets). Motions to move the capital were heard as early as Gates's day, but the colonists were preoccupied with surviving, making their livings, getting ahead. Then as now, life is what goes on while we're making other plans. If Jamestown was not an ideal city, at least, like Everest, it was there. If it escaped destruction by Indians in 1622, Englishmen running amok half a century later made up for that.

In 1676 a wellborn newcomer from Suffolk challenged his cousin-in-law, Governor Sir William Berkeley, over the latter's benign Indian policy, which successfully confined natives to reserved areas. Nathaniel Bacon inspired the massacre of tractable Indians, raised a rabble—some say rebel—army and laid siege to Jamestown. When Governor Berkeley fled to the Eastern Shore to marshal his forces, Bacon entered Jamestown and burned it to the ground in a nighttime blaze that struck fear into men's hearts as far as the glow was visible The firebrand might have reached greater heights, but a month later he died of fever—a case of Jamestown's Revenge?—and Berkeley reclaimed his ashen seat.

Taking vengeance, the governor hanged Bacon's followers, some at his estate and others at the place called Middle Plantation. This central site between two rivers on the high ground above the peninsula's narrowest spot already boasted a hamlet with a church and crossroads. It was the place where royal troops had been quartered and Indians agreed by treaty to live apart under English sovereignty. Then it was here that the Assembly, bereft of a capital in 1677, met at the home of one Captain Otho Thorpe and in its wisdom decided to restore the seat of government to Jamestown.

No portrait survives of Francis Nicholson, but the governor left his mark—on the city's plan and in this seal used to identify wine bottles from his private stock.

Given the magnitude of the troubles that befell his administration, it was inevitable that Berkeley would be recalled to England. He was replaced in 1677 by Thomas Culpeper, a baron and friend of King James for whom he performed one particularly noble service. Mindful that the Assembly had presumed the exclusive prerogative to tax Virginians since 1623, Culpeper nevertheless proposed a royal levy on exported tobacco. Predictably, the Assembly opposed it, but Culpeper had not been sent abroad because he was a fool. First, he promised certain rewards to certain burgesses if they would support his original bill—for example, to the elected Speaker of the House a lifetime seat on the appointed Council. Then Culpeper agreed to an amendment seemingly in a spirit of compromise: Tobacco carried in Virginia ships would be exempt from the new duty, giving the colony's captains a competitive edge. Through these maneuvers he got the bill passed subject to royal review. The king accepted the act, then exercised his acknowledged right to veto amendments, and the colony's advantage was annulled. Culpeper and his successors—uniquely in these colonies—were thus freed from having to bargain with the legislature for the funds to pay their salaries.

In the meantime, Jamestown was rebuilt on its ashes. The city grew beyond its original walls until the autumn of 1698 when disaster struck again. The statehouse, fourth building to fill that function since the colony's birth, burned in a fire of mysterious origin. For reasons unrelated to the fire, a new governor arrived a few weeks later and threw his considerable weight behind the logical decision to move the seat of government.

The new executive was actually returning to Virginia, so the tangled tale of his administration (and the founding of Williamsburg) starts earlier. First a soldier, then a professional administrator and prototype of the colonial civil servant, Francis Nicholson eventually governed English colonies as distant as Nova Scotia and South Carolina. Often champion of governmental reforms and a man of many talents, he seemed a paragon in some respects though he had three besetting sins: a chronic thirst, an apoplectic temper and an unrequited fondness for rich young women.

Nicholson had come to the New World in the 1680s as an infantry commander and served in New England under Governor Sir Edmund Andros. He swore loyalty to the deposed King James II in 1688 and opposed the succession of Parliament's choice, William of Orange, whose coronation signaled the end of royal rule by divine right. But he answered for that back in London and two years later was restored to royal service—this time in Virginia. Serving with distinction from 1690 to 1692, he opened new trade with Indians, inspected the frontiers, improved the militia, established a postal system and provided both moral and financial support to the idea of erecting a college. This last notion proved crucial.

A college for Virginia had first been envisioned upriver in 1617 by King James I (who won lasting fame for commissioning the English Bible's most poetic translation). Possessing missionary zeal and captivated by exotic Pocahontas during her brief stay in London, King James had wished to educate "the children of the Infidels"—before the massacre of 1622 dampened such ardor in English hearts. The college idea then lay dormant through the reign of James's ill-fated son Charles and the Puritan interregnum. It was revived in 1660 with the restoration of the martyred king's son Charles II, though by now its new goals had become "the advance of learning, education of youth; [to] supply the ministry and promotion of piety." Still it remained only an idea. Charles II's Catholic brother James II came to the throne and went into exile and King William was crowned before the idea arose again. Now it was championed by an ambitious minister trained at Marischal College, later a citadel of the Scottish Enlightenment.

The Reverend James Blair, the bishop of London's new representative in Virginia, won endorsements from the colony's clergy, the Council and notably Governor Nicholson who was then serving his first term. Possessed of persuasive powers that were nearly Rasputinian, Commissary Blair traveled to London where he won Queen Mary's support and through her King William's. In 1693 he convinced the monarchs to substantially endow the college that would bear their names. (The commissary also raised private funds, including a gift from imprisoned pirates as a quid pro quo for helping to secure their freedom.) Bearing the only royal charter ever granted a college in English America, he returned to Virginia where the Assembly named him president of the College for life and the king appointed him to the Council. The legislature then debated several Tidewater sites and resolved, according to Rutherfoord Goodwin, "That *Middle Plantation* be the Place for erecting the said College of *William and Mary* in *Virginia* and that the said College be at that Place erected and built as near the Church now standing in *Middle Plantation* old Fields as Convenience will permitt."

Meanwhile, in one of those shuffles that colonial administration was heir to, Nicholson was recalled to England, then named governor of Maryland while his old boss succeeded him as head of the Virginia government. Sir Edmund Andros was ensconced in Jamestown when Commissary Blair returned from England and the two quickly quarreled (as indeed Blair quarreled with—and bested—almost everyone who crossed him). When Blair fell sick and couldn't preach, Andros appointed another minister to fill the Jamestown pulpit; recovering his health Blair raged so violently about the affront that Andros suspended him from the Council. A witness observed that the first College building's foundation was laid "with the best Solemnity we were capeable" on August 8, 1695. But dignity deteriorated from there, when the king restored Blair to his Council seat and the feud between governor and commissary grew hotter.

Andros accused Blair of unbridled conduct and Blair replied with volleys of charges: everything from antipathy for the College in general to making off with bricks meant for its construction in particular. He spread tales of gubernatorial error as far as his pen could reach, writing Nicholson in Maryland that Col. Philip Ludwell, the best man to oversee the College's construction, had begged off. "The reason he gives out Publickly is his age.... But he sticks not to say among his Friends, that he sees no possibility of carrying it on in this Governors time." Journeying back to Virginia, Nicholson vainly tried to mediate and was once arrested by Andros for his pains. Blair went all the way back to England and brought charges against Andros before the archbishop of Canterbury. In Andros's place, Blair and such worthies as John Locke secured the reappointment of Nicholson, who had officially supported the College plan and personally subscribed £150 to it. For the moment, Williamsburg had champions at the head of both church and state.

The returning governor was as ambitious, able and headstrong as Commissary Blair, his patron pro tem—even if he was less adroit in their ultimate contretemps. Nicholson's principal accomplishment in Maryland had been to design the new capital city of Annapolis after he'd secured the removal of the capital from St. Mary's (a stronghold of Catholics whose loyalty was distrusted by the restored House of Stuarts). His plan for Annapolis far up the Chesapeake featured open squares and major buildings set in circles to command the views up radiating streets. The design, a mixed success, departed from English tradition to reflect new urban vogues exemplified by Sir Christopher Wren's ambitious (and unfulfilled) plans for rebuilding London after the Great Fire there.

Arriving in Jamestown weeks after the statehouse mysteriously burned, Nicholson willingly addressed the challenge presented by its charred remains. Knowing the old site, he disliked it. If a new statehouse were to be built, why not raise it in a pleasant and healthy place worthy of the distinction? There was already "the beginning of a town" seven miles away, as a student at William and Mary declared: "A Church, an ordinary, several stores, two Mills, a smiths shop, a Grammar School, and above all the Colledge." A goal clearly in mind, Nicholson began politicking to get his way, for though the governor's office had won certain new prerogatives after Bacon's Rebellion, his powers were limited to that of *primus inter pares* ("first among equals") as chairman of the Council. Perhaps he commissioned a survey without troubling other authorities about it. Certainly he consorted with Commissary Blair, still his ally, for on May Day, 1699, the College hosted a grand fête for the colony's populace and its establishment—the burgesses and Council with Nicholson at its head. The celebration featured student oratory to prove rhetorical prowess and one scholar's address offered persuasive arguments for locating the seat of government near the young institution: "The Colledge will help to make the town... [by] the very numbers of the Colledge who will be obliged to reside at this place viz. the president and Masters... with such servants as will be necessary for the kitchin, Buttery, Gardens, wooding, and all other uses." Further, the student declared, the institution would attract "Tradesmen, Labourers, Shopkeepers, perhaps Printers, Booksellers, Bookbinders, Mathematical instrument makers, nurses for the sick.... By this method we have an opportunity not only of making a Town, but such a Town as may equal if not outdo Boston, New York, Philadelphia, Charlestown, and Annapolis; and consequently such a Town as may retrieve the reputation of our Country." The colony "has suffered by nothing so much as by neglecting a seat of trade, wealth and Learning, and by running altogether into dispersed Country, [i.e.] plantations. If ever we would equal these our Rivals, we must contrive to joyn our heads and purses together,... learn to improve our shipping and navigation, our trade and commerce, our minds and manners, and what no man can do singly, by a friendly cohabitation and society to do jointly with one another."

Nicholson's plan vanished but Franz Michel, a Swiss traveler seeking a place for a settlement, sketched the town's landmark buildings in 1702: the College of William and Mary (above) in its original form before the first of several fires prompted alterations, the Capitol (opposite above) with its unique rounded ends and the first Bruton Parish Church (opposite below) within its enclosing wall amid a scattering of tombs.

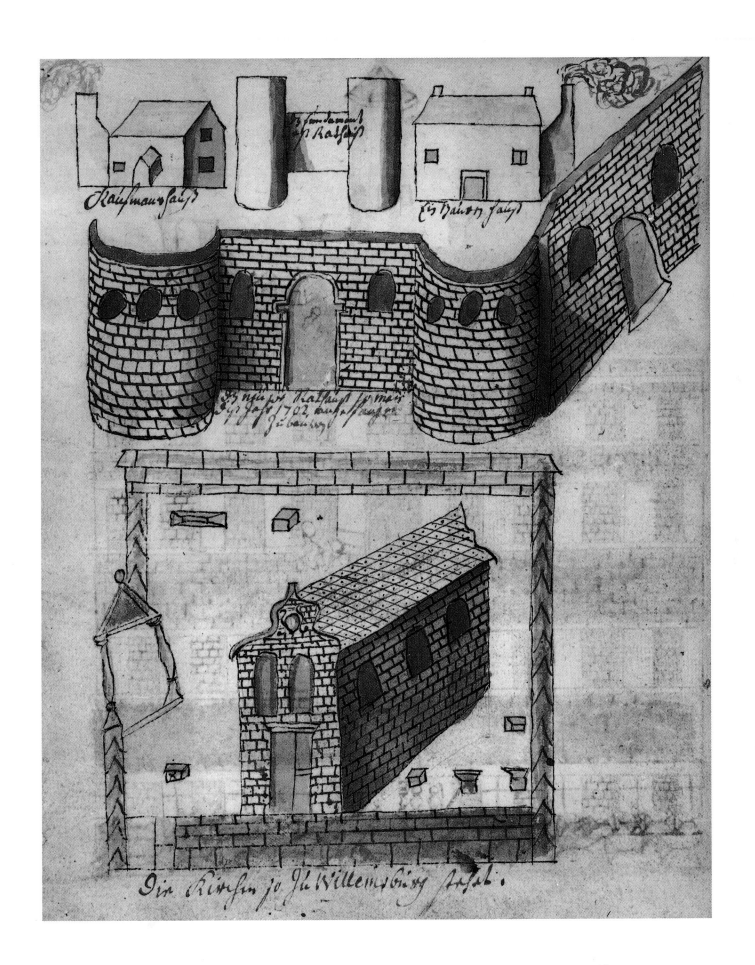

Kaufmanshaüs

Fundament zu Rathaus

Es hauon haüs

Neues Rathaus so man
im Jahr 1702 anfassangen
zu bawen

Die Kirchen so zu Willemsburg stehet.

A fortnight after May Day, one Benjamin Harrison, burgess, presented the student's prescient speech to the Assembly and formally proposed moving the capital to the College precinct. Meanwhile Theodorick Bland had surveyed the fledgling town's irregular boundaries and the miles-long ganglia leading to two landings on the nearby creeks. That task must have taken considerable time, yet Bland finished his survey map on June 2, 1699. Five days later the burgesses authorized the building of a city on the site his plat depicted. Nicholson signed the act into law the next day, as well he might, evidently having written a good deal of it.

This "Acte Directing the Building of the Capitoll and the City of Williamsburgh" at once stipulated the creation of both a building and the surrounding town. It is a remarkable document for its double focus and its syntax:

> And forasmuch as the Generall Assembly and Generall Courts of this his Majesties Colony and Dominion cannot possibly be held and kept at the said Capitoll [building] unless a good Towne be built and settled adjacent to the said Capitoll suitable for the Accommodation and Entertainment of a considerable Number of Persons that of Necessity must resort thither[;] and whereas in all Probability it will prove highly advantageous and beneficiall to his Majesties Royall Colledge of William & Mary to have the Conveniences of a Towne near the same[;] *Be it therefore enacted by the Authority aforesaid and it is hereby enacted*[:] that two Hundred eighty three Acres thirty five Poles and a halfe of Land scituate lying and being at the *Middleplantation* in *James Citye* and *York* Counties…shall be and is hereby reserved and appropriated for the onely and sole Use of a City to be there built and erected.

The act went on to reserve a specific plot 475 feet square for the structure to be "caled and knowne by the Name of the *Capitoll,*" a term not used in America before.

Nicholson's original bill—for certainly he was the principal author—was marvelous in its particulars as the act went on to read like a zoning code. It specified sixty-foot-square lots for warehouses and such at the public landings on the two creeks that led to the York and James rivers respectively. It directed that the town be divided into half-acre lots; that houses be set back six feet from the main streets; that dwellings measure at least twenty by thirty feet; that they stand at least ten feet high at the edge of the roof.

Building regulations would be written by "Directors appointed for the Settlement and Encouragement of the City of Williamsburgh." With Nicholson again the first among equals, these directors were empowered to "make such Rules and orders and to give such Directions in the Building of the said City and Portes not already provided for by this Act as to them shall seem best and most convenient." Twelve freeholders from the neighboring counties of York, New Kent, and James City were chosen to appraise the value of properties expropriated for the city; ownership passed to six trustees who were then commissioned to sell town sites and use the proceeds to repay the original owners.

Sales were conditional; a purchaser was required to build a substantial dwelling within twenty-four months or the land would revert to city ownership. While house size and material depended on the parcel—one needn't build two minimal houses on a double lot—all properties were to be fenced within six months of occupancy. Similar conditions could be applied to other parts of town at the discretion of the directors.

Having sketched the town in considerable if mutable detail and laid ground rules for its development, the act paid homage to royalty at home. It named Queen's Road, which led

His Royal Highness Prince William, Duke of Gloucester and heir to the throne, displays a regal bearing at the age of nine, about the time Williamsburg's main street was named for him. The lad died two years later and two years before the death of his godfather, King William III, for whom the city was named. Thus, the boy's mother, Queen Anne, assumed the crown in 1702 to become the second of five monarchs to reign while Williamsburg was capital. This portrait, attributed to Edward Lilly, hangs in the reconstructed Capitol, which bears Queen Anne's emblems.

to "Port or Landing Place" on Queen's Creek, "in Commemoracon of the late Queen *Mary* of blesed memory." It stated that Archer's Hope Creek, which ran to the James, "shall for ever hereafter be caled and knowne by the Name of *Princess* Creek... in Honour of her Royall Highness the Princess *Ann* of *Denmark*." It declared "the said main Street... in Honour of his Highness *William* Duke of *Gloceter* shall for ever hereafter be called and knowne by the Name of *Duke of Gloceter* Street." (This eleven-year-old princeling was heir apparent to the English throne by an act of Parliament which established the line of succession through deposed James II's fertile second daughter, a Protestant. Princess Anne conceived eighteen times but delivered only five children successfully, and none of them reached adulthood. The little duke died in 1700, and two years later the crown devolved to his mother—as Queen Anne—when King William died.)

Knowing that History does not reward the modest, the governor seized the prerogative to name the next largest streets Francis and Nicholson for himself. The rest took names of realms in the growing empire, for this royal governor was careful to observe appropriate amenities—often very grandly, as would happen when news arrived three months after the fact of King William's death and Queen Anne's coronation. Nicholson designated a holiday for some weeks off in order to have time to plan properly. As a Swiss traveler recorded, he hosted a day of both deep mourning and splendid revelry.

Most of the populace converged on Williamsburg for the occasion; two thousand militia from six neighboring counties were in attendance to say nothing of two Indian queens with two score "of their most distinguished warriors and servants." Grandstands were erected before the College, and musicians appeared on the College balconies. "On the uppermost were the buglers from the warships, on the second, oboes and on the lowest violinists, so that when the ones stopped the others began. Sometimes they played together. When the proclamation of the King's death was to be made they played very movingly and mournfully." Nicholson appeared in mourning astride a white horse draped with black and Commissary Blair's eulogy moved people to tears. "Considerable marching and counter-marching" continued until noon when the musicians abandoned dirges in favor of livelier airs. Riding a new horse, Nicholson reappeared in a blue uniform covered with braid and the new queen was proclaimed to rousing cheers and salutes from cannon. Nicholson refreshed his honored guests "right royally" while "the ordinary persons received each a glass of rum or brandy with sugar." The ceremony was then repeated at the building site of the Capitol and "the Governor entertained again as at noon" as toasts "were repeatedly answered by guns and buglers." That night when the master of ceremonies came a cropper at setting off the fireworks, the governor mounted his horse to oversee them himself. Nor did the revelry end there; it was all repeated the next day at Nicholson's grand behest.

Whether as governor of Virginia per se or executive director of Williamsburg, Nicholson claimed the role of urban planner even before the town was chartered. Given his worldly sophistication and experience, he was probably the most qualified man in town for the job, if hardly the most popular. The lay of the land physically limited the town's options, and traditions of English town design dating back to the period of Roman occupation dictated constraints at least as distinct.

Nicholson took it upon himself to design a city that was classic in some respects and progressive in others. While he had ideals, it was not to be an ideal city; the Tidewater was

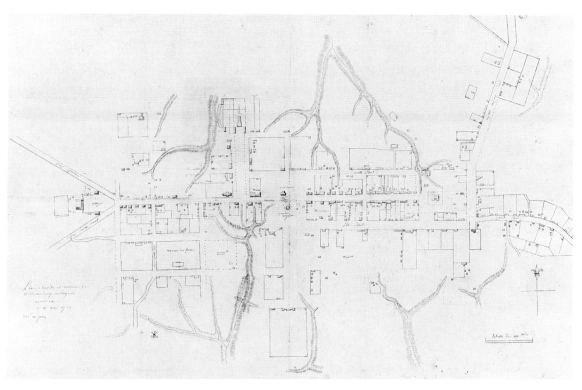

The "Frenchman's Map" of 1782 (above) shows Nicholson's grid plan of more than eighty years earlier. Roads slanting from the west end of town past the College may have figured in a cipher of royal initials, "W" and "M." No traces remain of similar ciphers—which early writers hint at—near the Capitol and Market Square, located on the map slightly left of center. One expert believes Nicholson originally offset the central green like a diamond; thus, the main street would have split to go around it, forming diagonals for another pair of ciphers. Probably drawn by French officers with an eye toward housing troops, the map shows topography, dwellings, even outbuildings. It proved indispensable to restorers, because it locates structures and, for instance, apparently confirms a report that catalpa trees lined Palace Green.

The Colles Map of 1789 (below) was the Triptik of its time—a convenient and easily carried edition of route maps published for travelers. Each sheet unfolded a stretch of main road, linking principal towns in the newly independent states.

Overleaf: North England Street passes the Grissell Hay Lodging House (built in the eighteenth century and long known as the Archibald Blair House) and its brick kitchen, one of the many residential complexes within the 173-acre Historic Area.

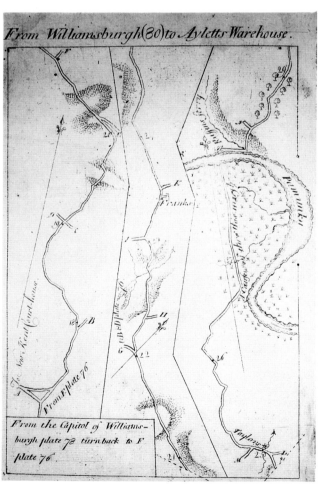

not Elysium after all but a ramble of woodland, pasture and gullies; his chalk was not indelible, nor was the slate perfectly clean when he began. The main building of the College, already in place, faced almost due east toward the old brick Church. A road, or horse path in some people's view, came north up the peninsula sensibly avoiding steep ravines by meandering along the top of the ridge. It followed the most level route, then split at the College, one path slanting off to Jamestown and the other toward Henrico and the eventual location of Richmond.

Topography and tradition combined with the locations of College and Church virtually dictated a central avenue running due east from William and Mary. Tradition alone dictated a grid pattern of parallel and perpendicular streets. But Nicholson was aware of the new aesthetics that architects and planners like Sir Christopher Wren were championing at home in the dawning of a newly urbane age. A principal tenet on the rise was the importance of the grand view to show off stately edifices and simultaneously bring order to their surroundings. With these principles in mind, Nicholson ordered a boulevard ninety-nine feet wide. It ended at the foot of the first College building which the colony's promoters soon insisted (misguidedly, as we shall see) had been designed by the master himself. As one correspondent described, "The Building is beautiful and commodious, being first modelled by Sir *Christopher Wren*, [and] adapted to the Nature of the Country by the Gentlemen there."

The street's other end, just short of a mile away, would be anchored by Nicholson's Capitol. Why didn't he place the latter building exactly a mile from the first? Alas, any rationale (if he had one) was lost scant years later. Even visitors, diarists and historians of his own generation could only surmise many details of his original plan once Nicholson had moved on. Nonetheless, his plan envisioned a main street linking the two premiere edifices of the town, nay of Virginia and of the English colonies in America. No other city of the period would boast such impressive buildings nor display them so grandly.

Cross streets would lead to large lots—sites for especially stately homes made all the more impressive by their placement—and Nicholson planned one site as grander than all the rest. Instead of an ordinary north-south passage across the main street alongside Bruton Parish Church, here his plan allowed a grand crossing with a ceremonial avenue twice as wide as Duke of Gloucester Street. This would provide a most spectacular vista when the inevitable governor's house would be built on the estate at the south end, a mansion the designer might have known he would never see.

At the risk of offending local tastes Nicholson embellished his grid design with diagonal streets to border open spaces and form royal initials. As College mathematician and cleric, Hugh Jones reported in his boosterish *The Present State of Virginia*, Nicholson "laid out the city of Williamsburg in the form of a cypher, made of W. and M." Gentleman Robert Beverley put the worst face on it in his *History and Present State of Virginia*, which suggested a plurality of cyphers: The governor "flatter'd himself with the fond Imagination, of being the Founder of a new City. He marked out the Streets in many Places, so as that they might represent the Figure W, in memory of his late Majesty King William, after whose Name the Town was call'd Williamsburg." If his statement sounds sour, Beverley had been burned by Nicholson's decision to move the government seat from Jamestown where he held considerable property. Further, he evidently coveted the return of the capital to its original site.

While much of his design would stand the test of time, Nicholson's royal cyphers disappeared—almost as quickly as he did. The reasons for his departure were trivial and political. The governor offended powerful competitors, among others Commissary Blair and Beverley who were his equal in nursing powerful grudges and engaging in mighty pettiness. Though he was gifted in several practical disciplines, Nicholson's violent temper and legendary thirst added fuel to his adversaries' fire.

In one recorded opinion, this worthy was "born drunk," an impression memorably strengthened when a naval officer requested money to service his ship for the voyage home. Then occupying apartments in the College, "The Governour flew out into such a Passion against the Comiss^rs of the Navy calling them all the basest Names that the Tongue of Man could express, & with such a Noise, that the People downe in the lower Roomes caime running up Stairs." The witness testified that others ran *down* as best they could, including one merchant captain wakened from sleep thinking that such a row could only mean the building was afire. He fled before putting on either his pants or his wooden leg. Yet another time, Nicholson suffered a famous "love-fit," forced presents on seventeen-year-old Lucy Burwell, and generally acted the fool. When she refused his suit he threatened her and the man she meant to marry as well as any minister who would perform the ceremony.

The business over Lucy Burwell was the last straw for Commissary Blair, who once again applied to his friends in high London places. (More important, perhaps, power in Parliament had changed hands twice and even the most adroit politician would have been hardpressed to keep his fences mended beyond an ocean that took one to three months to sail across.) So Nicholson was replaced in 1705 by Edward Nott, and the powers who remained in Williamsburg set about to undo what they could of the former governor's work. They removed his coat of arms from the Capitol and erased the cyphers that adorned his city plan. He wasn't gone a month when the Assembly amended his act, which directed the building of the city and Capitol in the first place.

In short order the Assembly and new governor appointed new directors, empowering them to make changes in the plan. They were authorized to "enlarge the Market Place and to alter any of the Streets or Lands thereof where the same are found inconvenient"—though Duke of Gloucester Street "shall not hereafter be altered either in the Course or Dimensions thereof." That course was straight in Bland's original survey plan, but the Reverend Hugh Jones hinted that it might not have remained so: The "noble street" became "mathematically streight" only after Nicholson departed and "the first design of the town's form is changed to a much better [one]." Whatever change occurred, it also pleased Robert Beverley who wrote in the second edition of his book that the streets were realigned "from the fanciful Ws and Ms to much more Conveniencies."

His considerable political accomplishments aside, this able if unbridled governor left legacies beyond his name on Francis and Nicholson streets. But for him there might not have been a college at Middle Plantation. (However powerful Commissary Blair might become, he was green when he first championed the borrowed dream of a college in his ecclesiastical domain.) In his first term, Governor Nicholson's gifts of money and support helped the idea become a reality; in his second term, his political gifts seated the government near the College. Finally, though his early plan for the town's design was altered, its basic form survived. It was Nicholson who sketched the town, made it Virginia's capital and drew Williamsburg around the seat of government. Whatever arose here grew from his brief vision.

The Cornerstones of Williamsburg

The new city, planned as a capital, soon boasted America's grandest buildings. Drawings engraved in copper about 1740 (opposite) and possibly intended to illustrate a history of Virginia show, top row, the front of the College with its flanking Brafferton and President's House and, middle row left to right, the Capitol, back of the College and Governor's Palace. Discovered two centuries after it was made, the so-called Bodleian Plate provided priceless information for the extraordinary enterprise known first as Williamsburg Restoration, Inc., and later as the Colonial Williamsburg Foundation. Said the architect who rebuilt the Palace (left), these buildings "stand as monuments to the prerogatives of power."

Sunlight plays on the checkerboard brickwork of the reconstructed Capitol, its walls laid up in Flemish bond. In each course or layer, "stretchers" (bricks set lengthwise) alternate with "headers" (bricks set end-to). The shiny headers owe their bluish color to natural glazing caused when handmade bricks are baked or "burned" with hardwood fuel. The window reflects a flawed image because, for the sake of authenticity, obsolete methods were employed in the 1930s to make panes resembling old "crown" glass. Early glaziers would blow a lump of molten glass into a five-foot bubble, then spin it so fast it flattened out. After cooling, the "crown" was cut into slightly rounded panes.

When Williamsburg became a city in name, it also instantly became capital of a strapping colony then on the verge of feisty maturity, a community of sixty thousand souls, the largest and most populous of the crown's American dominions. The new city was born as the intended hub of a vital and complex community. Like the scion of a noble family who comes into his inheritance before coming of age, Williamsburg was in charge of the place before it grew up. In a manner of speaking the city had been endowed an estate with a wealth of living traditions as well as all its burdens.

Chosen to play spiritual, intellectual and administrative roles—to fulfill many functions—the city had aspects of its eventual persona before it was born. What it lacked, of course, were the support structures both physical and intangible: first the major public buildings, then the offices, shops and dwellings along with a body politic to animate the idea of a capital.

This was an instant metropolis. Metaphorically speaking it did not have to invent the wheel; its coming residents, both rustic and passing elegant, had all sorts of working contrivances already: habits, ways of doing business, courts to settle disputes and the like. These people called themselves English and the gentry in particular identified with the mother country, looking more slavishly to London for guidance in matters of taste with each passing year. These emotional bonds were strengthened by the facts of economic dependence on England, a dependence that was reinforced by laws which favored the mother country as a trading partner. Both blood and banking—through the coin of tobacco, which earned its growers credit with English merchants—bound Virginia to Britain.

Yet things were also different here. While both "the finer things" and necessary hardware like hammers and nails came from across the sea, outlying plantations sustained life. The plantation had become the linchpin for city and colony, for the overarching economy and social structure alike. The royal government at home desired colonial communities to resemble those in England both socially and physically. But conditions often dictated otherwise, and even the most loyal leaders here often decided otherwise of simple necessity.

Climate alone made an enormous difference. Temperatures could range a hundred degrees in a year and humidity vary from arid winter to sodden summer; thus, some materials favored in England were virtually useless here. Then there was the shortage of other building stuffs: stone, for starters, which was simply not to be had around the Tidewater. Instead of solid rock, the peninsula was made of clay, which became bricks when shaped as mud in wooden molds, then air-dried and stacked into hollow "kilns" fueled with hardwood and burned for a week. There were also middens of oyster shells which were burned as well to provide lime, a *sine qua non* for vast quantities of mortar. Yet if the peninsula lacked stone for building, it possessed forests of such height and variety that the firstcomers thought they'd found an inexhaustible supply of ships' masts, building beams and firewood. Another difference was that English provincial capitals had grown helter-skelter for more than a millennium, while Virginia's was cogently planned and built in mere decades. The public buildings here would also receive very special display of a sort unknown in most English cities, where even the grander edifices tended to take their chances willy-nilly among the rest.

The College's original facade gained this taller cupola and right-angled pediment when it was rebuilt after the disastrous fire of 1705. Over the course of the next two centuries it burned at least twice more and was altered several times before the Restoration returned it to its eighteenth-century appearance. Traditionally called the Wren Building, it resembles some work of English master builder Sir Christopher Wren though no proof survives that he designed it.

Built in stages and intended as a quadrangle surrounding a central court, the Wren Building never received its enclosing fourth side. Seen from the rear (below), the restored main range shows odd gables suggested in the Bodleian Plate. The south wing on the right contains the chapel (above left and above right) now restored with graceful restraint. Cenotaphs on the walls commemorate colonial leaders like Commissary Blair and Governor Botetourt, whose remains lie in vaults beneath the floor.

If Williamsburg was rare in being designed, it was unique in that it did not have to accommodate the sort of commerce that choked growing New York and made Philadelphia a busy shambles. Their sites were chosen for their natural harbors; transportation was the key to these communities' very survival while growth and trade remained principal reasons for their existence. Here by comparison, the new capital did not need to manhandle and store huge amounts of goods (viz. tobacco) which were handled on plantation wharfs, in storehouses along Chesapeake tributaries, at the planned public landings on Queen's and Princess creeks. This infant, instant city could concentrate on better things than serving as a plain port and moving goods. Spared the need to be very muscular, instead she would be smart—both intelligent and chic.

Of course the young city would engage in some commerce, if only to cater to inhabitants, seasonal visitors and the curious travelers attracted by her growing reputation. But her forte was beyond business. Her cornerstones were found in the cerebral estates of College, Church and colonial government. Three cornerstones then? No, four, as it happened in a stroke both symbolic and ironic, because one of those estates would be made manifest in twain: government would be represented by the Capitol and by the residence of the royal governor.

The College, its construction slowed by Blair's quarrel with Andros and by a shortage of skilled workmen, was originally intended to be a quadrangle around a central court. But only the front range and one wing were built in those years, a chapel wing decades later and the enclosing fourth side not at all. (Academic instruction had not waited upon the completion of the first College building, however; classes were first conducted nearby about the time the foundations were laid in 1695.) Nonetheless with the handsome front and the northwest wing raised by the second year of the new century, Virginia's first historian Robert Beverley could report "In this part are already finished all conveniences of Cooking, Brewing, Baking, &c. and convenient Rooms for the Reception of the President, and Masters, with many more Scholars than are as yet come to it; in this part are also the Hall and School-Room." In 1702 it could be said that the College population included a chancellor, president, rector, schoolmaster, usher, writing master, registrar and twenty-nine students.

The Wren Building common room, originally used by professors for meetings and dining, appears as if the pedagogues had just stepped out. The walnut veneer English desk dates from about 1700; the red-checked "case covers" saved upholstery from wear. All rooms in the exhibition buildings have been given a lived-in-during-the-eighteenth-century look.

The building itself was laid up in English bond with alternate courses of stretchers (bricks laid lengthwise) and headers (bricks laid end-to). By one count it consumed 840,000 bricks, most of them "burned" nearby of clay dug on the spot. In appearance the building benefited from the application of a newly celebrated code of rules that harkened back to the Renaissance and even farther to classical times. Sir Christopher Wren had declared that beauty was to be found in nature, and his designing heirs concluded that nature was geometrical—hence the vogue for employing geometric forms.

However formally the building's design conformed to aesthetic formulae, the young College's small community didn't need such grand accommodations, which soon acquired other tenants as well. While the Capitol was being built, the Assembly, Council, General Court and governor found apartments here until they started using their own building in 1704 and occupied it fully the next year. Alas, they moved none too soon, for hardly had the lot of them moved than the College was destroyed in a fire of mighty spectacle.

Nicholson himself had warned that the College chimneys were too small: "A fire can't be made in them without running the hazard of its falling on the floor, as it once happened" in the secretary's office. In the Great Hall wooden girders ran "through the middle of the hearth whereby no use can be made of it." The room used by the Council had a fireplace with "some plank laid just under it insomuch that at Christmas 1702,...the wood under the hearth took fire & was almost all consumed before it was discovered."

It befell to Nicholson's successor, Governor Edward Nott, to inform the government in London: "I am sorry that I must give Your Lord[shi]ps the melancholy news of the burning of William & Mary College. On the 29th of October between 11 and 12 aclock at night, a fire broke out there, wch was got to that height before it was discovered, that it was impossible to save it, the building, Library, and furniture was in a small time totally consumed... I cannot tell what course will be taken to retrieve this misfortune."

Investigators heard hair-raising accounts: "Henry Randolph being one [student] that lodged in the College...doth testify that he was then in bed asleep, and one that lay in bed with him cryed out the College is on fire, wch awaked him, and looking up he saw the fire coming over the brick wall into his Room & so starting out of bed he ran down a back pair of stairs." Col. Edward Hill, a member of the Council and early backer of the College, "lay in Mr. Blair's Chamber." Aroused, he fled the building, and "made haste back into the Chamber" to save "what was most valuable." He lugged out his chest, then returned again for a sword, portmanteau, saddle, silver tankard and such truck. Carrying these things away, "If I remember well I had like to be knock'd on the head with something flung out of a window."

Hill's self-serving testimony included the routine admission that he'd gone to sleep with a small fire still alight on his hearth, which some thought started the conflagration. Others suspected foul play, as they had in Jamestown when the old statehouse had burned seven years and nine days earlier. College Master Mungo Ingles bruited the news that Robert Beverley and some others passed the rest of the night "drinking & ranting & carousing." One of them "(but I cannot learn who) was heard to say that if some Thunderbolt of lightning should destroy the Capitol, they might have some hopes of having the Seat of Governmt again at James Town. It's happening at so silent a time of the night, has left us all in the Dark about its cause and nothing but a large field for conjecture to loose it self in."

Nor was that field ever paled, for there were charges of dissembling and cover-up— "as Mr. Commissary gives it out, on purpose to divert peoples eyes." An official investigation failed to discover the fire's cause; Duke of Gloucester Street's western vista framed a gutted ruin where the thick walls stood charred and empty for several years.

The eastern vista presented the newly raised Capitol building, with Queen Anne's royal monogram on the weathervane atop the cupola and a stained-glass rendering of her coat of arms in the round window of the General Court's chamber. Decorations aside, almost every detail of the unique edifice was specified in advance by Nicholson: its H shape, its length of seventy-five feet, the twenty-five-foot interior breadth of each wing and fifteen-foot pitch to the second floor. In conformance with the enabling act, the foundations were four bricks thick to ground level, then in stages the walls became thinner by a half-brick as they rose to the water table, the top of the first floor, and to the cypress-shingled hip roof. (The waist-high water table, so named because its slope shed rainwater, was a course of specially shaped bricks that accommodated the change in thickness from broader foundation footings to thinner walls.)

The reconstructed Capitol (opposite) *stands on a rise at the east end of Duke of Gloucester Street. Destroyed by fire in 1747, the original was replaced by a building of which little is known except that it burned too (in 1832). Surviving records and pictures helped restorers build the first Capitol anew as a centerpiece of the resurrected town.*

Daylight floods the Hall of the House of Burgesses (above left) and the General Court (below), identical chambers save for their distinctive looks. The elected burgesses' plain domain has modest decor dominated by the imposing Speaker's Chair, which was saved from a fire. The box on the table holds a copy of Patrick Henry's famed "Resolves," which contributed to the movement that became a revolution.

The General Court chamber reflects the grandeur of the colony's royally appointed supreme tribunal. It features glass chandelier, raised bench, gallery and paneling painted to resemble marble.

The flagstaff atop the cupola (above right), bearing Queen Anne's coat of arms, awaits her banner, the Great Union flag, which flies nowhere else in the world today.

It had sash windows, not casements which were still more common, and ironwork, glass, paint and stone imported from England. Blithely referred to in the act as singular, the building became plural a few clauses later when it was ordered that "each building" would have flagstone floors. Further, a fifty-foot-long room at "one end of each p[ar]t or side" was specified for the ground floors. Graphically representing the bicameral order of the General Assembly, the building could easily be considered two: "One part or side of which building shall be and is hereby appropriated to the use of the Generall Court & Councill" (whose members sat *ex officio* for life as judges on the colony's supreme bench). The other wing "shall be and is hereby appropriated to the use of the house of Burgesses," the periodically elected legislative body, "and the offices thereto and to no other use or uses wtsoever." In size and layout each half (or single "building" if you will) closely resembled the earlier statehouse in Jamestown. This in turn had copied the prototypical Elizabethan guildhall by presenting to the world its widest side with a central door opening into the main room. Thus keeping tradition, the Capitol's broad "front" faced Duke of Gloucester Street. But as a twin complex, there was nothing like it—in Virginia or anywhere else.

The two parts or buildings were joined by a gallery "raised upon Piazzas." That gallery supported "in the middle thereof a Cupulo to surmount the rest of the building Wch shall have a Clock placed in it and on the top of the sd Cupulo shall be a flag upon occasion." Although the building that emerged was H-shaped, its initial plan appeared otherwise; originally the gallery that formed the bar of the H was to be crossed by an additional gallery. This extra "cross gallery" was abandoned and the main gallery—the bar of the H—further altered at the expense of symmetry. Once intended as a passage between the two *cameras*, it was redesigned as a conference room for joint committees and consequently widened, which nudged its center line to the north. This in turn moved the location of the cupola rising from the gallery's roof, placing it off-center to a man in the street. When an anonymous artist—possibly the traveling English illustrator Mark Catesby—prepared an engraving a generation later, he didn't depict the building from the "front" that faced Duke of Gloucester Street. Rather he portrayed it from the north side to reveal its twin piles and the gallery between them. Was the north side, analogous to the west front of a cathedral, meant to be the most imposing? Even then some gentlemen of taste thought so.

Perhaps with the lesson of the Jamestown statehouse fire in mind, the act had not provided for chimneys. At first there were neither fires nor smoking of tobacco inside, a prohibition that lasted only a few years until the secretary complained that dampness was injuring his precious records. Accordingly, chimneys were soon added so the place could be heated in winter. (Almost inevitably, it seems, the Capitol burned—on January 30, 1747.)

A committee named to oversee the construction had hired Henry Cary to do the work in the spring of 1701. Though he'd already built a Yorktown courthouse, he was required to start on a trial basis for a £50 fee, before he began collecting a salary of £100 a year. His first order of business was to collect materials: 600,000 bricks at 20 shillings a thousand, oyster shells for mortar at 1 shilling 3 pence per hogshead, and hardware worth over £100 from England. The foundation was laid August 7, 1701, six years to the day after the College. By autumn Cary began felling trees and laying lumber by for "fit scantlings sawd of high land white Oak for the Capitol doore Cases and windowe frames."

He was also ordered to get inch-thick pine planks for scaffolding, inch-and-a-quarter-

Governor Edward Nott failed to "season" well and died in 1706, the year after he arrived. His ornate tomb, imported at public expense and erected in Bruton's churchyard, bears the epitaph: "By the Sanctity of his Moralls and the Mildness [,] Prudence and justice of his Administration he was Deservedly Esteemed A Public Blessing while he Lived & when He Dyed a Public Callamity."

thick heart pine for flooring and a miscellany of victuals: 20 barrels of pork, 150 bushels of corn and 20 bushels of peas, all this "for diet for the Workmen." Six of them were brought from England and billeted in a kind of exile since a special bill prohibited the taverns from "entertaining any of them or selling them any drink." Other laborers were recruited locally, including four slaves which Henry Cary bought for £120 from his brother Miles, who was rector of the College, a burgess and clerk for the building committee. When the work was finished, Henry then bought three of the slaves back—at cost. (When the books were balanced *in medias res*, it was found that £3,822 had been spent and the project was over budget.) The Council first sat in its round-ended chamber on the second floor of the west building on October 20, 1704; the burgesses convened in their chamber on the first floor of the east building on April 21, 1705, and the builder's keys to the Capitol were ceremoniously broken on the last day of November.

In terms of time, Williamsburg's first cornerstone was Bruton Parish Church, which also became the first to disappear utterly and rise anew. By 1677 the parish boasted two churches in such sad repair that the vestry sought subscriptions for a new one. Councillor John Page gave sufficient land in Williamsburg for it with a churchyard sixty feet deep in every direction.

An "undertaker" (in that he would undertake a building contract, not consign a cadaver below) agreed to build the new sanctuary for £350. But he found himself in disagreement with two vestrymen and had them arrested. Another undertaker agreed to erect the Jacobean structure for a down payment of £150 cash and "sixty pounds of good sound, merchantable, sweet scented Tobacco and Caske" from every tithable parishioner for three years running. Mr. Rowland Jones, the "first and most esteemed pastor" according to his epitaph, hired on in 1682 at a salary paid in tobacco (or the currency of tobacco notes) and dedicated the new sanctuary two years later. (At about this time deaths were registered for three pounds of tobacco, while the sexton got ten pounds of tobacco for the necessary digging. One could be buried in the chancel for one thousand pounds of weed or five pounds sterling.)

Alexander Spotswood, the next royally appointed governor after Nott, became Williamsburg's second master builder. Born in Tangier, the son of a soldier and a career officer himself, he was hit at the Battle of Blenheim by a cannonball, which he kept as a souvenir. An active and amiable man, after serving here and acquiring vast estates he found a bride in England, then returned to Virginia for the rest of his days. Colonial artist Charles Bridges probably painted this oft-copied portrait.

The new church was a plain brick affair with shallow buttresses, a roof slicked with two barrels of tar, and doors specified to be a foot higher and half-foot wider than the church at Jamestown. Never a very sound building, it required such regular repairs that by 1706 the vestry levied a collection of twenty thousand pounds of tobacco to build anew rather than patch the old. Now the parish fathers sought help from the government as they petitioned: " 'Tis very Apparent [that] the Parishioners are very much straightened & often outed of their places & seats by...allowing room for the frequent resort of strangers, & more particularly at the meetings of the Generall Assemblies; Courts; Councells & other public occasions." Variously waiting upon each other, the men of Bruton Parish and the burgesses in due time agreed that a grander church was needed than the parish could afford, largely because visitors and transient public officials swelled the congregation mightily. In 1710 the Assembly contributed two hundred pounds sterling from duties on liquor and slaves "Towards the building [of] a Church in Williamsburgh And for Making Conveniencys Therein" for royal officials and elected legislators. Further, it was decided that the new church should be designed by a new governor who had only just arrived.

Alexander Spotswood was an affable and able soldier who lacked the connections at court to rise above the rank of colonel. Son of an army surgeon born in Tangier, he entered

Bruton Parish Church (opposite), one of America's oldest Episcopal sanctuaries, again appears much as it did when consecrated in 1715.

The governor's pew (above left) was paid for by Spotswood, who designed the building to accommodate parish members, College students, legislators, government officials and visiting strangers.

Out of sight within the brick tower, a forest of handhewn timbers (above right) supports the spire erected by Benjamin Powell in 1769. A new rope serves the original bell bought for Bruton Church by merchant James Tarpley and cast at Whitechapel Bell Foundry by the man who made Philadelphia's Liberty Bell.

Seen from the west gallery, the nave (below) stretches past high-backed pews resembling those in which Washington and Jefferson knelt to pray. Here a day of "Fasting, Humiliation and Prayer" was observed in 1774 to protest the closing of the Boston harbor after the Tea Party there. In this century Presidents Roosevelt, Johnson and Reagan have heard sermons from the cantilevered pulpit, which is dedicated to the memory of the Reverend James Blair, fifth of the parish's thirty-one rectors.

the army at seventeen and fought at the Battle of Blenheim where he was hit by a cannon-ball, which he kept as a souvenir. Like Nicholson in his first term he was actually lieutenant to an absentee governor who'd been favored by the crown with a sinecure. (Spotswood served from 1710 to 1722 at a yearly salary of £2,000, of which he paid his superior in London, Lord Orkney, £1,200.) Also like Nicholson, he was a man of diverse talents who would leave his mark on the town. If his predecessor had made the plan, this Scot would perfect it by making Duke of Gloucester Street "mathematically streight" and by adorning the city with several outstanding buildings.

Notably he was invited by the burgesses to "take the trouble of laying it out for Enlarging the said Church and building pews" for all officials. The Council recorded that "the Governor was pleased To answer that he thanked the house for the confidence they had in him, that tho he had never been concerned in business of this nature, he would use his best endeavors." Despite the ubiquity of his efforts, he was more of a seat-of-the-pants army engineer than architect; the felicity of his designs arose from a devotion to mathematical order. As a critic later opined, "It would be wrong to say that in designing Bruton Church Spotswood called Geometry to his aid: he practically handed the job over to her."

Spotswood designed the church in the shape of a cross that lay, by tradition, with its altar to the east. His original plan owed its dimensions to simple geometric ratios; he may have started by making one internal diagonal sixty-six feet—the length of a surveyor's chain. But when it came time to build, the plan was altered. Having agreed to pay for twenty-two feet of the building's length himself, Spotswood then informed the burgesses that since visitors would be "Contented with less Room" he would "Diminish the Wings projected for Publick use." These transepts would be open to strangers while the "church" proper, or nave, was to be reserved for parishioners with men seated on the north side and women across the aisle. Students from the College would use the rear gallery. When the Church opened in 1715, the governor's elevated state pew in the chancel was "covered with a canopy" on which his name was "written in gilt letters." (When the Church proved too small, it gained galleries in the transepts, then in 1752 an eastern extension that made the chancel as long as the nave. It also got a tower with steeple and spire at the west end in 1769.)

Meanwhile, Spotswood had been busy elsewhere: enlarging the Gaol; designing the octagonal Magazine, where the colony's arms and ammunition were kept; rebuilding the College; and finishing the governor's residence so grandly that it would henceforth be known—scornfully at first—as the Palace. The Magazine could hardly have been simpler given its elegant octagonal plan: The walls are twenty-four feet high and the roof twenty-four feet more; the diameter of the building, thirty-four feet, is the size of a square whose diagonal is forty-eight feet, or the structure's height.

As the Reverend Hugh Jones wrote, Spotswood also turned his constructive attention to the ruined College: "Since it was burnt down, it has been rebuilt and nicely contrived, altered and adorned by the ingenious Direction of Governor Spotswood." The walls still stood on the original foundations, and they were repaired. To make a more distinguished central entrance, he designed a shallow pavilion below a right-angled pediment. Redesigning the roof, he added a new cupola shorter than the original; now its apex stood sixty-eight feet above the ground, or half the building's length.

Spotswood's crowning architectural work was the Governor's Palace, which had been

Wine barrels again lie beneath the Governor's Palace. In 1781 the building burned, collapsing into the original vaulted cellars, which became crypts for many artifacts and for much physical evidence of the structure's appearance—the pattern of its exterior brickwork, for example.

The Governor's Palace was—
and is again—the apex of this
colonial town. Jefferson, who
lived here when he was the Virginia Commonwealth's second
governor, wrote, "The palace is
not handsome without, but it is
spacious and commodious
within, is prettily situated, and
with the grounds annexed to it,
is capable of being made an elegant seat."

Royal governors received visitors in the privacy of the middle
room (opposite above), *its*
walls again covered with
embossed leather as they were
during Governor Botetourt's
residency from 1768 to 1770.
The gilt "chimney glass" resem-
bles one he owned; the chande-
lier was "standing furniture"
owned by the colony.

A bridge in the Chinese style
(opposite below) *spans the*
"canal," one of the many ameni-
ties that Governor Spotswood
designed—and paid for out of
his own pocket when colonial
representatives deemed them too
extravagant.

A wrought-iron gate (left)
bearing the monogram "GR,"
George Rex, frames the wing
containing the ballroom and
supper room, an addition built
more than thirty years after the
handsome house. A short dis-
tance from the path, a dozen
tall native yaupon hollies stand
like sentinels; the so-called
"Twelve Apostles" are named
after trees found in contempo-
rary English gardens.

Vignette outside the Palace supper room door: Myriad details enrich this colonial city incarnate. Williamsburg's restorers decided that as in colonial times, steps must be made of imported Portland stone; that a railing must be wrought iron with a finial of brass. Even the path shows clever fidelity: Early gentry paved their paths with marl, the crumbled fossil oystershell found in ancient deposits. When marl became scarce recently, a landscaper suggested spreading new shell, then crushing it with lawn rollers. This cheap substitute can hardly be told from the real marl.

a gleam in every gubernatorial eye for decades. A century earlier Sir Thomas Gates had built an official residence of wood, and a brick one followed until it was sold in the 1670s when Sir William Berkeley lived at his own estate, Green Spring. Thereafter, resident governors received housing allowances for rented lodgings while London prodded them to build an official house which the burgesses insisted they couldn't afford. Nicholson had made no progress in the matter during his first term in Jamestown, but during his second term in the new capital he persuaded the Council to buy a sixty-three-acre parcel at the head of the broadest cross street. Still, royal and local authorities didn't agree on a way to pay for the residence until Governor Nott had arrived in 1705 and a duty was levied on imported slaves and liquor, like that instituted to pay for the Capitol. The Council invited Nott to design the residence in 1706, but the man was not "seasoning" well in the new country that was hard on immigrants, even aristocratic ones. In June an enabling act was approved by the Assembly, in August Nott's personal constitution gave out and he was buried in Bruton's churchyard.

This act authorized £3,000 for a two-story brick building fifty-four feet long and forty-eight wide with "convenient cellars underneath and one vault." Specifying sash windows and a slate roof, the act further called for a kitchen and stable and directed that "in all other respects the said house be built and finished according to the discretion of the overseer"— Henry Cary again. He turned out to be somewhat liberal in his interpretation of what constituted an overseer's duties when no royal representative was in the land to oversee him. After spending more than the allotted funds, he moved his family into the premises and went so far as to charge the colony with their victualing.

In any event, when Spotswood arrived on the scene in 1710 he found the residence insufficient and took it upon himself to oversee extraordinary improvements to bring it up to what he considered a reasonable level of elegance. He ended up paying for such amenities as gardens and "canal" out of his own pocket, though arguments over who should foot the rest of the bill went on and on. Nevertheless, when completed in 1720, the Palace was the grandest residence in the colonies. (Like the Church, the Palace would grow even grander over the years. Extensive repair work was completed and the interior most likely remodeled about 1751; a new wing containing a ballroom and supper room was added by 1754.)

The "cittie of Williamsburgh" was coming into its own. As Beverley wrote, "There are two fine Publick Buildings in this Country, which are the most Magnificent of any in America," the Capitol and College. The Reverend Hugh Jones added the Palace to the list: "These buildings are justly reputed the best in all *English America*, and are exceeded by few of their kind in *England*." (He may be excused the hyperbole; he could not have seen Blenheim Castle, which was begun the year the Palace was first finished.) By the end of Spotswood's term in 1722, the town of 220 acres administered a strapping colony with a population approaching 90,000, and it dominated the local landscape. Where primeval forest lately stood, one could climb any of three cupolas—in Capitol, College or Palace—and see both rivers bounding a peninsula bereft of trees which had been felled for firewood and lumber. By 1716 it had boasted that pantheon of artifice, a theater, the first one west of the ocean. Yet the town still showed remnants of its natural beginnings. If governors decreed a "mathematically streight" street, nature declared it could not yet be level: a carriage negotiating the stately distance between College and Capitol would disappear twice from view, so deep were the remaining ravines.

A Capital Becomes a Town

This capital never lived by politics alone. Its builders made a place of commerce and habitation too, with homes abutting stores or workshops and buildings that served several purposes. Thus, all in a row on Duke of Gloucester Street today (opposite) stand, left to right, Russell House, Margaret Hunter Shop millinery, the Golden Ball silversmith, Unicorn's Horn apothecary and its twin, John Carter's Store, and Raleigh Tavern (partially visible). As colonists built deftly, so did their successors (left): Five of these are "reconstructions" built anew on original sites; only Hunter's millinery is a "restoration," a surviving eighteenth-century building renovated in our time.

Outbuildings behind the George Wythe House now serve diverse domestic arts: weaving cloth, making baskets, smoking meat. Colonial Virginians did a brisk business exporting hams to Europe, where they were called delicacies because—so the lore went—pigs that roamed free in Virginia woods fattened on wild acorns and tasted best. The smokehouse door in the fore-ground bears the householder's monogram, "GW," traced in nailheads. Buildings in colonial Virginia displayed a strict "hier-archy" in terms of decorations and architectural detail: Homes were adorned as richly as the owner could afford; kitchens near the house had poorer paint and fewer details; work buildings farthest away had none at all.

*A*s the May Day orator had predicted, "friendly cohabitation" of academe and government combined to make "such a Town as may retrieve the reputation of our Country." The College attracted students, masters, servants and merchants who sought their custom. The government seat drew a year-round population of civil servants, along with seasonal tides of legislators and men seeking influence and opportunity along with those bound to them by blood, business or bond. As the Capitol rose, lesser structures multiplied—dwellings that like as not served the dweller's livelihood be he artisan, hosteler, scholar or jack-of-several-trades. These buildings were raised by skilled men, who borrowed English design traditions and later found general plans and fine details alike in printed manuals brought from England. To suit the new place they bent these Old World notions into an architecture that simply didn't exist elsewhere.

On many levels this architecture was a marriage—shotgun perhaps or one of convenience—between substance and style. It joined English forms and traditions with native materials like "heart" pine, superbly straight-grained and everlasting wood cut from the center of trees that had grown slowly for centuries in the Tidewater's dense forests. It suited not only Virginia's climate, with high-ceilinged rooms and one-room-deep plans that fostered ventilation, but also the social lives and mores of its new client-inhabitants. As Hugh Jones wrote twenty-five years after Williamsburg's founding: "Here, as in other parts, they build with brick, but most commonly with timber...cased with feather-edged plank [unplaned boards], painted with white lead and oil, covered with shingles of cedar, etc. tarred over at first; with a passage generally through the middle of the house for an airdraught in summer. Thus their houses are lasting, dry, and warm in winter, and cool in summer; especially if there be windows enough to draw the air. Thus they dwell comfortably, genteely, pleasantly, and plentifully in this delightful, healthful, and (I hope) thriving city of Williamsburg."

The developing architecture reflected an evolving society in ways both huge and subtle. Since full two-story homes were taxed more heavily than ones with lofts, builders learned to get the most out of attic spaces by changing the roof slant: Instead of a plain peaked roof with dormers, for instance, they adapted the Dutch or gambrel roof which had two pitches: on the upper part a very shallow slope, on the lower part a nearly vertical slant. It contained almost as much space inside as a full second story but qualified for the lesser tax rate. As both the economy and social order became dependent on black slavery, the architecture developed ways of keeping the slaves apart. Domestic work came to be performed in detached dependencies—kitchens, dairies and the like—outside the homes of owners who paradoxically felt uneasy at the growing numbers of racially distinct people on whom their economy and comfort depended. Outbuildings also left the house free of cooking odors and heat.

The new architecture did not spring full-born from the brow of some designing Zeus. Instead it was firmly rooted in the tradition of English buildings both humble and grand, though at first it stressed pure utility. The earliest settlers at Jamestown probably built with mud and timber, using rafters cut from saplings to hold their thatched gable roofs aloft. No matter how humble the structure, its single room was called the "great room" or "hall." One of the long walls was broken by an off-center door, while the short wall farthest from it had

Clad in colonial garb, two modern Colonial Williamsburgers (opposite) pass the time of morning over a porch rail—as the Hunter sisters doubtless did after Jane married a wigmaker and spinster Margaret bought this millinery shop by 1774. Near the Governor's Palace stables (above), a coachman drives the blue phaeton. Facing Market Square, the St. George Tucker House (below) wears the red-and-white colors that Tucker himself ordered in 1798, according to a painter's contract found by scholars.

It takes two men to work a lathe in the Anthony Hay Shop (opposite), typically a journeyman or master wielding the chisels to carve the wood and a muscular apprentice to drive the "great wheel." Some interior balustrades were perhaps turned better by Restoration carpenters than their predecessors. For example, the stair to the reconstructed Capitol cupola (left) was built with lavish care and attention to detail, even though it was never meant to be seen by visitors or anyone but the lad who tends the flag.

A wealth of fine detail adorns the better homes, and none more than the house that "undertaker" (eighteenth-century parlance for "builder") Richard Taliaferro is said to have designed for his daughter when she married burgess George Wythe. The outer edge of each stair tread (opposite) has nosing with double molding; each ornamental "bracket" displays a graceful triple curve.

Palace inventories noted the use of delft tile in fireplaces (left) and excavators found many pieces in the building's cellar hole. The tin-glazed earthenware decorations, their scenes painted with cobalt before firing, were supplemented with new tiles of identical style to decorate the reconstructed building.

a hearth and exterior chimney. The floor was packed dirt, the walls daubed clay though some walls would soon boast painted plaster. A flat ceiling was introduced to serve as the floor above for the simplest of attics reached by a ladder.

The first grand house in Virginia was Governor Berkeley's Green Spring, built on an English model in the 1640s. Called by his wife "the only tollerable place for a Governour," it was among other things the spot where Berkeley hanged some of Bacon's followers and received the royal commissioners sent to investigate the rebellion that blotted his long record of service. (The king's agents would see him recalled to England—after Lady Berkeley saw to it that they left the estate in a coach driven by the local hangman.) The house burned and was replaced by an even grander one that stretched almost a hundred feet along a riverside rise. This one had two rows of dormers and four downstairs rooms (plus a wing probably containing a kitchen). The front door, set dead center, opened into an almost square "hall," the most public and ceremonial room in the house, perhaps in the colony.

In 1649, less than a decade after the original Green Spring was built, Arthur Allen raised an equally impressive house across the James River. Inherited by his son, a Speaker of the House of Burgesses, it was seized by insurgents in the 1676 rebellion, and though their leader may never have darkened its door, it was henceforth known as Bacon's Castle. Shaped like an unbalanced cross, its broad arms contained both the largest room belowstairs, the hall, and a less formal, slightly smaller chamber. The shallow arms, which were the home's front and back, accommodated stairs in the rear and in front a closed "porch" upstairs and down. Fully a century later any small room on the second floor above an entrance would be known as the "porch chamber," even when there was no longer a protruding porch per se.

Baronial country houses aside, by century's end and Williamsburg's birth the plainest home was still very simple indeed: one oblong room with a loft under the peaked roof reached by a ladder. The outside door was still placed off-center on one of the long walls, the fireplace and outside chimney in the middle of the far short wall. This kind of building could grow, as the house bought by General Court clerk and entrepreneur Benjamin Waller later tripled in size from one-room simplicity to genteel complexity. Waller bought a large tract of land east of the Capitol and sold off the lots piecemeal as a distinct new district of the town. The lot he took for himself had a basic house on it, which then gained additions.

Even as most Williamsburg houses became more sophisticated, the most simple and useful form would abide or often return in such ubiquitous outbuildings as kitchens. Unadorned, the basic building would return in a little bootmaker's shop that would one day stand on Duke of Gloucester Street, a house big enough for two or three men to "stick to their lasts" by the windows.

In one early stage of development, the simple building—whether workshop, store, tavern or most likely a dwelling with a commercial use as well—acquired an inside partition. Thus the Virginia yeoman entered a narrow "passage" containing a stair to the loft above. The "hall" remained the major downstairs room, still boasting a fireplace on the far short wall. Another practical design, this one never quite vanished either, but was adapted for use into the twentieth century.

During Spotswood's term, one John Brush paid £4 to buy his freedom from apprenticeship in London. He was admitted as a journeyman into the Gunmaker's Company, a guild, whence he made his way to Virginia. Perhaps he came at the behest of the governor

Governor Sir William Berkeley's Green Spring, long a paradigm of the grand Virginia home, intrigued Benjamin Latrobe, later architect of the United States Capitol. He sketched it in 1796 and wrote: The building's "inconvenience and deformity are more powerful advocates for its destruction," though "the antiquity of the old house...ought to plead" for its renovation. In this he anticipated the spirit of historical preservation for which Colonial Williamsburg would become famous. Berkeley, who governed Virginia from 1641 until 1677 (save during England's Commonwealth), was not such a conserving soul. He tidied up after Bacon's Rebellion so brutally that Charles II complained: "That old fool has hang'd more Men in that naked Country" than the king "done for the Murther of his Father."

who found that "the great part of the Arms in the Magazine and at the Governor's House were much out of repair and unfitt for Service." It was Brush who refurbished them as "Publick Armorer," keeper of the new Magazine and a signal member of the community. In 1717 he acquired a choice Williamsburg lot: the one closest to the governor's residence facing onto Palace Green.

Looking ahead, Brush built his chimneys at the rear, anticipating the addition of more rooms into the yard toward the separate kitchen, "necessary" outbuilding (i.e. privy) and other dependencies. The armorer's residence also embraced some new ideas and spaces. As he built it, three rooms probably graced the ground floor: the centered front door opened into the passage with its stair; to one side was the all-purpose hall for formal entertaining (now called the parlor), and to the other side was the new "chamber" (today's library), a more intimate room where the family took their meals and leisure.

At about the same time that Brush was building his house, William Robertson was raising his own on nearby Nicholson Street. Clerk of the Council, gentleman and factotum for a succession of governors, he kept in step with new style—or perhaps barely astride of changing fashion. Looking backward, he borrowed a jutting porch like the one at Bacon's Castle for his otherwise cubical dwelling. Looking forward, he built a gracious curiosity that boasted a stair passage and three rooms downstairs, all of them heated by fireplaces serving a single chimney. In addition to the more formal hall (parlor) and informal chamber (small parlor), it had a new amenity called the dining room.

About 1726 the Nicholson Street property was bought by John Randolph, later the only Virginian ever knighted and an eminent man of law whose son Peyton would become president of the First Continental Congress and whose other son John "the Tory" would return to England on the eve of the Revolution. Such a distinguished family required a grander domicile than even the Council's clerk, and the two-story house that Robertson built gained an extension that joined it to a one-and-a-half-story dwelling on the next lot. The work was done with such notable care that the beaded boards on the new wing's facade lined up with those of the older cube. A visitor had to look twice to see that the chimneys didn't match.

In 1727, by the time the Randolphs were firmly ensconced, Sir William Gooch came to govern an increasingly prosperous and peaceful dominion. The colony's shipping was no longer beset by pirates; Spotswood had seen to that when an expedition he'd mounted trapped Edward Teach (more commonly known as Blackbeard) whose head was nailed to the bowsprit of the ship that brought his henchmen to Williamsburg for trial and hanging. The Indians were reasonably tractable on both sides of the Alleghenies (until the French would foment them some years later). The tobacco business was hampered by overproduction more than anything else, and locally grown food was plentiful. The old adage that a mother should not get too fond of her baby was almost forgotten as more children began to survive infancy than perished. Periodic famine was no longer a living memory and family life among the gentry was more gracious. The continent's first theater had been built on Palace Green by one William Livingston, sometime dancing master and musician, who briefly staged plays by Shakespeare and other entertainments. Virginia was coming of age.

As in England and Europe, most people had more of the amenities once considered luxuries and more leisure. People of middling circumstances were on the rise and Gooch's twenty-two-year administration seemed a period of prosperity and peace. (This notwith-

By the middle of the eighteenth century, Virginia's gentry coveted domestic "decencies" both old and new to augment the "necessities" in their homes. Furnished again as the nonpareil colonial lawyer might have had it, Peyton Randolph's library (above left) now features an "easy chair" covered with rare needlework upholstery from the previous century. It also boasts a painted floorcloth and two "book presses" like the six cases that held his treasured tomes. (Randolph had such a fine library that upon his death in 1775, his cousin Jefferson bought it; Jefferson's books in turn became the core of the Library of Congress.) The Brush-Everard House dining room (above right) reflects aspiring taste and amenities for "polite living": the fireplace with marble surround, the floorcloth and, over the mantel, allegorical figures of the "Four Seasons"— glass transfers—set in a carved gilt frame. The revolving brass plate stand, another luxury item, was made in the 1760s and imported from England. Everard's parlor (below) has Venetian blinds but, in keeping with fashion, no curtains. When not in use, the English mahogany side chairs would stand against the walls.

Handsomely paneled with red oak from floor to ceiling, this Peyton Randolph House bedchamber (above) is unique in all Virginia, where most walls were plastered or paneled in pine and then painted. The mahogany chairs were made in Williamsburg about 1770; the dressing table in the Virginia Piedmont about the same time. The Randolph parlor (below) has a pair of elaborately carved and gilded rococo looking glasses and a Wilton carpet imported from England. Set for tea, the table bears a Chelsea tea service like one Betty Randolph bequeathed in her will.

standing his foray to the Colombian port of Cartagena in 1740. Leading four hundred Virginians against the Spanish stronghold in the War of Jenkins's Ear, Gooch was hit by a cannonball that passed between his ankles. Adding insult to injury, he caught a fever. The expedition was ill-starred from the start; it was to have been led by former governor Spotswood, who died while embarking at Annapolis.) More thought, however collective or unaware, went into designing the family context, the home. Houses came to be more carefully and artfully planned and, as a result, more distinctly different from other buildings.

Conversely, workshops and commercial buildings became distinct too. On Duke of Gloucester Street, Dr. Archibald Blair built a store that was soon purchased by William Prentis and his stockholders. This handsome establishment, Prentis & Company, acquired "neat and plain" features. For one, down to the water table the bricks were laid in Flemish bond to make an appealing checkerboard of red rectangles and gray-glazed squares. Between brick courses, the shell mortar joints were struck with straight lines to make the walls appear more uniform. Unglazed bricks chosen for doors and window margins and building corners had their surfaces rubbed perfectly flat. The jack arch above each opening was pieced together out of specially tapered bricks to serve the same purpose as keystones in older arches—to form a downward-pointing wedge that could not fall out. To heighten the tidy appearance, these finely finished bricks had the very thinnest joints, paper-thin white lines of pure lime-paste mortar.

Unlike residences which sat broadside on their lots, Prentis's store and many others presented their narrow, gabled ends to the street. This practice evolved for the sake of common-sense practicality. English experience had proved that commercial buildings virtually filled their lots. With only the narrowest of alleys running beneath the overhanging eaves of crowded buildings, little light filtered down so there was little use for windows. Further, inside a shop the space for shelves to hold a merchant's wares was far too precious to surrender to windows along the long walls. There was room enough for windows on either side of the main door at the front, which offered passersby a look at the goods for sale. In the triangular gable above, another door opened directly into the loft where more goods were stored and an apprentice slept at night, perhaps with an ear alert for the sound of burglars.

The main room downstairs took most of the space, in keeping with plans provided by the most popular technical manual, Joseph Moxon's *Mechanick Exercises.* In short order this borrowed plan would be amended—in the Nicolson Store closer to the Capitol and in the twin stores which the brothers Carter raised. Robert sold general merchandise while James Carter, a physician and apothecary, vended medicines and herbal cures under the sign of the Unicorn's Horn. Their three-story brick building contained two complexes, mirror images of each other. Each front salesroom had a bay window overlooking the street. The back "counting room," boasting the only fireplace, served as office and living room for the family that slept in chambers abovestairs. As was the pervasive practice by now, cooking and other domestic tasks were performed in outbuildings.

In 1738 Henry Wetherburn, operator of the Raleigh Tavern, bought a lot on Duke of Gloucester Street across the last ravine from the Capitol. Within a few years he built a tavern at the eastern side of his lot, an intentionally commercial structure that resembled a fine house of its day. This rectangular building had four rooms on the ground floor, plus the passage. Patrons entered through a door that centered the welcoming facade with two windows

Like many colonial buildings, the Wythe House (even from the rear) displays a stately symmetry based on simple geometry and the repetition of plane dimensions. The facade is as wide as the chimneys are tall. The height of the roof equals the distance from the centerpoint at ground level to each cornice. The height of the roof edge above the water table is the same as the depth of the house. Below the roof, the facade is twice as wide as high—a double square, one of the tidy forms based on neat ratios that Georgian builders favored. Also popular was the "root-two rectangle," in which a square was enlarged by taking its diagonal as its new length.

on each side. The four rooms boasted fireplaces set diagonally in the corners; these hearths shared two interior chimneys. Upstairs the bedchambers, where guests slept three or four to a bed, also had the luxury of fireplaces. A front room, too narrow for anything but a servant's cot and chamber pots, was still called the "porch chamber."

The new tavern featured a jerkinhead, or gable roof shortened at each end by a sloping face. This was covered by courses of juniper shingles riven by hand, their butt ends rounded to retard curling and splitting. It had sash windows with lead weights and applewood pulleys. It had sawn weatherboards, not clapboards (which were split from sections of oak log). Planed smooth for appearance sake, these boards were "beaded"—their lower edges grooved and rounded with a molding plane—once perhaps to prevent splitting and possibly to shed the rain better, but now primarily for looks. Out back were a dairy and the inevitable kitchen which featured an unusual room for sleeping, no doubt for the chattel help.

Wetherburn took advantage of all opportunities. When another tavern keeper died, he married the widow—not once but in two instances, thus acquiring his competitors' properties, which included the Raleigh Tavern. Enhanced by the practicality of his sworn affections, his business boomed. His clientele included not only travelers and transients attending the Public Times, but also College scholars and gentry, the new aristocrats of burgesses and Council members. The latter kept impressive part-time residences in the capital for when the General Court was in session and the Assembly convened but lived in distant manors for the rest of the year. Flush with success and eager for more, in the 1750s Wetherburn expanded his facilities by adding a wing to the west. It was not enough to have the Bull's Head Room to serve private dinners and "clubs" of men who met for an evening of food, drink,

For all its Georgian grace, the Wythe House is a practical place. Its serviceable kitchen (left)—located in a separate building, as was the norm—boasts a huge fireplace and few decorations other than edible ones, now made daily during cooking demonstrations. Flooring in the house's central passage (above), *made of heart pine planks from the Tidewater's centuries-old trees, still resists wear after more than two hundred years of use. Doors front and back in the passage improve air circulation.*

gaming and conversation. Evidently hiring the man who'd built for him originally, he commissioned the city's largest public reception chamber, the Great Room that spanned twenty-five feet and could accommodate a hundred revelers at subscription balls.

Spanning such a distance required an expensive system of heavy beams and girders and a trussed roof. Like the floorboards of heart pine, the main beams were handhewn with adze and broadax. Planks and joists from squared logs were cut in a sawpit with a two-man pit saw, one sawyer standing in a trench and his partner above him on a raised trestle. Like as not the heaviest work was done at the carpenter's yard: the beams hewn, the joists sawed and planed, the mortices notched with long straight chisels, the tenons carved to fit into them. Then all the members were pieced together and their ends marked with easily cut Roman numerals—as amended by the carpenter's tradition. (Eleven was VVI, not XI, which upside down could be misread as nine.) This way the frame could be built wherever the carpenter liked, then dismantled and carted off for rebuilding on the client's ground; indeed colonial carpenters served customers as far away as the Caribbean by building here and shipping prefabricated houses to the wood-poor islands.

In 1754 John Palmer, bursar of the College, built a new brick house on the main street lot closest to the Capitol, a lot he and others had occupied before. Nearly twenty years earlier, a jeweler named Alexander Kerr incurred the city's official ire by "setting a Brick-Kiln upon the Capitol Bounds." Thus the Council "*Ordered* That the Directors of the city of *Wb* take care to remove the Nuisance." Kerr nonetheless built "a well finished Brick House" with "a convenient Store, Coach-House, Stables and other Office-Houses." In the late 1740s Palmer moved in, then one night in 1754 rushed out when another of Williamsburg's plaguing fires wrecked the neighborhood. It destroyed the store where it began and spread to two dwellings, causing damages rising beyond £5,000.

Palmer replaced his house with a new one of brick that resembled the town houses of London and Bristol in its urbane asymmetry. The front door stood atop a short flight of stone steps at the left of twin windows. The door opened into a deep passage, with the stairs rising at the back of the house. This was a "double pile" home, one two rooms deep. On the ground floor the hall and parlor each had a diagonal fireplace which shared a single chimney. Outside, the proud facade rose a full two stories from the water table to a steeper, taller roof than the colonial norm. At ground level, the basement windows were guarded with wooden bars. Once the house was raised, workmen failed to fill in the widely spaced gaps in the brickwork where the scaffolding had been anchored, leaving "putlog holes" which birds nested in.

Within a year of the fire, Palmer's peer and Virginia's ranking legal scholar, George Wythe (pronounced "with"), took a wife in Elizabeth Taliaferro. Her father, Richard, was a planter and notably a builder of sufficient reputation to design and construct the new ballroom and supper room wing of the Governor's Palace. It is thought that he raised the splendid double-pile house facing Palace Green, which he then offered to the newlyweds with the provision that it pass to their children at their death, or to his other grandchildren if they died without issue. In effect, his wedding present was life tenancy in the house that became one of the most celebrated in Williamsburg for both its elegant architecture and its enlightened occupant.

This was a builder's building, one most likely intended to prove Taliaferro's competence to the world as well as his affection for his daughter. The facade exemplified the new

This fireplace at Wetherburn's Tavern was apparently altered into its present, unusual configuration in the 1780s by Williamsburg brickmason Humphrey Harwood, perhaps to improve its draft.

colonial style: balanced, symmetrical and geometric. The imposing double door opened into a central stair passage leading to another double door at the rear which opened onto the gardens. Four commodious rooms—the formal hall, family parlor, dining room, and professor's study—graced the first floor and each was served by an ample hearth. Upstairs were four bedchambers, one of them often occupied by resident students and eminent guests in later years. (The Wythes lived long, but, sad to say, Elizabeth died childless and the widower came to a sorry end. He died in 1806—almost certainly from coffee laced with arsenic by a grand-nephew intent on getting his estate. George lingered long enough to disinherit the venal kinsman who went scot-free because the only witness to his crime was a slave and thus could not testify in court. But these events happened in Richmond a half century after Williamsburg's architectural flowering.)

Williamsburg still had its debunkers of course, like itinerant clergyman Andrew Burnaby who visited the city in the late 1750s and damned it with faint praise: "Although the houses are of wood, covered with shingles, and but indifferently built, the whole makes a handsome appearance. . . . The governor's palace, indeed, is tolerably good, one of the best upon the continent; but the church, the prison, and the other buildings, are all of them extremely indifferent. The streets are not paved, and are consequently very dusty, the soil hereabouts consisting chiefly of sand: however, the situation of Williamsburg has one advantage, which few or no places in these lower parts have; that of being free from mosquitoes. Upon the whole, it is an agreeable residence; there are ten or twelve gentlemen's families constantly residing in it, besides merchants and tradesmen: and at the times of the assemblies, and general courts, it is crowded with the gentry of the country: on those occasions there are balls and other amusements; but as soon as the business is finished, they return to their plantations; and the town is in a manner deserted."

For most, however, it seemed a capital town. Witness the rise in real estate values: Robert "King" Carter (whose nickname reflected his grand manner and regal three-hundred-thousand-acre domain) left a lot on Palace Green to a son whose estate sold it to a London merchant in 1746 for £104. The next year apothecary Kenneth McKenzie bought it for £224, then sold it in 1751 for £537—doubtless with the substantial improvement of a double-pile house which Governor Robert Dinwiddie used while the Palace underwent extensive repairs. Two years later the government sold it for only £450 to Robert Carter Nicholas who turned a neat profit of £200 in 1761. He sold the place to his cousin Robert Carter as a home away from Nomini Hall, the plantation where Philip Vickers Fithian would teach Carter's children and keep a diary that became famous centuries later.

Further downtown in the commercial district near the Capitol end of the main street, a lot went for £350 in 1760. Ten years later it was bought for £600 by James Anderson, the public armorer who owned an adjacent lot and must have seen the writing of revolution on the wall. Quite soon he began throwing up a warren of forges—five connected shops before he was done—to produce nails, gun mounts and other ironwork useful to an army. While he laid stout wooden sills on brick foundations, his walls were most likely covered with rough boards; as an architect Anderson was something of a throwback. He built on the old plan: four walls with a loft and peaked roof overhead. The noises of war were loud in the land, and gracious Williamsburg, a century of evolved architecture notwithstanding, could still employ forms as simple as those found in the colony's rude beginnings.

Commercial purposes prompted innovative design: Wetherburn's Tavern had the largest public room in Williamsburg, thanks to clever bracing of the ceiling beams. Sometimes the scene of subscription balls, the Great Room was expensively furnished and generally reserved for private functions.

Set sideways on Duke of Gloucester Street, Prentis Store (below) makes efficient use of both its lot and its interior space. Front windows admit light while displaying choice wares; long, windowless walls hold storage shelves.

Apothecaries and surgeons (above left) also sought off-the-street custom; one practitioner in town is known to have owned a human skeleton to enhance anatomical study—or perhaps to display his erudition.

The wigmaker (above right) served a wide clientele. The rarest wig, such as one ordered by Governor Botetourt for £60, was made of "virgin white" human hair that had never been bleached or dyed. Tradesmen and burgesses favored brown and gray perukes, each one made by hand to fit the customer's head.

Signs of the times emphasize visual symbols, since many colonial folk could not read. Thus (clockwise from far left), the barber displays a wig on its stand; Hartwell Perry, an innkeeper of good repute, hangs a rebus of his Christian name; John Greenhow displays a ship to stress that his store carries imported goods; a pork vendor advertises his cured wares with an iron cutout.

The Lives of Williamsburg

While Virginia remained a colony, this capital knew vibrant vitality: gentlemen betting fortunes on blooded horses racing head-to-head, and common folk plying commonplace crafts to serve domestic needs. Such doings come again to the pretty city, whether during each autumn's renewed tradition of the Colonial Fair with its specially vigorous activity (opposite) or day-to-day behind the Wythe House (left), where dexterous hands weave wicker baskets from slender oaken splints.

America's first playhouse opened on Palace Green, where colonial Virginians attended plays by Shakespeare and others. A second theater, near the Capitol, announced the New World debut of London's hit The Beggar's Opera, which a modern company would present here in robust manner two centuries later.

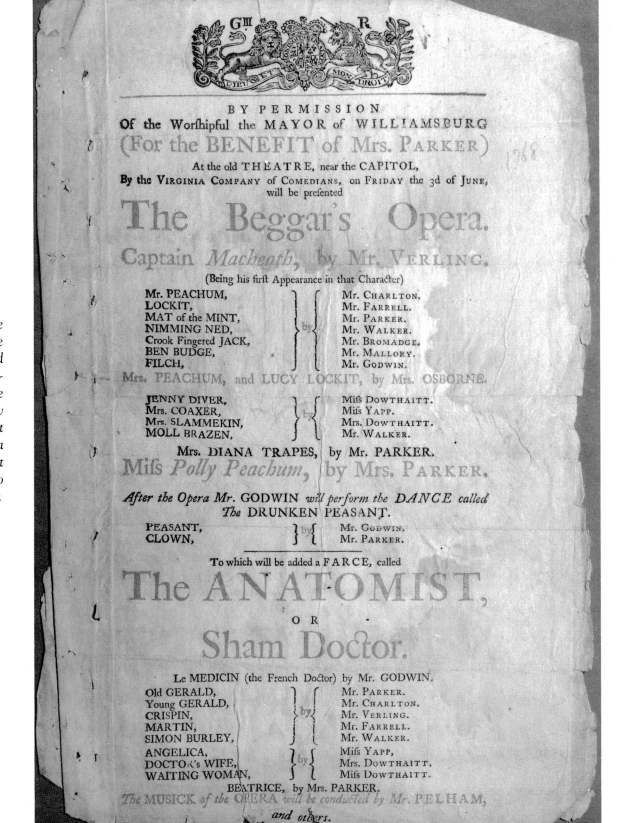

BY PERMISSION
Of the Worshipful the MAYOR of WILLIAMSBURG
(FOR the BENEFIT of Mrs. PARKER)
At the old THEATRE, near the CAPITOL,
By the VIRGINIA COMPANY of COMEDIANS, on FRIDAY the 3d of JUNE,
will be presented

The Beggar's Opera.

Captain *Macheath*, by Mr. VERLING.

(Being his first Appearance in that Character)

Mr. PEACHUM,	Mr. CHARLTON,
LOCKIT,	Mr. FARRELL.
MAT of the MINT,	Mr. PARKER.
NIMMING NED,	Mr. WALKER.
Crook Fingered JACK,	Mr. BROMADGE.
BEN BUDGE,	Mr. MALLORY.
FILCH,	Mr. GODWIN.

Mrs. PEACHUM, and LUCY LOCKIT, by Mrs. OSBORNE.

JENNY DIVER,	Miss DOWTHAITT.
Mrs. COAXER,	Miss YAPP.
Mrs. SLAMMEKIN,	Mrs. DOWTHAITT.
MOLL BRAZEN,	Mr. WALKER.

Mrs. DIANA TRAPES, by Mr. PARKER.

Miss *Polly Peachum*, by Mrs. PARKER.

After the Opera Mr. GODWIN will perform the DANCE called
The DRUNKEN PEASANT.

PEASANT,	Mr. GODWIN.
CLOWN,	Mr. PARKER.

To which will be added a FARCE, called

The ANATOMIST,

OR

Sham Doctor.

Le MEDICIN (the French Doctor) by Mr. GODWIN.

Old GERALD,	Mr. PARKER.
Young GERALD,	Mr. CHARLTON.
CRISPIN,	Mr. VERLING.
MARTIN,	Mr. FARRELL.
SIMON BURLEY,	Mr. WALKER.
ANGELICA,	Miss YAPP.
DOCTOR's WIFE,	Mrs. DOWTHAITT.
WAITING WOMAN,	Miss DOWTHAITT.

BEATRICE, by Mrs. PARKER.
The MUSICK of the OPERA will be conducted by Mr. PELHAM,
and others.

*T*he colonial capital became a metropolis in form and function if not in size, the epi-center of Virginia if the home of only two thousand souls. Preeminently and inevitably a place of politics, and mecca for everyone having business with the government, the capital was nevertheless a civil, social and economic community as well as a collection of buildings. What then of the life of the town? Or rather its many lives? And what role did Williamsburg come to play in the drama of a new nation's birth?

Williamsburg was the precinct of scholars and scoundrels, of gentlewomen and slaves, of indentured servants working off the price of their passage to the New World through years of service to masters who had bought their certificates of indenture. There were gentlemen whose lust for games of chance cost them fortunes; fortune hunters who thrived by investing more daring than capital; Capitol clerks and officials who saw their public duty as a means for private gain; gainsayers unwilling to let Britain call every shot who resisted such measures as the ban on farmers raising sheep for local wool; sheepish debtors whose kin brought them delicacies and firewood to wile away their prison terms; wily innkeepers who accommodated guests three to a bed; lawyers who had trained at London's Inns of Court; courtly thespians who staged such imported dramas as *Richard III* and *The Beggar's Opera* at the colonies' first theater on Palace Green and then at the Play House near the Capitol; a church musician who became the jailer at £40 a year to augment his organist's income of £25; printers who served as postmasters, assuring their publications a wider circulation; a black preacher with the engaging name of Gowan Pamphlet. Severally and separately, they made a town.

The center of their city was central to everything except politics (which had its nexus at the Capitol). Here stood the Magazine beside the field where the militia mustered, and where revelry and bonfires celebrated royal births, coronations and the arrival of the crown's new governors. The Customs House was also here. A James City County courthouse stood nearby across Francis Street until it was replaced by one on Duke of Gloucester Street that served both county and city. Misdemeanors and civil disputes were settled in this edifice; burgesses were elected on its steps as freeholders cast their votes aloud for all to hear before balloting became a secret act. Near its portals miscreants found swift justice at the whipping post, stocks and pillories. (Since a felon could lose an ear for theft, a man who parted with one in a tavern brawl often came to court to seek a writ proving he wasn't maimed by judge's order.)

Market Square itself was self-evidently named. Governor Nicholson planned its use, which the city charter ratified in 1722, designating Wednesdays and Saturdays as market days. Farmers and vendors gathered to sell food and goods of all sorts—first in rude stalls, later in a two-story building of some rough dignity. Slaves and land were also auctioned here (and at the Exchange between the Capitol and Raleigh Tavern which dealt in tobacco and livestock as well). Here too occurred the three-day fairs mandated by the city fathers to start on April 23 and December 12 each year. Swine roamed the streets and fowl ranged free (fences required by law did more to keep animals *out* than anything in), yet human affairs were actively and strictly regulated by government in the eighteenth century. Witness the all-important taverns, institutions of singular significance in a town whose population

Raleigh Tavern, once owned by cabinetmaker Anthony Hay and frequented by George Washington, boasts the famed Apollo Room (above). Here Thomas Jefferson "danced with the fair Belinda"; students from the College founded Phi Beta Kappa in 1776; men of boisterous business and politics met for diverse purposes.

A table in the fireplace corner of the gentlemen's reception room (below) awaits patrons given to an eighteenth-century addiction: gambling—whether on cards, dice (sometimes loaded), a horse's speed or cock's ferocity.

A bar cage (left), open as if for business, again secures the Raleigh's stock of spirits. In colonial Virginia, local courts regulated the taverns, or "ordinaries," by deciding who could operate them and who could be served. All prices—for drink, room, board and even a horse's keep—were set by law each year and proprietors who overcharged faced severe penalties. Today the Raleigh invites guests to drink only from history's cup; for real potables and meals served in colonial style, visitors patronize operating taverns.

An inventory of Anthony Hay's worldly goods suggests his tavern had the finest appointments, such as this matched basin and bottle of Worcester porcelain (above). Though guests slept three and four to a bed, they dined with silver-mounted cutlery and English pewter like this plate dating from 1770.

would swell during Public Times. Year-round the taverns were social centers and business places as well as way stations.

After 1638, when the Assembly first set the price for a meal or a gallon of beer at six pounds of tobacco (or eighteen pence in "ready money"), Virginia's inns, taverns and ordinaries—call them what you will—were closely overseen. At first the royal governor granted commissions to innkeepers, then the prerogative to license them passed to local courts. By the time the Capitol was dedicated, regulations governed the sale of bottled drink and established true weights and measures (e.g. four gills made a pint, two quarts a pottle). Limits were set on credit, with none allowed to customers who owned less than two servants or £50 in property. Penalties were established for illicit sales, and punishments fixed for gambling and drunkenness. Sailors, servants and students were barred from taverns lest they incur debt or cause damage that could not be recovered in a lawsuit.

Before an inn opened, a court reviewed its location and the character of the proprietor, who was required to post a substantial bond. Each March the Hustings Court in Williamsburg set prices that taverns could charge for food, drink, lodging, even for a horse's keep. Those who overcharged were fined, those who reported scalpers were rewarded. By mid-century the annual license fee was thirty-five shillings or fifty pounds of tobacco; the bond was fifty pounds sterling or ten thousand pounds of "bewitching weed"; and the proprietor who failed to post security could be sentenced to a whipping.

The fare was varied. In the Bull's Head Room Henry Wetherburn served turkey, veal, chicken, fowl, calf's head, chicken and asparagus, lamb, tongue, pork, Scotch collops, fish, venison, beef, mutton, bacon. The celebrated diarist and gentleman William Byrd II, who daily recorded even his diet in code, dined at Jean Marot's ordinary variously on roast goose, roast beef, fricassee of chicken, mutton, fish, roast veal. To drink, Marot offered wines from Madeira, the Canaries, Portugal, and Germany; brandy from France; English and Bristol beer; cider; and aniseed water in addition to the spirits he produced in two stills. Another hosteler served imported red and white wines, Hock, shrub, arrack, cherry brandy, raspberry brandy, and citron water in addition to the inevitable rum made from molasses and a rum made from cherries too. There were ales and porter to be had, along with beers made not only from barley but persimmons and corn husks. The diverse punches—one recipe called for beer, brandy and sugar—were served by the bowl. Drinking was the pastime of colonists of every station, while gambling was considered the privilege of the better folk and taverns were where they gamed.

Virginia gentlemen played whist, billiards, dice, backgammon, draughts and "the royall and most pleasant game of the goose"—often for stakes as high as whole plantations. Many were ruined. When Williamsburg butcher John Custis lost heavily one night and died of a cut throat by morning, a coroner's jury ruled his death felo-de-se—a suicide—and his estate was confiscated by the crown. William Byrd III, who would hazard £500 at a time, gambled away his inheritance, ended up bankrupt thanks to his addiction and also died by his own hand. Loaded dice were not unknown, nor was violence. Col. John Chiswell, in-law to the distinguished Randolphs and a burgess, killed a rude Scot in a country tavern. Jailed in Williamsburg and then bailed out, he took an overdose of laudanum to avoid the shame of trial. Whatever personal prices were paid by sporting men, the proprietors of the inns profited from their custom.

It was the tavern keepers who organized subscription horse races at the track just outside town. "Quarter racing" was the early eighteenth-century rage, and Virginia horsemen developed a famous breed of sprinters, the first quarter horses, until longer distances became popular for racing. By mid-century, Williamsburg had a mile-round track, and match races of three four-circuit heats attracted bettors from all over, which just increased the taverns' business. Innkeepers, who sold a variety of imported goods on the side and forwarded mail, also profited from the trade attracted by cockfights. On the whole theirs was a very busy and lucrative trade. The value of one proprietor's bed linen amounted to £20, nearly the annual salary of a skilled tradesman. Several innkeepers owned as many as twenty slaves, or more than enough to work a country plantation.

Every class of traveler patronized these establishments. As acting governor in 1726, Robert "King" Carter stayed in a tavern when business kept him in Williamsburg though he was the most extravagantly landed gentleman in Virginia. George Washington patronized Mrs. Vobe's establishment on Waller Street and then followed her to the King's Arms; for a time he favored Christiana Campbell's where tips ran up his bill to more than £4 in 1768. When his wife and stepchildren accompanied him, he stayed at Richard Charlton's across from the Golden Ball. A few years later a German traveler found his lodging expensive but elegant: "Black cooks, butlers, chamber-maids, make their bows with much dignity and modesty; were neatly and modishly attired."

As habits changed so did regulations. By the 1760s the Raleigh Tavern served as a lecture hall (hosting one notable discourse "on heads," or phrenology). With taverns increasingly becoming the meeting places of men's social clubs and intellectual societies, so too students came to frequent them legally; thus Phi Beta Kappa was founded by College men in the Raleigh's Apollo Room in 1776. In celebration of one event of public importance, a newspaper reported, "there was a ball and supper at the King's Arms tavern which the Ladies graced with their company; during which the populace concluded their rejoicing, by a repetition of the healths round a large bonfire. The whole day passed with the greatest joy, decency and unanimity." (Few ladies stayed overnight in taverns. By and large these were rowdy places where men caroused late into the night, often passing out before making it upstairs to a shared bed.)

If gentlemen frequented the taverns for recreation, they also entertained at home. In part this tradition arose out of practicality; the three hundred families who ran Virginia's society, economy and politics all knew Williamsburg, but lived on their far-flung estates for most of the year. To visit a friend or cousin like as not meant spending the night; to celebrate a wedding meant a house party that lasted several days. In this era of rising aspirations, middling folk, like their social superiors, devoted greater energies to finely orchestrated recreations in a manner that was quite new. After reading Greek and Latin on arising, William Byrd II danced in the morning; it was his exercise. For others it was a social activity—what quality people *did* when they got together.

To entertain themselves and each other they also made music by singing, bowing, strumming, plucking and blowing as the instrument demanded. Robert Carter of Nomini Hall and Palace Green, according to his children's tutor, Philip Vickers Fithian, owned and played "*Harpsichord, Forte-Piano, Harmonica, Guittar, Violin & German Flutes.* [The latter were later known as recorders. Despite having been perfected by Benjamin Franklin, the

In Hay's time the Raleigh Tavern even offered the entertainment of a billiard room (left), now equipped with a twelve-foot table built in England in 1738 and brought to Williamsburg in 1965. The satiric engraving on the left wall (enlarged top), printed in London in 1780, sports a wigged hustler and his dupes. Fortunes also changed hands over draughts (now checkers) between gamblers who like as not sat in chairs similar to this New England Windsor (above) made for the coastal trade late in the century.

Engraved forever, a gentleman and his lady leave a squiggly trail across the floor (right) to edify subscribers in the mysteries of the minuet. Virginia gentry learned many arts through printed manuals and leaflets imported from England, font of manners and social conventions. This plate, from Kellom Tomlinson's The Art of Dancing Explained by Reading and Figures (1735), is dedicated by the British dancing master to his patron. It diagrams the final steps and arm positions the partners must perform. George Booth (opposite above), *a young Virginia planter, stood in an approved posture—with one leg cocked to display a well-turned calf—for his portrait by artist and dancing master William Dering in the 1740s. The plaster busts may be purely fanciful, accessories added to the scene to prove the subject's aspiring gentility. Social intercourse also involved intellectual exercise and the study of natural philosophy (opposite below) in the era that saw the death of comet predictor Edmund Halley.*

"Harmonica" fell into disuse. It comprised a set of spinning glasses which made crystal notes when touched just as wineglasses vibrate when one runs a finger around the lip.] At Williamsburg, [Carter] has a good *Organ*, he himself also is indefatigable in the Practice," observed the tutor. Fithian, a candidate for the Presbyterian ministry from New Jersey, was commissioned to teach Carter's two sons, five daughters and one nephew everything from the English alphabet to Greek grammar in addition to reading, writing, "Cyphering" et academic al. Itinerant specialists instructed the Carter clan—and many others—in the social arts of musical performance and dancing.

Not only did people entertain at home, they adorned their residences with furnishings imported from England (shipped by agents who bought the tobacco that provided the colonists their distant credit). Fine porcelains, tall clocks, mirrors and rich fabrics all came from England; so did the styles of furniture, clothing and manners which the colonists copied almost slavishly. By mid-century, imported brocade and chintz were preferred fabrics; a choice Chelsea serving piece or figurine graced tables and mantels in every modish home. This was an age of balance and delicacy, of Handel, Mozart and the minuet, of Thomas Chippendale's chairs and Josiah Wedgwood's tureens. Virginia's aristocracy had the leisure and wherewithal to indulge in all these and more while middling folk cultivated their own heightening sensibilities.

As the colonists looked to England for guidance in the finer things of life, they also learned to provide them for themselves. A royal governor might bring suites of elegantly decorated hunting arms with him, but Virginia gunsmiths also made beautiful (and very serviceable) rifles, tools that combined base metallurgy with pure artistry in form and decoration. The councillor who sent abroad for a serving table and chairs had to wait six months or more, and then perhaps got only what the cabinetmaker happened to have on hand. To get exactly what he wanted, he'd pay *more* for local cabinetry because skilled labor was dearer in Virginia than England (while freight charges were absurdly low in empty westbound ships that had come to fetch tobacco). But growing demand supported growing industry. Men like Benjamin Bucktrout and Anthony Hay made up elegant pieces to precise specifications; if so ordered, they could borrow the selfsame devices of pattern and adornment that their peers in London used. Often using native woods and locally developed techniques, they made chairs, tables and sideboards that resembled London's latest—as described in Thomas Chippendale's *Gentleman and Cabinet Maker's Director*—and sometimes surpassed them in quality.

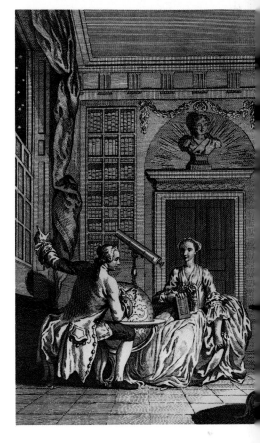

Clearly, accomplished artisans were at work in Williamsburg, despite the absence of guilds, which controlled crafts and professions in the Old World. James Geddy and his sons cast brass and bronze fittings, silver candlesticks, pewter plates and tankards. Unable to legally import raw silver from England—one of the many trade restrictions imposed by the crown—James Craig did a handsome business nonetheless. His patrons brought in salvers and coffeepots of dated design and bade him melt them down to make new ones in the latest style. He also wrought gold and made jewelry too.

If the colony had imported taste, it nonetheless found native talent in Williamsburg to produce desired amenities. There were wigmakers, milliners, tailors, bootmakers, bookbinders and shopkeepers of all sorts selling local notions made after English models. Apothecaries who imported the latest medicines from England also pushed homegrown cures such as rattlesnake root and ginseng, native drugs claimed to be as potently all-curing as any bot-

Propertied people coveted—
and gained—a growing array of
possessions during the last decades of British rule. The Peyton Randolph House Lafayette
Room (above left) disports a
lady's dressing table with English dressing glass and accoutrements for her toilette. The
elegant French fan (below) with
gilded and silver sticks unfolds
an idyllic pastoral scene printed
on parchment. A bedchamber
in the James Geddy House
(above right) has a child's
scattered toys, including a puzzle of royal portraits published
in 1788. Both in Europe and
America, this era saw the flowering of family life and the new
phenomenon of middle-class
parents taking pleasure in
their children.

The desk-and-bookcase (left), made in England in the first quarter of the eighteenth century, graces the library of the Peyton Randolph House. Peyton's father and the room's previous occupant, Sir John Randolph, was the only colonial-born Virginian ever to be knighted.

George Wythe, lawyer, scholar and the city's burgess for whom an exhibition house is named, took in promising boys and gave them houseroom along with academic instruction. For one, he tutored a black lad to test his belief that all races had equal potential to become learned. The Wythe House students' room contains tools of early science (above): a celestial model used to demonstrate the movement of the planets, a globe and a telescope resembling one owned by Wythe's protégé, Thomas Jefferson.

tled potion for everything from snakebite to social disease. Like innkeepers the apothecary, surgeon and "practicer of phisic" had their fees regulated by law though not until 1736, a year also notable for a new sort of license—the permit to publish.

For a century and a quarter Virginia was barred from producing one sort of commodity—the printed word. Gentlemen owned books; some libraries contained several hundred volumes, most of them classics and all of them imports. Governor Berkeley had railed in the seventeenth century that "learning has brought disobedience, and heresy, and sects into the world, and printing has divulged them." Further, he believed that publishers' stock-in-trade was "libels against the best government." In England the printing press was allowed in only four cities before 1695; the Old Dominion did not have one until Governor Gooch's time. In 1730 William Parks came from Annapolis to take up the duties of public printer for Virginia. First his work was confined to printing official documents, laws enacted by the Assembly and the like; in time he built a paper mill to make his stock and published all manner of material: medical manuals, agricultural tracts, political pamphlets. These proved Berkeley's infamous point: A publisher could criticize governments or governed alike, spread seeds of dissent or contentment, disseminate ideas and even misinformation.

In 1736 Parks established the weekly *Virginia Gazette*, the colony's first newspaper, which survived him and two subsequent owners, each of them employees who bought out the business that enjoyed monopoly status. In 1766 Alexander Purdie ran the *Gazette* and favored the royal governor's view of news and events. Yet there were other sides of the story to be told, and enough interest in goings-on around America and elsewhere to support competing journals. By 1776 Williamsburg boasted three independent papers, all of them named *Virginia Gazette*. Berkeley might have anticipated the results of so many published voices and no doubt he would have dealt with them summarily a century earlier. However, many things had changed in the generations following Berkeley's rule: among them the methods of governors (who had to rule largely by persuasion rather than fiat), economic conditions, intellectual attitudes and political relationships both within Virginia and with the mother country.

The parental metaphor is telling; the colonies were growing up and like adolescent children becoming impertinent, even rebellious while England became less permissive, indeed more demanding of her offspring. Always the most populous of the British colonies, by 1750 Virginia had more than 230,000 inhabitants. She had come a cropper in terms of mineral wealth and exportable natural resources, but tobacco proved an immensely valuable crop. (This despite the fact that its market price could vary more rapidly even than its growth could wear out the land.) The evolving plantation system that produced it depended on vast tracts of virgin land or fallow ground and on a perennial supply of cheap labor. As indentured servitude provided less and less manpower, slavery became the keystone of the tobacco economy, and blacks accounted for forty percent of the population. Among worse things, this meant that farming had become a capital-intensive business since slaves were expensive to buy, if cheaper to maintain than free men. All this tended to concentrate economic power in the hands of a relatively small number of families who by now were all related by marriage several times over. As this coterie came to dominate the colony's economy, so these men also controlled politics. A virtually hereditary aristocracy had come to rule Virginia, and struggled to keep that power just as others tried to seize a share through hard work, shrewd investment or marriage.

The "Manor Plantation," seat of influence and source of wealth, was a microcosm in many respects. Fairly self-sufficient, it resembled a feudal fiefdom. As William Byrd II mused at his plantation home Westover on the James River, "I have a large Family of my own, and my Doors are open to Every Body, yet I have no Bills to pay, and half-a-Crown will rest undisturbed in my Pocket for many Moons together. Like one of the Patriarchs, I have my Flocks and my Herds, my Bond-men and Bond-women, and every Soart of trade among my own Servants, so that I live in a kind of Independence on every one but Providence....I must take care to keep all my people to their Duty, to set all the Springs in motion and to make every one draw his equal Share to carry the Machine forward."

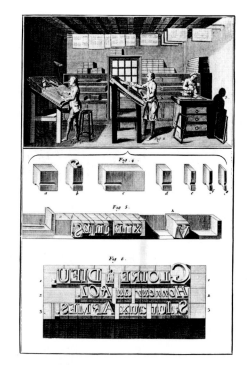

In such a place, the scions learned about governing early. A young Byrd's supremacy over personal servants was obvious in early childhood, while his liberal education was geared to provide all the sorts of knowledge required to oversee agriculture, operate businesses, invest money and govern the folk of this New World Elysium. The boy raised to run a Virginia estate was also expected to do his share beyond its borders—initially by overseeing the temporal affairs of the established church. In this era church and state were closely joined and the two heavily influenced each other. Not only was church attendance required of all freemen by law, but gentlemen with any political ambition at all began their careers on church vestries, where they conducted the business of the parish. Vestry seats were held for life; vacancies caused by death were filled when the surviving vestrymen chose their late colleague's successor. The gentry came to control each parish (as soon as there came to be a gentry), and power in parish affairs became all but hereditary too. The young aristocrat—even one with the most lackadaisical sense of *noblesse oblige*—would then seek out a post as a justice of the peace from which he would administer the temporal affairs of his community. Most young gentlemen took commissions in the militia and thus acquired military influence as well. As soon as he was able, the ablest of the lot would seek election to the House of Burgesses.

While nobody was looking, it was in this House that the first American revolution occurred. In Sir William Berkeley's day, the governor's appointed twelve-man Council held sway over the lesser chamber, which comprised two members elected from each county. But as the number of counties increased to 59 by the 1770s, the number of burgesses swelled to 122—118 from the counties plus 4 from the College, Williamsburg, Norfolk and Jamestown. The Council of gentlemen chosen by royal governors (and thus likely to be sympathetic to royal causes) never grew in size; it soon lacked the manpower to dominate the business of colonial government as it had previously. After 1750, only three laws were initiated in the Council; by weight of numbers and other changes the freeholders' chosen representatives had essentially assumed control.

The master of the Printing Office (above), *still using muscle power to strike proofs, practices the same trade as William Parks, who founded the Virginia Colony's first newspaper at Williamsburg in 1736. Americans could study almost any industry known to Europeans— even printing—via such works as Denis Diderot's* Encyclopédie (top), *first published in 1751.*

Modeled on the House of Commons, this was a deliberative body. As it grew its more numerous members voiced more varied opinions, which were carried farther and wider both in private letters and in the growing public press. The colonists, firm in their belief that they were loyal Englishmen, also believed that tradition and the common law conferred upon them rights and privileges that could not be overruled by a distant Parliament or colonial administrators. Ever since civil war had rocked England in 1649, deposing the king (to whom Virginia remained loyal), Virginians had demonstrated their willingness to differ

with political leaders at home. They called themselves Englishmen and honored whoever wore the crown while they learned to demand rights due them as royal subjects. (All agreed they couldn't reasonably be represented in the national legislature that sat an ocean away.)

There was a mortal ambiguity in all of this. The key to wealth and opportunity still lay in land, and the land lay in boundless tracts to the west. Though London repeatedly tried to prohibit it, westward expansion occurred willy-nilly despite threats from French colonists beyond the Alleghenies. King George II rushed in both to defend his interests and to provide the royal protection that intractable pioneers had come to expect. Thus began the French and Indian War, a New World manifestation of the Seven Years War that involved all Europe. Simultaneously, this period saw new leaders coming to Williamsburg which, as the capital, was centrally involved with goings-on in the west and everywhere else for that matter.

In 1755 Gen. Edward Braddock marched grandly on Fort Duquesne (later the site of Pittsburgh, Pennsylvania) only to have his troops surrounded by an Indian force who butchered those that didn't flee in panic. Braddock was killed, and Governor Dinwiddie then named the most proven Virginia officer, George Washington, commander of all the colony's forces. Three years later British and colonial troops retook Fort Duquesne (which was renamed Fort Pitt in honor of the king's minister), as the tide turned against the French and their native allies. In the same year, Frederick County sent Washington to Williamsburg as a burgess.

In 1760 the king died, to be succeeded by his grandson George III. Two years after that William and Mary student Thomas Jefferson started reading law with the multitalented George Wythe—Williamsburg's burgess, a leader in its intellectual establishment, eventually the first law professor in an American college and first among Virginians to sign the Declaration of Independence. In 1763 the Treaty of Paris certified Britain's victory in the Seven Years War; France ceded Canada, and Spain abandoned her claim to Florida. That same year the young lawyer Patrick Henry gained fame as an orator in a celebrated lawsuit known as the Parson's Cause, a tangled affair that saw the Privy Council intervening in the matter of Virginia ministers' salaries. Henry soon became a burgess too.

Meanwhile, the king and Parliament were seeking new sources of revenue. Hard economic times had fallen on Europe; Britain's national debt had doubled as a result of the recently won war, which had been all the more expensive for the defense of the distant colonies. After a series of lesser money bills imposed new duties on goods, word came that Parliament meant to pass a Stamp Act requiring that documents such as deeds, licenses, newspapers and whatnot bear a stamp, for which the colonies would have to pay. Patrick Henry, though burdened by an upstart's reputation, delivered his Caesar-Brutus speech in the House of Burgesses. He railed against the act as a tax imposed by England's legislature, Parliament, despite the Virginia Assembly's presumably exclusive right to levy taxes in the colony. Henry offered a series of resolutions, the most extreme of which passed by only one vote. So hotly worded that some thought them treasonous, these resolves were opposed by such resolute men as Wythe and Peyton Randolph, who exclaimed in Thomas Jefferson's hearing "By God, I would have given 500 guineas for a single vote." Next day Henry was absent, the five resolutions were reconsidered and one, the most extreme, was repealed— by a single vote. The editor of the *Virginia Gazette* had considered them too harsh to print, but all Henry's proposals quickly found their unexpurgated way into a few other newspapers

Students and other poor colonists enjoyed spare furnishings and wardrobes, witness the scant apparel in the clothespress of the Wythe House students' bedchamber (opposite and top) *and the meager objects found in one in a nearby kitchen* (above), *home of slaves.*

and spread throughout the colonies. In the meantime Governor Francis Fauquier, one of the most able to serve the crown in Virginia, dissolved the Assembly for challenging the constitutionality of Parliament's legislative supremacy. Legally emasculated by the governor's order, this colony's leadership could not send representatives to the Stamp Act Congress. Nonetheless Fauquier sent word to London that the Stamp Act, which by now had been passed, could not be enforced.

Henry's sentiments, if not his expressed resolves, found support in Virginia and elsewhere throughout the colonies. Opponents said the Stamp Act written by a distant legislature, imposed a de facto local tax—contrary to precedents established in Jamestown. For months the Stamp Act was the main topic of conversation. In Williamsburg it was debated in the Capitol, in the taverns and around the polished tables of the city's leading citizens over their long midday dinners. When a hero of the recent war returned to Williamsburg from England as distributor of the stamps, he had the ill luck to arrive during Public Times. A crowd followed George Mercer to a coffeehouse hard by the Capitol where he was greeted by Governor Fauquier; the crowd became a mob, and Mercer only escaped injury or worse when the governor escorted him away personally. Next day Mercer resigned his commission and the hated stamps were placed for safekeeping on one of His Majesty's ships at Norfolk.

In some instances opposition to the Stamp Act was more subtle. Virginia justices of the peace and judges declared their hands were tied; since Mercer failed to deliver the necessary stamps, they could not conduct court business. While they continued to try murderers, probate wills and such, they declined to handle civil suits to the despair of colonists' creditors in England.

In 1766 Governor Fauquier received word and announced the repeal of the Stamp Act, prompting revelry in the streets, an illumination of the town and grand celebrations in the taverns. All seemed forgiven for the historical moment; Fauquier clarioned the king's benevolence in resolving the crisis (and invoked good Enlightenment principle to propose the building of a mental hospital, the first in the colonies). The Assembly proposed raising a statue of King George to honor his beneficent wisdom in repealing the improper tax. Still, that year was pivotal in several respects.

A cabal of "hot burgesses" invited printer William Rind to relocate from Maryland, since they could not trust the present *Gazette* publisher to air their opinions fairly. Also, Peyton Randolph was elected House Speaker after a most remarkable revelation. His political patron, John Robinson, long Speaker-treasurer of the colony, had very generously abused his official duty of retiring dated currency or tobacco notes (the certificates of ownership of tobacco casks that were used as money). Robinson had provided funds from this pool of supposedly obsolete money to various gentlemen in need. After his death it became clear that more than £100,000 in bad debts were outstanding. Robinson had not taken any of it for himself nor profited—except by winning friends and perhaps their votes. The most direct result of this revelation was the corporate decision to separate the duties of treasurer and Speaker. Thus Speaker Randolph saw Robert Carter Nicholas, long a leader of the conservative faction in the House of Burgesses and an antagonist of perfect probity, take the mantle of treasurer. (Like every colonial officer from county clerk to governor, he was entitled to a small percent commission on all the work he performed; but he never took a penny more than his due.) Thus, power in the liberal House was diffused.

Relations might cool between crown and colony but English factors still catered to American markets, even advertising the likes of this inflammatory vessel in 1760s newspapers. The creamware teapot probably comes from Cockpit Hill, Derbyshire.

While many problems and misunderstandings exacerbated relations between the several colonies and England in the next few years, Virginia remained closer to London than most. Alas, her good governor Francis Fauquier died in 1768, though he was succeeded by a most congenial and elegant gentleman in Norborne Berkeley, Baron de Botetourt, who arrived in a royal coach drawn by six matched grays. The new governor impressed the hoi polloi and won the affectionate admiration of finer folk like Anne Blair, an avid correspondent who spread Botetourt's fame through her letters. A man of dignity and protocol, he presented himself at the Capitol, heard his commission read and took his oath there. When he banqueted at the Raleigh, the town was illuminated for him.

It was a lovefest; as one paper declared "All ranks of people vied with each other in testifying their gratitude and joy that a Nobleman of such distinguished merit and abilities is appointed to preside over, and live among, them." For his part, Botetourt declared he would defend the traditional rights of colonial legislators: exemption from arrest, protection of their estates, freedom of speech and debate. As he had been a favorite in the royal court, so too he became remarkably popular in Virginia. If the colonists learned that he'd been involved in a financial scandal and tried to bribe the lord privy seal to save his fiscal skin, they didn't care. The bachelor governor was almost instantly the most beloved in Virginia's memory. He endowed gold medals at the College "for the honour and encouragement of literary merit." Until he'd furnished the Palace to his taste, the leading lights of town took him to dinner. He captivated the populace with his gilded coach displaying Virginia's coat of arms and silver-mounted harness—gifts from the king who evidently hoped to save his able and hardworking friend from the worst rigors of his recent financial ruin.

But trouble had been brewing elsewhere. Since Parliament's passage of more revenue measures in the form of the Townshend Acts in 1767, colonists and British authorities were clashing with greater frequency and rancor. One of the acts forbade the New York legislature to sit, and in 1768 Massachusetts called for concerted action by all the colonies in a pamphlet that Parliament banned. Despite the prohibition, Virginia's burgesses—which Jefferson joined in 1769—debated the Massachusetts proposals; in response to a new threat they passed resolves much like those that had answered the Stamp Act, albeit in more respectful terms. The king's ministers had unearthed an ancient law: men accused of treason outside the realm could be taken to England for trial. The burgesses reiterated their exclusive right to tax Virginians, their right to petition the crown and to communicate with each other. Pledging their loyalty to King George, they also begged him to abandon the notion of spiriting Americans to London for trial, an act that could bring only "dangers and miseries." Under orders to suspend any Assembly that endorsed the Massachusetts proposals, Botetourt summoned Speaker Randolph to the Council Chamber and with memorable dignity declared: "Mr. Speaker and Gentlemen of the House of Burgesses, I have heard of your Resolves and auger ill of their Effect. You have made it my Duty to dissolve you; and you are dissolved accordingly."

Quite simply he had invoked the royal prerogative to dismiss a legislature, a prerogative that was the linchpin of the king's power. That might have been that—had the House stayed dissolved, as it did when Fauquier dismissed it a few years earlier. But the burgesses adjourned to the Raleigh Tavern down Duke of Gloucester Street and resumed their colloquy in the Apollo Room. Electing Peyton Randolph as their moderator, they declared themselves

Dedicated, politic and able, Norborne Berkeley, Baron de Botetourt, arrived in 1768 to assume the governorship. Despite the troubled times, he became a most popular royal agent and was honored in death with burial beneath the Wren chapel.

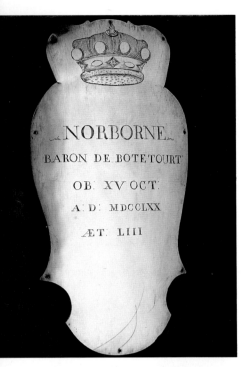

Extravagance followed aristo-crats to the grave but might not remain there. Lord Botetourt's sterling silver coffin plate van-ished during the Civil War; a jeweler in upstate New York returned it to Virginia gratis in 1889. The engraving displays Botetourt's baronial coronet and, in roman characters, the information that he died October 15, 1770, at the age of fifty-three.

an association and deliberated a proposal brought down from northern Virginia to ban the import or use of British goods. Once fully drafted and debated, eighty-nine members of the "dissolved" House signed it. On that afternoon, May 17, 1769, elected representatives of an American citizenry defied royal authority with remarkable effect: They constituted *themselves* as a self-sufficient instrument of representative government. They demonstrated that they didn't need the king's permission to act or represent the people.

Nonimportation became a matter of fact; the governor reportedly said privately that he supported the demand for repeal of Parliament's "obnoxious acts," and life went on. When Botetourt marked the king's birthday with a sumptuous Palace ball, "a numerous and very brilliant assembly of Ladies and Gentlemen attended." When the burgesses held a ball at the Capitol in the governor's honor, their ladies attended in gowns made of homespun. (The boycott seemed a promising economic weapon, but its first casualties were those Britons most sympathetic to Virginians' interests, namely their agents and suppliers. This led to the charge that rebellious acts were being inspired by deadbeats who meant to welsh on their English bills.) When the Assembly convened again the following winter, Botetourt predicted a happy resolution to past problems and swore to faithfully present the colony's cause to Lon-don. Virginians believed him true to his word, but he could not be so for long.

Botetourt fell ill of a fever in September 1770. When he died Williamsburg's three bells—in the College, Capitol and Bruton Parish Church—all tolled. Six members of his Council and Speaker Randolph bore his pall; Norborne Berkeley was buried in a vaulted brick crypt beneath the chapel of the College of William and Mary. To celebrate his memory, the Assembly commissioned a splendid marble statue of him to be placed outside the Capitol.

John Murray, Earl of Dunmore, a Scottish peer descended from the royal Stuarts, was appointed to become the next governor. His selection seemed to prove London's growing insensitivity to the colonists and ineptitude in coping with an already inflammatory situa-tion. As patriot Richard Henry Lee wrote a few years later, "If the administration had searched through the world for a person the best fitted to ruin their cause...they could not have found a more complete agent than Lord Dunmore." Having just recently been named governor of New York, he got off to a bad start before he even reached Williamsburg by trying to wriggle out of the assignment. (It didn't help that his letters on the subject were published and Virginians found them insulting.) When he arrived in 1771, he rudely summoned the Council to the Palace—contrary to tradition—and took the oath of office there. As custom dictated, the town was illuminated for him; his only bow to precedent was to call for new Assembly elections.

Dunmore, who liked high living and brought an immense amount of luggage to fur-nish the Palace, was known as a philanderer by the time his wife and children joined him. As averse to hard work as Botetourt had been dedicated, he declined to meet visitors until he was forced to establish office hours. Oddly, he struck a friendship with Washington who found him an able man despite appearances and called him potentially "the most formidable enemy America has."

When a ring of counterfeiters was discovered in Pittsylvania County, Dunmore had them haled into Williamsburg before they'd been examined by a local court. The burgesses approved jailing the men whose bogus notes had nearly paralyzed business. But they pro-

Following military tradition, the chaplain of a visiting regiment—albeit in postcolonial uniform—delivers a drumhead sermon during the Colonial Fair. Because this was the capital—and because the Magazine held gunpowder, which Botetourt's successor purloined—Williamsburg saw much saber rattling before the outbreak of war.

tested Dunmore's abandonment of due process (no doubt apropos of Parliament's threat to take accused patriots to England). Strictly construing legal precedent and tradition, the burgesses objected that appropriate steps had been skipped by Dunmore's summary prosecution. They then wrote: "The duty we owe our constituents obliges us, my Lord, to be as attentive to the safety of the innocent as we are desirous of punishing the guilty" lest arbitrary justice threaten "the safety of innocent men." Within days the Assembly resolved to establish a Committee of Correspondence to share news of events in England and other colonies.

The pace of escalating events still reflected the distance in nautical miles between the mother country and the colonies and the months of sailing time it took for news (and official dispatches) to cross the Atlantic. The Boston Tea Party, first notably violent response to a change in taxes levied in the colonies, occurred December 16, 1773. London replied by ordering Boston's harbor closed. When word of that response reached Williamsburg, the burgesses hastily deliberated. They resolved to dedicate June 1 "as a day of fasting, humiliation and prayer, devoutly to implore the divine interposition, for averting...the evils of civil war." Dunmore reacted by dissolving the House, to little practical effect. After assembling in Bruton Parish as planned, the burgesses scheduled a convention in Williamsburg for August and called for a congress of representatives from all the colonies. Convention delegates reviewed Jefferson's lately written *Summary View of the Rights of British America* and agreed to strengthen the nonimportation agreements. They chose Peyton Randolph to lead a delegation to the First Continental Congress in Philadelphia, and he was elected its president by acclamation.

In the meantime, Dunmore's one success came from capitalizing on trouble in the west. Settlers were ignoring royal orders and crossing the Alleghenies into land reserved by treaty for Indians; the Shawnees retaliated with raids and massacres. Dunmore marched to Fort Pitt (which he renamed for himself) while an army of militia under Andrew Lewis met Chief Cornstalk at Point Pleasant. Outgunned and outnumbered, Cornstalk fought to a standoff but sought peace when Dunmore arrived with reinforcements. Having planned a campaign in which Lewis took all the risks, Dunmore managed to win brief popularity in Virginia and London, while drawing attention away from more serious problems. For instance, in November of 1774 a band of patriots dumped two chests of tea consigned to Prentis Store into the York River.

By Christmas Dunmore was warning his superiors at home that Virginia was armed to the teeth and recommending that the navy blockade every colonial port. In March Patrick Henry declaimed "Give me liberty or give me death" at the Second Virginia Convention in Richmond. The governor soon found it prudent to remove a wagonload of powder from the Magazine. This was discovered and Williamsburg's mayor, accompanied by militiamen, went to the Palace and demanded it back. When Dunmore refused, Peyton Randolph and Robert Carter Nicholas managed to disband the angry throng. But a militia force was reported marching from the north to seize the powder, and the governor, who had no troops to speak of announced he'd put the torch to Williamsburg if they threatened him. When Patrick Henry mobilized another militia army to demand either the powder or reimbursement, Dunmore finally defused the situation by paying for the purloined powder.

In the meantime he'd boobytrapped the Magazine and laid plans to flee the city. After convening the Assembly in June he made the empty gesture of suggesting that voluntary pay-

British satirists saw Virginia's gentry as a mob bent on coercing their betters to support nonimportation pacts—or be tarred and feathered (opposite). Events in the colonies supplied comic fodder for London wags before hostilities broke out during the administration of John Murray, fourth Earl of Dunmore (above). Virginia's last royal governor, he appears as haughty as his critics thought in this portrait by Sir Joshua Reynolds. Still, the English lord earned Washington's respect as a dangerous adversary.

Cannon smoke billows on Yorktown's heights as French and American ships blockade English forces in this original watercolor from the period.

ments to the king's treasury might replace taxes imposed by Parliament. Then he fled to an English warship in the dead of night, leaving a regal array of possessions in the Palace: paintings and furniture enough to fill 25 rooms, a personal library of 1,300 books, an orchestra of musical instruments including 3 organs and a pianoforte; 42 barrels and 2,000 bottles of wine, 480 gallons of vintage rum, 300 head of cattle and sheep, 19 horses, assorted coaches, carriages and other vehicles, 56 slaves and a dozen indentured servants.

The burgesses sent an envoy asking him to turn over arms and powder that he'd cached in the Palace. When he declined, colonists broke in and took the ordnance. (Later his personal property was auctioned off to aid the war effort.) After sending his family home to England, Dunmore would further infuriate Virginians by skirmishing below Norfolk and offering emancipation to any slaves who would join the British side. But by now events had fled Williamsburg as well, though men who had frequented the town were in the thick of them.

The Second Continental Congress had convened in Philadelphia in May and Peyton Randolph was elected president again. George Washington had been appointed commander in chief of the fragmentary Continental Army. The Battle of Bunker Hill had been joined in June; that same month the Fifth Virginia Convention met in Williamsburg to adopt a new constitution, and Patrick Henry was elected first governor of the Commonwealth. The Convention also adopted a resolution drafted by Edmund Pendleton instructing delegates to the Continental Congress "to declare the United Colonies free and independent States." Jefferson put his pen famously to work and on July 4 the Congress adopted the Declaration of Independence. The next month King George declared the colonies to be in a state of rebellion.

Jefferson would succeed Henry as governor and live in the Palace he'd sketched during Dunmore's time. But because of its easy accessibility to the York and James rivers, Williamsburg was deemed too vulnerable to attack by naval forces, and in 1779 Jefferson supported the plan to remove the capital north to Richmond. Indeed, the little city on the peninsula was taken by Lord Cornwallis (as was the new capital) on a trek that led him to camp at Yorktown where he meant to find a royal fleet bringing reinforcements. The British used the Palace as a hospital and, leaving an epidemic of smallpox in their wake, retreated down the peninsula, putting the torch to forges and foundries before they left. Washington's troops—Continentals and French volunteers under the Marquis de Lafayette—followed Cornwallis. They stayed in Williamsburg long enough for the commander in chief to plan his next move. Awaiting massive reinforcements in 1781, Washington accepted George Wythe's invitation to stay at his stately brick house on Palace Green. From there, he marched south and laid the seige that forced Cornwallis's surrender at the Battle of Yorktown which won the War for Independence. Thus, British power hereabouts went the way of Williamsburg's: It ended.

122

Each year companies of volunteers muster and camp in the old colonial capital, recalling scenes that led to America's Independence. In 1781 General Washington marshaled his troops at Williamsburg, where he awaited reinforcements before marching down the peninsula to Yorktown. There his superior forces besieged Lord Cornwallis's army, whose surrender led George III to sue for peace and acknowledge his loss of the thirteen colonies.

PART TWO

The Phoenix Years: Decline and Resurrection

Slumber Time

Abandoned by history, the erstwhile seat of empire seemed as ruined as Lord Botetourt's once gracious statue in the crumbling Capitol (left), where itinerant architect Benjamin Latrobe sketched it in 1796 "deprived of its head and mutilated in many other respects." Richmond became capital of the newly formed Commonwealth, and Williamsburg lapsed into the dusty semblance of a one-horse town (opposite)—except in this late-nineteenth-century scene the horse was an ox.

Virtually every business would abandon Williamsburg when the government of Virginia moved up the James River in 1779. Only the College and what might be called the health industry remained. The colonial pharmacopoeia included mineral, vegetable and animal cures: pills containing ground gold, potions of native herbs and bloodsucking leeches to restore balance among a too-sanguine patient's humors. Apothecaries treated every conceivable complaint, even de facto mental ones. By the 1760s the idea spread that madness was a form of sickness and amenable to scientific treatment (given the standards of the day). In 1773 Williamsburg opened the first hospital in English America devoted exclusively to mental illness, the Public Hospital for Persons of Insane and Disordered Minds.

The ravages of the rude hand of time meet the eye in every quarter of the town.... I never walk the streets without experiencing the most gloomy sensations, but it is a kind of pleasant melancholy, that the mind rather courts than despises. It is a dignified pleasure that is always experienced in the mind when viewing the vestiges of departed greatness.

—A Student in 1804

*I*f there was no good "natural" reason for Williamsburg to be here in the first place—no strategic, commercial, or geographical, advantage that dictated her location—therein lay her tragic liability, an almost fatal flaw. Having been created by the stroke of a pen, she could be erased by fiat too. The removal of the capital to Richmond in 1779 was such a stroke. It left Williamsburg bereft. Designed to govern, the city lost its *raison d'être*. The charter had been annulled, and Williamsburg began its long, slow decline into virtual village status. Once a seat of empire, it became a backwater bench. The Capitol building, which had burned in 1747 and been rebuilt along very different lines six years later, stood empty. If a symbolic event were needed, the year after the departure of Virginia's new state government another conflagration lighted up the sky in 1781: the Palace, symbol of the royal presence, burned in a fast hot blaze and simply collapsed into its ample cellars.

With neither industry nor commerce to speak of, the people who had frequented Williamsburg in political seasons went instead to the new epicenter of the growing Commonwealth. Men involved in the business of government, like George Wythe, abandoned the place for the new capital city. Men of business who depended on the patronage of government per se or the custom of government people, like blacksmith and armorer James Anderson, followed them there. The courthouse remained, as did the city's first cornerstone, the College of William and Mary which fell on very hard times. But for these two old institutions, and a new one, the city could have wasted away. One needn't look farther than five miles away at Jamestown to see a place that perished when human events took a new course and fickle history turned her back.

The younger institutional neighbor in Williamsburg had its ups and downs in a kind of counterpoint to the city's fortunes. As Shomer Zwelling illustrates in his history, *Quest for a Cure,* the Public Hospital for Persons of Insane and Disordered Minds went through many transformations. Happenstantially founded—as *invented* perhaps as the town itself—it was the brainchild of one generation of Virginia's enlightened leaders.

The Hospital's first champion—back in 1766—was Governor Francis Fauquier, a member of the Royal Society in London and once he reached Virginia a leading light in the colony's intellectual fraternity. As a man of the Enlightenment (which knew no geographic bounds), Fauquier was a student of science and natural philosophy, a devotee of music and good works. No doubt he knew that a new sort of institution was rising elsewhere and thought to place his city in the vanguard of social progress. London had raised Bethlehem Hospital, better known as Bedlam; France had opened madhouses; Pennsylvania Hospital was reserving separate wards for deranged patients.

Fauquier proposed this Hospital to the House of Burgesses under curious circumstances—right after word arrived that Parliament had repealed the hated Stamp Act in re-

Governor Francis Fauquier, whose likeness was painted by Richard Wilson, first voiced the enlightened notion of building a hospital for the mentally ill.

Dr. John de Sequeyra (above) treated Washington's stepchildren and introduced the tomato to America (according to Jefferson). He arrived in Williamsburg about 1745, when William Dering may have painted this portrait. Almost thirty years later he was named the Public Hospital's first physician. Treatment of the insane was problematical even in the most famous institution of the time, London's Bethlehem Hospital, whose nickname became synonymous with clamorous madness. William Hogarth depicted "Bedlam" in his Rake's Progress series (opposite) several decades before Williamsburg's madhouse opened.

sponse to the uproar it had caused in the colonies. The governor's address to Virginia's legislature began by espousing lofty sentiments about how beneficently the crown and royal ministers had responded to the Stamp Act crisis. It ended on a very different note, indeed a sort of tangent, as he recommended building America's first public hospital exclusively for mental patients. The governor endorsed "legal confinement" for those who "cannot help themselves" and medical efforts "to restore to them their lost reason"—all this after putting as handsome a face as possible on England's surrender of principle in the recent Stamp Act showdown. Were the disagreements between king and colony akin to common lunacy? Weeks later the burgesses passed a pair of resolutions that suggested the legislators might have linked these issues too. First, they proposed to erect a statue honoring the king who'd restored "ease and happiness" to his colony; second, they hoped to improve the lot of "persons who are so unhappy as to be deprived of their reason." By 1770 no less a moralist than Treasurer Robert Carter Nicholas expressed the fear that "Lunaticks and other unhappy objects of insane minds...will multiply too fast in this country." All was not right in the mind of the body politic.

After Fauquier's death in 1768, Norborne Berkeley, Baron de Botetourt, arrived to represent the crown, becoming a governor of incomparable *noblesse oblige*, political politesse and popularity. His gilded coach wowed the populace; his gracious gifts to burgesses' wives won their husbands' gratitude; his condescension pleased all, as when he happened upon a gaggle of sweltering gentry one summer evening and joined their songfest. A winning politician, he went out of his way to oblige. When the colony's legislators deemed a madhouse reasonable, he graciously endorsed their bill—since granting this desire could not hurt the king's interests.

The Hospital's design was drawn by Robert Smith of Philadelphia who had raised Carpenter's Hall there and Nassau Hall for a young college in New Jersey. The building contract called for "hard well burnt Bricks and laid with good Mortar," a cypress-shingled roof and inch-and-a-half-thick flooring. The commission for construction went to Benjamin Powell, the able builder who repaired both Capitol and Gaol and raised Bruton's tower from his own design. Though this first-class building took longer to build and cost more than planned, the asylum accepted its first patient in the fall of 1773.

The building was an imposing edifice, proof positive of the colony's enlightened sense of social rectitude. It contained all of twenty-four cells, an apartment for the keeper and meeting room for the supervisory court of directors who numbered such luminaries as Wythe, Nicholas, brothers Peyton and John Randolph, and John Blair Jr., nephew of the celebrated commissary. Serving gratis, these gentlemen as a group reflected Virginia's tradition of responsible leadership as well as any and better than most. So too the protocols they established made manifest the best thinking of this time and place. As the final arbiters over who would be admitted and who released, the directors accepted only those patients considered dangerous or curable. They would not admit chronically harmless lunatics, alcoholics, paupers and the like; this was neither prison nor extended-care facility.

The first visiting physician was Dr. John de Sequeyra, who in 1770 attended Botetourt's last illness ("a bilious fever and St. Anthony's fire"). By birth an Englishman (of Portuguese Jewish descent), he'd earned a medical degree at the University of Leiden and been in Williamsburg since 1745. He examined patients upon their admission and once a week

thereafter; since the patient population was rarely more than fifteen, he continued his private practice. By the end of his twenty-year tenure, patients were receiving such state-of-the-art treatment as diagnosis by phrenology and therapeutic jolts from a static electricity generator. The full-time resident keeper (at £100 a year) was James Galt, who qualified for the post by having been keeper at the Gaol. His wife came with him as matron (at £25). Thus began a connection between this family and the Hospital that lasted for generations.

Until the Hospital opened, people of unsound mind had been lumped with paupers, beggars, vagrants, orphans, et al.—haphazard wards of a parish. Some were placed under the care of people who took in unfortunates for pay; others were imprisoned for lack of an alternative, such as the Virginian "under great insanity of mind... [who] was committed to the publick Gaol for preventing mischief he might otherwise have done, and which everybody apprehended he would commit." Now as in London and Philadelphia there was a special place for such woebegones. Now there were coming into being procedures that doctors prescribed for persons whose illness was impalpable—although these treatments were naive and often contradictory.

William Galt, who succeeded his cousin James as resident keeper, in 1800 became second dynast in the family of keepers and physicians at the Hospital.

The "unhappy object" of a patient might be made more tractable by a baleful stare since "dread of the eye was early imposed upon every beast of the field" and mad people were considered bestial in some respects. Since the humors were still blamed for almost any human irregularity, "mania" and "melancholia" were seen as the results of one internal imbalance or another. Thus mental patients were variously bled or blistered with salves. They were given drugs; if opiates or sedatives didn't prompt the right results, stimulants were administered. If induced constipation didn't balance the humors, the answer might be found in a laxative. Since one school of thought held that madness was voluntary (albeit a malady that could cause brain lesions), harsh treatment was encouraged to help the mad choose rationality. The "plunge bath" or dunking chair involved the patient's total immersion and might quiet the violent or stimulate the lethargic. When the patient was not undergoing one of these regimens, he was allowed brief exercise in the "mad yard" and then left alone—often for long periods. Those who couldn't be trusted were restrained in irons affixed by the blacksmith.

As for the Hospital's success in restoring reason to the mad and the once-mad to the world, there was some. In its first five years, thirty-eight patients were received. Eight were "restored" to sanity and discharged; four were released to friends or family and ten died. Of the rest, fourteen were still confined in 1778. Whether or not these results satisfied the community, the coming war soon took its toll and in 1782 the Hospital was closed for want of funds. A traveler at the time wrote that the "Bedlam-house is desolate, but whether because none are insane, or all are equally mad it might, perhaps, be hard to tell."

Reopened a few years later, the Hospital notably became a state-supported facility. James Galt remained the keeper until his death in 1800 when his cousin William took the job. Upon Dr. de Sequeyra's death in 1795, the medical work was accepted by Dr. Philip Barraud (who left for Norfolk a few years later) and by James Galt's brother, Dr. John Minson Galt, who'd studied in Paris and Edinburgh. He was succeeded in turn by his son, Dr. Alexander Dickie Galt, who was visiting physician until his death in 1841 when his son, Dr. John Minson Galt II, took the new title of superintendent.

During the first quarter of the nineteenth century, nearly forty percent of the Hospi-

Conditions changed over time—
a bit—as exhibited in the reconstructed Hospital. An
eighteenth-century cell (above)
has little more than a pallet on
the floor. A century later, more
sympathetic keepers provided
patients with beds, even fiddles,
in their rooms (below).

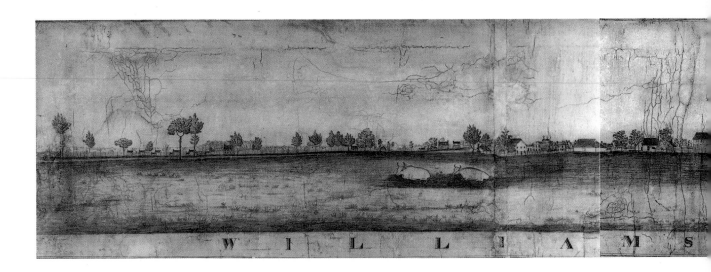

tal's patients were ultimately released as cured; then the rate started falling off even as the size of the inmate population grew. Alexander Galt kept up with the latest medical literature and was aware of new European notions that insanity was an illness that could be cured by "moral management" and kind treatment. But change was slow in coming, especially since the state redefined the Hospital's role and enlarged it as a custodial facility. It grew to four major buildings by 1833, a year after Williamsburg lost the last vestige of its former political greatness when the second Capitol burned. During Dr. Galt's tenure, however, and spurred on by concerned legislators, treatment became more humane. The more reliable patients were encouraged to take Sunday excursions, play musical instruments and work in the keeper's vegetable garden which led to charges that the keeper, cousin Dickie Galt, was taking advantage of them.

Andrew Jackson's Populism spread in many directions as the second quarter of the century gathered steam; one was to improve the lot of prisoners and patients, even those in the newly named Williamsburg Lunatic Asylum. Here John Minson Galt II became the man of the hour. He organized activities from lectures to carpentry and fancy needlework, one of the manifold expressions later called "folk art." He trained his staff to concentrate on a patient's sane features rather than insane aberrations. He treated the inmates with kindness, mesmerism and warm baths. He replaced restraints with opium and claimed to cure almost half his patients (though it's fair, if sad, to say that his knowledge of addiction and pharmacology proved wanting). Accepting slaves as patients, he trained one of his cured blacks as an attendant. The doctor himself became a charter member of an organization that would become the American Psychiatric Association. The Enlightenment was long gone, but this Galt was an enlightened practitioner in the early days of a discipline that would seek to ease needless human suffering, psychiatry.

John Minson Galt II was also a loyal and devoted son of the new Confederacy. When Union forces finally captured Williamsburg at the end of the devastating Peninsula campaign in 1862, he was distraught. To calm his nerves, he took a dose of his own medicine, laudanum, the heady blend of opium and alcohol which seemed so felicitous for his patients. The prescription might have served a de facto addict, but it killed good Dr. Galt.

There were nine buildings now, with nearly three hundred patients, and the Hospital

132

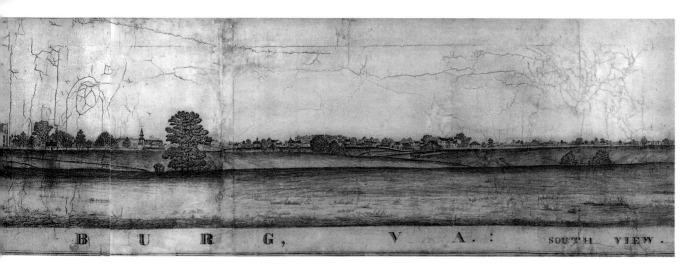

B U R G, V A.: SOUTH VIEW.

was sacked during the Yankee occupation. When it was repaired and reopened in 1866, the most common cause of mental breakdown among new patients was now the ghastly trauma of "the war." Soon the place was racially segregated, and while some therapeutic programs came into being, ten years after Appomattox only five percent of the patients were considered curable. When a new superintendent instituted furlough programs, he was forced out and Williamsburg's once progressive institution became almost exclusively custodial. In early summer of 1885, when the population was approaching five hundred, a fire broke out in the old main building and destroyed it—remarkably, with few human casualties. The original edifice, dedicated to the enlightened treatment of lunatics, was razed at a time when the "warehousing" of mad patients came into vogue. Virginians who went "to Williamsburg" were not expected to return; about the only destination for outsiders here was a place to which most were committed for life.

In a manner of speaking, things were even worse at the College. When war broke out between the states, William and Mary's president, professors and every undergraduate answered the call to the colors. For all but one of them the shade was gray, according to oral lore. During the war the Wren Building was variously fortified, fitted out as a Confederate barracks, equipped as a Union hospital, and burned (for the third time since Nicholson's day) by a mutinous cavalry unit from Pennsylvania. The president, Benjamin Stoddard Ewell, spent two decades vainly seeking reparations from Washington. While classes had been suspended for various periods during both the Revolution and the Civil War, in 1881 William and Mary closed for lack of money. But Ewell (whose brother had been a general at Gettysburg) kept the charter alive by ringing the bell at the start of each academic year. Briefly, the insane asylum was about the only game in town. In 1888, the College reopened with a state appropriation to train public school teachers. So it went for Williamsburg: down, up and down again until the next century.

One child who must have heard Ewell's annual tolling of the bell was Catherine Brooke Coleman, whose mother was descended from St. George Tucker, an illustrious alumnus and law professor at the College. Living just down Nicholson Street from her ancestor's old house, the eleven-year-old girl was stricken with appendicitis (probably) and died during one of those Septembers when William and Mary was closed. A year after her daughter's

By the 1850s an engraving depicts the enlarged Hospital (above), *complete with new name, as a spa with gentlefolk strolling the grounds—no doubt to ease the minds of patients' kin. By 1884 the main building had gained a third floor* (below). *The enlarged structure soon burned to the ground but the institution as a whole continued to grow.*

EASTERN LUNATIC ASYLUM

North View

death, Cynthia Beverley Tucker Coleman invited the girl's playmates to form the Catherine Memorial Society in remembrance. In the habit of southern gentlewomen, the young ladies learned to sew for charitable profit; they sold their stitchery and in springtime collected ivy sprigs and daffodils to sell as well. The girls sent the proceeds of these activities to Bruton Parish Church. Indeed, within two years of their first meeting the Catherine Memorial Society had donated $300 to buy a communion table and repair the heating system. By 1887, the girls were striking further afield. Mrs. Coleman appealed through the Christian journal *Southern Churchman* and raised enough money to repair the churchyard's round-crowned brick wall and restore the broken tombstones. The Catherine Memorial Society's name came to be carved in the stone of several markers.

Bruton's churchyard might look better than it had in decades, but the town was still a shambles, the dimly remembered capital of an erstwhile colony whose heirs had not yet recovered from losing America's most devastating war. The Palace and Capitol both lay in ruins. The Magazine was now a storage shed. Various lots had been sold off from the public greens. The College boasted all of six professors plus a president, no more than in the seventeenth century. The most viable institution was a madhouse complex of such miserable repute that town residents traveling elsewhere would tell strangers they came "from near Richmond" rather than admit that Williamsburg was home. This was the place where "two thousand lazy lived off one thousand crazy" according to local wags. All this had come to pass because of the loss of capital status, the loss of the war and, perhaps, the loss of Williamsburg's self-respect. Still, all was not lost.

Intrigued by the Catherine Memorial Society's success in restoring shards of Williamsburg's once proud heritage, Mrs. Coleman got together with Miss Mary Jeffrey Galt of Norfolk, a kinswoman of the medical dynasty. Through the good offices of Governor Fitzhugh Lee—his wife was keenly interested—they chartered the aptly named Association for the Preservation of Virginia Antiquities. Though its headquarters would soon be removed to Richmond, it gained a statewide membership. And for obvious reasons the A.P.V.A. became a substantial property owner in Williamsburg—or perhaps insubstantial comes closer to the mark, given that its acquired properties had greater symbolic value than practical worth. A real estate firm, for example, willingly gave the Capitol site to the new association, which capped the foundations with concrete lest scavengers continue to rob the bricks. The group's first purchase was the "Powder Horn" (as the Magazine was then called) which was soon repaired and opened as a simple museum. Within a decade, Mrs. Coleman's group was given twenty-two acres at Jamestown where it restored the most ancient church tower (dating from about 1639) and began work on a sea wall to save the island from encroaching tides. Virginia's heritage was being resurrected.

The A.P.V.A. was founded in 1889. That year one William Archer Rutherfoord Goodwin, a twenty-year-old orator and moralist from the Blue Ridge foothills set out in the world. He sojourned in Richmond to test his vocation and decided to enter the ministry.

The "new" Public Hospital, reconstructed to its original eighteenth-century appearance, opened as an exhibition building in 1985.

The Visionary and the Angel

One man dreamed of restoring this "Cradle of Liberty" to its former state and grace. But dreams require money to become real—and the bigger the dream the larger the bankroll. The Bruton Parish rector's vision intrigued one of America's most celebrated millionaires, and an informal partnership was struck. Together the Reverend William A. R. Goodwin (left in both photographs) and John D. Rockefeller Jr. (shown in both photographs) embarked on a venture that was nothing short of remarkable.

The sun rises on a garden beside Benjamin Powell's erstwhile home—and on a new day for Colonial Williamsburg.

*W*hat had once been Virginia's colonial capital would never—could never—have become Colonial Williamsburg but for one man's dream and another's fortune. The two prime movers were not related like the proverbial chicken and egg. One undeniably came first; the city's resurrection was conceived by a minister's remarkable imagination.

As he himself declared in *A Note-Book of Memories,* years before he met his patron, the Reverend William Archer Rutherfoord Goodwin was a man "possessed." First there were the binding legacies "of a southern temperament and a New England conscience" which he likened to a "combination of rheumatism and St. Vitas dance." Afflicted by contrary drives from birth—and pursuing every interest with monastic intensity—he was both mystic zealot and Episcopalian patriarch, antiquary and trendsetter, unabashed patriot and a bit of a bigot. He was a tireless builder whose joy came in the work itself; rarely would he enter the edifices he'd raised. A cleric dedicated to worthy works (and finally to one cause), he was to have been remembered in a son's memoir entitled *My Father Was a Beggar.* So be it (though the filial biography was never written). He didn't beg for himself, but strenuously for good causes: missionaries abroad, William and Mary's endowment fund and finally for the historical rebirth of historic Williamsburg.

In pursuit of these interests, he seized likely benefactors by the emotional throat and throttled them, or mesmerized them, holding them transfixed like the Ancient Mariner. If that didn't work, he seized their lapels and held them fast while he talked. "He wouldn't let you go," says one man he often collared. "Begging" for him was like mending bicycles for the Wright brothers; he elevated a greasy business to a new vocation and changed the world somewhat. To his credit and undying memory hereabouts, he invented Colonial Williamsburg as surely as Wilbur and Orville put together the first airplane with horse glue and baling wire. It simply could not have happened without him. To get things started, on the basis of nothing more than a handshake and a dream, this man of the threadbare cloth persuaded John D. Rockefeller Jr. to parcel out more than $2 million. With this pre-Depression fortune he bought a town lot by lot in his own name in order to raise the colonial capital like a phoenix. In short, Goodwin was a genius. As Hamlet was "to the manner born," this man drew breath to resurrect the colonial capital. It was almost in his genes.

"Inheritance has made me constantly mindful of the rock and the stream from which I sprang," he wrote, tracing his Virginia lineage to a Yankee grandfather who came south in the 1830s to study theology. "A man of austere piety" according to the heir who had a nose for metaphor, grandfather possessed a doctrine "strongly perfumed with the mingled odors of the Mayflower and of brimstone that had come out of hell." Entering missionary work for the diocese of Virginia, grandfather Goodwin married an army surgeon's daughter, Mary Archer, and settled in the Blue Ridge Mountains to raise four sons. Half of them became ministers in turn; this clan's men took to pulpits like mockingbirds to treetops. A third son went west and became a judge in the Arizona territory; the fourth, John Francis Goodwin, entered business in Richmond before the Civil War "in partnership with his uncle, Mr. William Archer, after whom I was named." Their business was iron, which no doubt seemed promising stock at the time. But "in after years, when making love to several Richmond girls," the heir would write in 1924, "I often looked down from Gamble's Hill at night into the seething and molding masses of iron which continued to flow through the furnaces after my father and uncle had retired from the Vulcan Iron Works." Retired? More likely Messrs. Archer and Goodwin had been ruined by the war, if not the peace called "Reconstruction," a word then innocent of architectural meaning.

Like the flower of his generation's gentry, John Francis Goodwin had answered the call to arms. He took a captain's commission in the Confederate Army and was never the same again, "his health having been undermined during the War." As his firstborn son explained it, he followed doctors' orders "to remove to the country" with his wife, née Letitia Rutherfoord. He packed the family back to Norwood, in rural Nelson County below Charlottesville, where one of his sisters had married the local doctor who promised expert medical care gratis. There they lived in genteel poverty, farming poorly and collecting rents from tenants. Captain Goodwin, CSA ret., served as senior warden in the local parish and his wife ran the Sunday school.

Born in Richmond June 18, 1869, "Will" was a babe in arms when the family moved. His only brother didn't survive infancy; one of his sisters "died of sunstroke" at seven. The scion lived through a smallpox epidemic, measles and a seemingly deathly regimen of chores until at sixteen he ventured off to Roanoke College in Salem, Virginia, where one of the ubiquitous priestly uncles offered free room and board. Testing his possible vocation, he led religious services at the jail, and one Sunday was locked in for his pains. He sold books door-to-door—the Bible and Mark Twain. He toyed with the idea of studying law.

At prosperous Uncle Thomas Rutherfoord's behest he went to live in Richmond for a year. This benefactor had a motive: It was to give his impecunious nephew "a taste of city life. . . . He sent me to the theater, entertained me sumptuously. . . paid all my expenses. . . and gave me the opportunity of studying Greek. . . . I did my best to suppress any. . . clear call to the ministry of the Church. I stopped going to the YMCA. For a time I entirely stopped going to Church. I danced furiously. I tried to be mildly wild (although I was never led at any time to resort to strong drink)." But his calling was clear.

In 1890 he entered the Virginia Theological Seminary in Alexandria. "On the first night at the Seminary I climbed the cupola and looked down upon the forest in which the Seminary is embossed, and out to the lights of Washington gleaming in the distance. I can well recall the thoughts and feelings which came to me in those silent moments lit with the light of spirit-enkindled emotions." Alas, he did not specify what those thoughts and feelings were. As would often be the case, when it came to patriotic matters Will Goodwin assumed everybody knew what he meant at the drop of a rubric. He left the particulars unstated, perhaps lest they prompt avoidable discord.

Ordained a deacon, he was assigned to St. John's, a poor parish in the middling city of Petersburg, south of Richmond. The neighborhood boasted five saloons within a block of the church. It was here that one of his most remarkable talents blossomed: he became a fundraiser. Preaching that "most of the poverty in the parish resulted from the drink evil," he persuaded one bar owner to give up the business. He established a "dry" social club and said men flocked to it. Finding the wherewithal to replace the plain wooden church with one of brick, he left the tower a blunt stub for reasons of economy—until a shopkeeper across the street paid for the steeple to save himself from facing an eyesore.

Dr. Goodwin sports a mustache and steady gaze in 1901 (left) shortly before his first call to Bruton Parish. About to venture North several years later (below), he ponders a tome on heretics in the rectory building that would later become "Restoration House," first headquarters of the experiment ultimately known as Colonial Williamsburg. The scene includes his first wife, Evelyn, and eldest son, Rutherfoord, who became a newspaperman, then returned to Williamsburg, where he married a member of Peyton Randolph's clan and grandniece of the bishop who first called Dr. Goodwin to Williamsburg.

The young minister supported the Bishop Payne Divinity School to the tune of some $8,000 a year, a sizable sum in the Gilded Age. This little seminary prepared "colored students" for the ministry and Goodwin found teaching there an experience of "invaluable benefit." Ahead of his time in many respects, he would testify in favor of a law "prohibiting little children from working all night in the cotton mills" and lecture the Masons on religious tolerance when Al Smith ran for president. But in matters of race, he walked in step with most white Virginians of his day. Of his divinity school pupils, he wrote, "Truth had to be made very simple" to them. "The thought and study necessary to present the truths of redemption to these earnest but uncultured people demanded clearness of thought and simplicity of language, or else there was a complete failure to secure results." He called one of his teachers "an ignorant Yankee" for fraternizing with blacks and inviting them home for dinner. "This, however, did not last very long, as one of them stole all of his silver spoons ...which resulted in his conversion to the southern point of view."

In 1895 Goodwin married a local girl, Evelyn Tannor, with a bishop and six clerics in attendance, two of them Reverends Goodwin. In the next six years two daughters and a son were born, the last of them (notably for this narrative) the remarkable Rutherfoord who was "so impatient to begin his varied human activities that he arrived before the doctor did." A second son died in infancy leaving Evelyn with the kidney ailment that shortened her life.

Meanwhile, far across the James River, trouble was brewing in Bruton Parish. Advertised as "the oldest [Episcopal] church in constant use in America," it had a future less promising than its past. For reasons lost in the undusted crannies of parochial history, a rift in the little establishment had developed between minister and vestry, becoming an abyss deep enough to engulf the entire congregation. With actions threatened in civil and ecclesiastical courts, the bishop opted for a change in personnel and called Goodwin to Williamsburg in 1902.

The new rector seized the challenges that lay ahead, especially in the red letter year of 1907, which marked the tercentennial of Jamestown's founding—perhaps the event that addicted the young minister to historical commemoration. There was much to be done. As he'd remember, "The old town became very much agitated over the question of paving the Duke of Gloucester Street, someone having presumed to suggest that this should be done. [Goodwin himself perhaps?] By many the suggestion was repudiated with indignation. They said that WASHINGTON, and JEFFERSON, and MARSHALL, and MONROE, had walked in the mud...[Emphasis in the brittle-paged original, now faithfully preserved by a daughter-in-law.] It was presumptuous for the modern upstarts to insist they were too good to do it." When this grumbling died down, there remained the problem of paying for the job, for this was a most parsimonious town. But the impasse gave Goodwin the golden opportunity to prove his ability to move mountains—a mountain of gravel in this instance. Determined to see the street paved, he persuaded the owner of a distant quarry to donate the stone and talked a railroad president into freighting it to Williamsburg free of charge. Then he convinced the governor to assign prison gangs to do the shoveling.

Having literally paved the way, the good rector saw to it that Williamsburg would play a key role in the coming festivities, which centered around Norfolk. It didn't hurt his cause that there was virtually nothing left in Jamestown to serve as a focal point, nor any facilities there to accommodate the expected throngs. Neither did it hurt that the Bruton Parish ves-

Bruton Parish Church was the first building to be renovated by the energetic young rector before he even dreamed of restoring the town as a whole. It was refurbished in 1907 to celebrate the three-hundredth anniversary of the first successful English settlement at nearby Jamestown. King Edward VII wanted to send a Bible embossed with Virginia's seal, but Dr. Goodwin pointed out that the state's emblem (above left) was hardly appropriate to adorn a monarch's gift. Instead, Goodwin found a seal conferred by the crown in the seventeenth century (below). To hold the book, President Theodore Roosevelt presented the lectern (above right) that adorns the crossing still.

143

The city might become a national shrine, yet it had been many people's hometown for generations. Destined to become "museums," its antique dwellings were homes to plain folk. The dining room in the Tayloe House (above), like many others that would be restored, reflects the busy taste of Victorian America early in this century. The once "neat and plain" residence built by the Magazine's first armorer—and later called the Brush-Everard House (below)—got a veranda long before Miss Coral Smith stood in a dark dress behind the gate about 1920.

try had already agreed "to restore the old Church to its Colonial form and appearance." (Partitions had divided the interior into several rooms, the tower had become a coal bin, etc.) Raising donations "from far and near," Goodwin hired architect J. Stewart Barney to perform Bruton's first renovation in time for the tercentennial; the General Convention of the Episcopal Church recessed its Richmond meetings in order to witness the dedication.

The restored Church was reconsecrated with all due pomp and ceremony. President Theodore Roosevelt sent a brass lectern in the shape of an angel (labeled *PAX*) standing on a globe the size of a volleyball; it was "commemorative of the three hundredth anniversary of the permanent establishment of English Civilization in America." The angel's rampant wings shouldered a Bible given by the king of England to honor the planting of the Anglican faith in the New World, and even here Goodwin's adroit hand had been at work.

When Edward VII instructed the archbishop of Canterbury to secure a copy of Virginia's state seal for the Bible's cover, the pastor of Williamsburg found himself engaged in "a somewhat embarrassing correspondence.... I replied that I hesitated to comply with the request of His Majesty" because the state seal displays "a very arrogant Virginian" standing as rampant as Teddy's angel over a newly decrowned king and the motto *Sic Semper Tyrannis*. "I ventured to suggest, through His Grace to the King that he might be pleased to use the colonial seal of Virginia which Charles the Second had given Virginia permission to adopt."

Goodwin unearthed this seventeenth-century seal and sent it to Canterbury whence it reached the royal bookbinder. In turn the bishop of London—successor to the divine who sent Commissary James Blair hence—presented the suitably embossed King James Bible to Bruton Parish. To mark the occasion the princes of Episcopalianism filled the Church, along with a host of notable laity including the likes of J. P. Morgan, while a few thousand faithful gathered outside. The immediate celebration was marred only by the bishop of Washington's announcement that the new Bible was given by "King Henry the Eighth" who, alas, had been dead for 360 years by then. The larger occasion was marred by what Goodwin might have considered a personal defeat: Morgan failed to become a major benefactor. He'd arranged for the millionaire to ride between Church and train station in Williamsburg's finest vehicle, a wagon. The robber baron noted the shabby condition of the harness, and hinted at donating new tack; Goodwin told him that the owner was a college professor and Morgan wrote only a thank-you note, not a check.

Approaching forty, the minister went to England the following year as a delegate to an Anglican congress. He preached at St. Mary's, a fourteenth-century church in Bruton, Somerset, which gave the Williamsburg parish its name. The duchess of Marlborough invited him to a garden party and his old correspondent the archbishop of Canterbury presented him to the reigning king. Edward asked about his gift of the Bible and Goodwin replied that Williamsburgers listened more devoutly when read Scripture from that copy.

Goodwin was traveling in such lofty circles that his days in Williamsburg were numbered. In 1909 he was called to a far more prosperous parish in Rochester, New York, where his fund-raising techniques blossomed. (Preaching his first sermon on the Fourth of July, he recorded for posterity that his choice of a Gospel reading that particular Sunday enabled him to begin his Yankee ministry with "the southern use of the words 'I reckon.'") A silk parish in a burlap town, his new church, another St. John's, was led by "men of wealth" whom the

The Brush-Everard House was also enhanced by a ship etched on a windowpane by Miss Coral's brother H. B. Smith, a boy in 1873.

Backyards and the ravine called
Ginny's Bottom would in time
become the site of a sort of
colonial industrial park comprising Printing Office, Bookbind-
ery and Post Office. The
shed in back now shields paper-
makers in summer.

young rector visited individually. His message to each of them: "I was not willing that the fact that they had money should stand between us or hinder me from the freest possible conference and intercourse with them." The man who'd eventually spend a patron's millions politely demanded that his Rochester vestry vote policy on its merits and not its price. He even tangled with his bishop by advocating more active support of foreign missions abroad. For this he ended up in the diocesan doghouse—barred from conferences—until the mitre was passed to a new bishop.

Goodwin's Rochester ministry was just a sojourn; Virginia remained home. When his wife, Evelyn, died in 1915, he returned to Williamsburg and buried her in Bruton's churchyard. When he sought a second bride, he found Ethel Howard in Ashland, Virginia, north of Richmond, and married her in 1918. He took her back to Rochester, where she bore the first of their three sons a month before her husband turned fifty. Then in 1923 the president of William and Mary invited him to organize an endowment fund and teach religion courses. Once back in Williamsburg, he was called to serve as rector of Bruton Parish a second time.

He had come home again and set his boundless imagination on familiar tracks. As he'd later speculate: "Perhaps it was on one of those mild, clear, Virginia nights when I roamed the streets of the sleepy town, and felt the stir of ancient thoughts, visions, prophesies, that arrested the men who lived here, who walked these streets and gazed in admiration at the very same stars that shone on me.... How shall we keep forever the vision of those men? How can we impress upon the coming generations their deathless ideals? Why not a shrine to their memory, a living shrine that will present a picture, right before our eyes, of the shining days when the great idea was in the crucible of freedom."

On another occasion he would write of Williamsburg and his neighbors: "Memories lingered here of the things which had been said by those of the olden times. The ghosts of the past haunted the houses and walked the streets at night. They were glad and gallant ghosts, companions of the silent hours of reverie. They helped to weave the stories of the past which have found their way into fiction, into current traditions, and into history. While these stories may not have been always entirely true to fact, they were true to life. They grew as they were told on moonlit verandas or on winter nights by those gathered around a blazing fire whose flickering light illumined the faces of ancestral portraits which still graced the Colonial walls. These ancient personages had been too long silent...."

Whenever these lofty notions first came to mind, in February of 1924 Dr. Goodwin traveled north to attend a banquet celebrating the newly chartered Phi Beta Kappa Foundation. Wearing his cap as William and Mary collegian, the Virginian thanked the assembly for its support of the proposal to build Phi Beta Kappa National Memorial Hall at the College. The building would contain an auditorium, guest rooms and a reconstruction of the Raleigh Tavern's Apollo Room where Phi Beta Kappa had been founded in 1776. One Dr. George E. Vincent spoke on the educational ideals that the revived honor society would pursue anew. It bears mention that he was president of the Rockefeller Foundation; and that Mr. Rockefeller Jr., who'd earned his Phi Beta Kappa key at Brown University, was chairman of the committee to raise funds for the building. Goodwin met him and, ever the Old Dominion's champion, invited him to Williamsburg. The invitation was politely declined.

Four months later, the energetic cleric was back in New York, this time calling at

Rockefeller's Broadway offices with the hope of soliciting a gift for William and Mary, perhaps to restore old buildings. Received by a secretary who heard him out, he soon got a note from another aide: "The letter which you addressed to Mr. Rockefeller, Jr. . . . has received his consideration. He appreciates the circumstances you present, and regrets that he could not wisely make an exception to his policy in the matter of personal gifts to educational institutions." He had foundations to do that sort of thing, and do it in a rather grand manner.

Four days after receiving this news, Goodwin directed his energies elsewhere with a remarkable sheaf of letters to Michigan. First he sent a copy of a booklet on William and Mary's "Romance and Renaissance" to Henry Ford in the "hope that it will be of interest to you." The same day he addressed to Henry's son, Edsel, an epistle that opened: "Seriously, I want your father to buy Williamsburg." He went on to explain that the city had been capital of a colony that "included the land on which the Ford factory is now located" when Virginia stretched to the Great Lakes. After waxing patriotic about town and College, he enthused: "Other men have bought rare books and preserved historic houses. No man has yet had the vision and the courage to buy and to preserve a Colonial village, and Williamsburg is the one remaining Colonial village which any man could buy. . . . It would be the most unique and spectacular gift to American history and to the preservation of American traditions that could be made by any American." Assuring Edsel that he had "no financial interest whatsoever in this matter," he then exercised what could be called prelate's license: "Unfortunately you and your father are at present the chief contributors to the destruction of this city. With the new concrete roads . . . garages and gas tanks are fast spoiling the whole appearance of the old streets and the old city, and most of the cars which stop at the garages and gas tanks are Ford cars!"

The proselyte of patriotism received a letter of thanks for the pamphlet, and shortly thereafter a three-sentence response to his accusatory epistle from Henry Ford's amanuensis: "Your letter of June 13th has been received. We regret that Mr. Ford's many activities are absorbing his entire attention. He is, therefore, unable to interest himself in the matter mentioned." (He was already embarking on some building restorations in Massachusetts and a museum in Dearborn, Michigan.) Goodwin next wrote Henry's brother William Ford, this time omitting mention of the family's culpability in Williamsburg's destruction. Instead he suggested that they come visit, promising the titans of horseless carriages a ride in a horse-drawn one. If he received the courtesy of a reply, it is lost to history.

But the *Detroit Free Press* got hold of the letter and published its particulars, including the notion that the town could be restored for some $5 million. Papers around the country joined in the hilarity; the *Baltimore Sun* wrote an incredulous editorial, but at Goodwin's invitation sent a man to look around and recanted. The year wound down with little more activity on this front and no further progress, so the next February the cheeky cleric again wrote Rockefeller, recalling their meeting a year earlier. "I am writing to renew the invitation and to suggest that you try to plan to come to the College, if possible, early in May. . . . You can bring your pocketbook, or leave it behind." He got another refusal but at least it was signed by Rockefeller himself.

Another year passed and Goodwin busied himself with other things like forestalling the destruction of the old Magazine and contemplating the uses to which he could put the brick mansion built for George Wythe. This home shared the block with Bruton Parish

Church and Goodwin coveted it as a parish house. Then in March 1926, word came from the head of Hampton Institute thirty miles south that Mr. Rockefeller would visit there in a fortnight with his wife and sons in tow. That was hardly surprising; Rockefeller generously supported this and many other Negro institutions throughout his life. What delighted Goodwin was the second-hand news that the family wished to tour Yorktown, Williamsburg and Jamestown on their way back north. He responded that College President J. A. C. ("Blackjack") Chandler would roll out the red-white-and-blue carpet.

(Goodwin's reply to the Hampton man is interesting in another respect. Half its length is devoted to a separate visit in April by another group of "northern friends," i.e. Hampton Institute benefactors, who wanted to see William and Mary. Chandler would assuredly "entertain the party at lunch at the College," Goodwin wrote. "We take it for granted that the party will be composed exclusively of white persons. It would otherwise occasion you grave embarrassment and criticism, which we would not be willing here at the College to bring about or be responsible for." Thrilled at the prospect of the Rockefeller visit, Goodwin was nonetheless compelled by his sense of southern propriety—and by the Gordian protocols of segregation—to make certain that those other Yankees observed the rules.)

After a flurry of letters up and down the peninsula, Goodwin stood by the side of the road on the morning of March 29 waiting for Rockefeller's car. The spot he chose for the pickup: outside Bassett Hall, a house that would figure prominently in years to come. The minister guided the party to the site of the erstwhile Capitol, to Bruton Parish Church and then on to the College for lunch. In the course of the tour young David Rockefeller played the clown and enchanted Goodwin, begging some old photographs for his collection. In the course of the day, Mr. Rockefeller expressed interest in the antiquities and asked if any plans were afoot to preserve the older buildings. Just that once, the voluble minister bit his tongue.

In September Goodwin's request for "a brief interview" with Mr. Rockefeller was fielded by his aide-de-camp, Col. Arthur Woods, who agreed to see him at his convenience in New York. The surrogate interview took place the following month and Goodwin outlined his plan to resurrect Williamsburg. According to Goodwin's faithful secretary, Elizabeth Hayes, "Colonel Woods asked many searching and thoughtful questions, listened attentively, looked with interest at the photographs presented, and, while courteously expressing his personal interest, remained entirely non-committal."

But Rockefeller returned to Williamsburg in November for the dedication of Phi Beta Kappa National Memorial Hall. Between the morning ceremony and evening banquet Dr. Goodwin escorted his celebrated guest around town in a chauffeured limousine borrowed from a Norfolk judge. They stopped at the Wythe House, then being restored, and encountered the caretaker who gave the millionaire some handwrought nails found in the woodwork to take back to son David. Miss Hayes reported, "They talked of the educational value which would come from the perpetual preservation of the buildings and colonial greens. Driving down to Bassett Hall, they walked into the woods, past the gigantic oak tree which Mr. Rockefeller greatly admired.... After this he said he wanted to walk alone over the ground ...in order that he could better study the houses and grasp the situation." That night at the head table, Rockefeller whispered he'd put up seed money—a mustard seed amount really—to pay for some architectural sketches of a restored town and Wren Building.

His first day back in New York, the benefactor wrote two long and precise letters to

Farmers' fields near Bassett Hall, eventually the Rockefellers' home at Williamsburg, would become pastures (opposite) after Dr. Goodwin's dream took shape.

Goodwin. The first asked for photographs of the town and an encyclopedia of information about the Williamsburg buildings and their historic importance. He requested a prioritized list and "a memorandum in regard to the several houses which could most speedily and easily be secured, because of a desire to sell on the part of their owners, because of mortgages or other obligations." Further, he wanted "the financial facts" regarding historic buildings that Goodwin already "had tied up or gotten a hold on." Reviewing "other important points in our conference," Rockefeller seemed interested in "the assembling of this interesting historical material around one or two centers," the Capitol neighborhood and the vicinity comprising Bruton Church, the Wythe House and Palace Green. In closing he reiterated "the complete and frank understanding that nothing may come of it and that I am committed to nothing, either now or later on, except as such committals are definitely made in writing."

The second letter anticipated a very preliminary study into the feasibility of restoring "the Sir Christopher Wren building" which the College wanted to modernize. Rockefeller stated with unmistakable clarity that he was only interested in the building from a historical standpoint—not in aiding William and Mary per se—but if the College wanted a feasibility study to learn whether the building could be saved, he'd help out to the tune of $10,000. He stipulated two conditions to Goodwin: "(1) That such assistance should be rendered through you; (2) That it should be rendered anonymously."

On the same day, Dr. Goodwin was writing Rockefeller a letter of plaintive thanks and hard data: "Today 'I feel like one who treads alone/Some banquet hall deserted.' But in Williamsburg we always have the ghosts which abide, even when the distinguished men of the present come, stay for a day, and depart. I have always felt sorry for the people who live in Williamsburg who are incapable of holding companionship with the ghosts, and who do not feel their presence hallowing their ancient haunts. It has been a great pleasure to me to have been privileged to help introduce you to the haunts and homes of these departed spirits...

"You were good enough to ask me to send you a memoranda [sic] of the indebtedness incurred by me up to this time... incident to the preservation and restoration work which I

have ventured to undertake." Goodwin wrote that he owed $22,000 on the restoration of the Wythe House, its purchase of $15,000 having been underwritten by the Colonial Dames of America. There was $6,000 outstanding on the Jonathan Blair House which he and friends had "rescued from being torn down for a garage" and turned over to the College. "To save the Powder Horn from being crushed in by two buildings, I got a gentleman to buy the lot immediately in the rear of it for $500, and I bought the corner lot in back of it for $1000 (giving my note in the bank). I hope for an additional $1000 to get control of the lot immediately to the west. . . . I have said nothing about the study of the Christopher Wren Building, and will say nothing about it until I receive the letter which you said that you would write, . . . with the perfect understanding that it carries with it no further committal whatsoever on your part. In the meantime [watch this switch!] I wish you would buy Bassett Hall for yourself. It would give you a charming vantage point from which to play with the vision and dream which you see, and it might give me the joy of being your 'playmate' in this dreamland playground."

These men—so often described as opposites—forged a partnership by each one being himself: Rockefeller the circumspect executive, financial administrator and practical philanthropist; Goodwin the visionary and persuader. They did become playmates—sometimes opponents at tug-of-war, sometimes teammates at capture-the-flag. When Goodwin waxed too euphoric, vague or ambitious, Rockefeller knotted his purse strings more tightly even as he encouraged his protégé to reach his stride. (Once Goodwin pleaded that his duties as William and Mary's fund-raiser were distracting, and said he could quit that work if Rockefeller would make a major gift. The patron called his bluff by suggesting that the restoration could wait until Goodwin discharged his obligations to the College.) When Goodwin got wind of a historic residence coming on the market, their pact was put to the test.

The handsome brick house on Duke of Gloucester Street had once been owned by Philip Paradise, a Virginia gentleman living in London when the Revolution broke out. Virginia's new government had confiscated it, which led the owner's friend Samuel Johnson to make a memorable quip about "Paradise's Loss." (After the war, Paradise's widow, the eccentric Lucy, returned to Virginia, reclaimed the house and lived there in her dotage. She was old and some say addled. Inviting visitors to take an outing, she led them to the porch where her carriage stood and when all were seated inside bade her butler to stand in the traces and jostle them up and down. Two nieces, perhaps greedy for her estate, had her committed to the mental hospital across town.)

On December 4, 1926, Goodwin wrote Rockefeller that distant heirs wanted to sell the house immediately for the "exceedingly low" price of $8,000. His supplication described the house in detail, noting that a poster announcing Lord Botetourt's funeral had been removed from a wall to the College library. Though the conspirators had not arrived at a firm plan, on December 7 Rockefeller fired back a telegram authorizing "purchase of antique... at eight." To hide his identity from Williamsburg's Western Union man, he coined a code name but his chosen nom de plume communicated something more than anonymity. Rockefeller signed his first Williamsburg purchase order "David's Father."

The Ludwell-Paradise House was the first building acquired for the future Restoration.

The informality, which seemed to invite intimacy, was particularly telling, since Rockefeller was habitually formal in the extreme. Unfailingly polite, he called only one associate by his first name, and then because they'd been friends in college. At the office he suffered the sobriquet "Mr. Junior," just as his sons would be called "Mr. David," "Mr. Nelson," etc. to avoid confusion. Yet in later years around Williamsburg, he would always be called "Mr. Rockefeller." Here he was uniquely his own man rather than his father's son, which might have been one reason the place came to have such special meaning for him.

John Davison Rockefeller Jr. was born cautious in 1874, the youngest of five children and only son of the self-made Midas of Standard Oil. His father, John Sr., had been sternly reared by an all-sufferingly Christian mother and a wayward entrepreneur. (Working upstate New York out of the back of a wagon, "Doctor" William Avery Rockefeller sold patent medicine. He often stayed away from the homes he bought with cash for months at a time—in part because the law was looking for him. After dodging a felony indictment by moving his family to Ohio in 1853, the snake-oil salesman taught worldly lessons to young John by lending him money with interest, then pointedly calling the loan when he thought the boy was strapped.) If the father was a philanderer and mother a devout recluse, their heir was a deeply religious monomane possessed of a gift for making money. A tithing Baptist from the day he went to work as a teenager, John Sr. let discipline govern his life and the rearing of his children, especially the boy.

Never robust, John Jr. was small, sedate and shy. Following his father's orders and example, he faithfully kept an account of every penny he spent and only began to blossom after going off to college where he got along well enough socially and excelled scholastically. Even at Brown, his biographers describe an overweening desire to please his adored mother and stern father. It was here that he met Abby Aldrich, daughter of the senior senator from Rhode Island, Nelson W. Aldrich, whose political influence almost rivaled his eventual in-laws' financial clout. Married in 1901, Mr. and Mrs. John D. Rockefeller Jr. settled down in New York hard by his parents' home on West Fifty-fourth Street.

There seems to have been little question about his life's work: to manage his father's empire and achieve the public rehabilitation of the man who had come to personify (somewhat unfairly) the evils of great wealth. The scion devoted most of his considerable and highly disciplined energies to the systematic support of worthy causes—always in his father's name. By the time he was fifty, and agreed to help build Phi Beta Kappa National Memorial Hall, he had earned the reputation of a singular philanthropist who was as realistic as he was generous. (When one worthy organization asked for one-tenth of the $1 million it needed, he instructed an aide to restudy the matter: "Mr. Chorley it's not a question of money, it's a question of what's right.") He had also developed efficient office protocols and clear policies, in part no doubt to see that his father's money was dispensed efficiently, and in part to discourage gold diggers. Typically, Goodwin's first solicitation of a gift for the College had prompted a secretary's formal refusal.

If Goodwin had a dream, Rockefeller had the money and something more, a method of spending to achieve almost any painstakingly defined goal from restoring the roof at Versailles to making insulin available for American diabetics. This approach was a nebulous asset of almost inestimable value. From the beginning the cautious patron took just one step at a time while keeping the parson on a very tight rein as their common interest progressed. Not that he adopted a special method of dealing with this visionary dynamo; systematic caution was his wont. As an associate would say years later, in dealing with Mr. Rockefeller "one never ventured beyond the scope of the subject of the day." Yet here he found himself working with a zealot who "could leap on his horse and ride every direction at once" as a Restoration executive put it. By habit, Rockefeller would weigh his options, then decide the direction of the next step, take it and pause again. Had they looked far ahead at the outset, it seems unlikely that Williamsburg would ever have been restored. In later years a consensus emerged among the two men's associates, in the words of Kenneth Chorley, the man who ran the Williamsburg show for twenty-eight years: Mr. Rockefeller "had no conception of what he was getting into. Neither did Dr. Goodwin as far as that goes. . . . Nobody really knew what was going to happen" as the pretty dream evolved into a reality of labyrinthine complexity and institutional proportions.

If Rockefeller was a paragon, he nonetheless was a mortal man of his time. By the mid-1920s, America had been seduced by two fickle mistresses, brazen prosperity and the liberating automobile. Never before had people been so mobile or so affluent. Flush from victory in "the war to end all wars," the nation had turned its back on international affairs and taken its own heritage to its bosom in orgies of jingoistic enthusiasm. Further, interest in the arts was on the rise. New York's Metropolitan Museum, a Sunday afternoon stroll up Fifth Avenue from the Rockefeller residence, opened its celebrated American Wing in 1924. Across the land interest was growing in restoring historic buildings and raising new ones in old architectural styles. Mrs. Rockefeller was in the vanguard of cognoscenti; a founder of The Museum of Modern Art, she was also a collector of art, both "modern" masterpieces and the seemingly accidental masterworks of unschooled "folk artists." Meanwhile, as Kenneth Chorley would remember with uncharacteristic whimsy, "Mr. Rockefeller had a great many people sitting around more or less with wet towels on their heads trying to figure out how he could give his money away intelligently."

It was in this atmosphere that the philanthropist haltingly embarked on the miraculous enterprise of Colonial Williamsburg.

Mr. and Mrs. John D. Rockefeller Jr. in 1901, shortly after their marriage. A generation after the patron's death, one crusty old Williamsburger told the author, "I never heard one mean thing said about him, except that he didn't drink."

The Secret Start

Perhaps only a dreamer could see antique beauty here in 1928 (opposite) when Dr. Goodwin persuaded an Army Air Corps commander to send a biplane aloft with a photographer aboard to take this picture. As for the town's other denizens, some seemed content to sit in the shade on Duke of Gloucester Street (left) and watch the telephone poles grow.

Like any county seat in Dixie, Williamsburg boasted a courthouse (above)—indeed one built in 1770—and a hotel with verandas, this one the Colonial Inn, which had seen better days. Meanwhile the store once owned by William Prentis (below) had chased time's winged chariot often enough to abandon its original horse-drawn carriage trade and serve less gracious vehicles.

*E*arly in 1926 two hunting partners left Boston "in a new Marmon car" for a North Carolina bird shoot. Though no one knew it—least of all the gunners—they were the first gentle wave in "the second Yankee invasion of Williamsburg." William G. Perry, an architect interested in period buildings, persuaded his friend to pause on their return trip and visit the colonial capital. They found "a country town" straddling a concrete highway with a median strip punctuated by utility poles and put up at a guesthouse kept by one of Governor Spotswood's descendants.

It was a town where "life was very pleasant," said one native son. "You could almost count the population every morning at the Williamsburg Drug Company." Dr. H. M. Stryker, the dentist, and young Vernon Geddy, a lawyer descended from the clan of smiths and farmers, shared a floor of the local skyscraper, a three-story walk-up. When business was slow they played checkers. The Reverend John Bentley, then curate at Bruton Parish, thought the town "dilapidated in many places. For the most part Williamsburg was a community of people who were just able to make ends meet and live with some sense of dignity and pride. People lived quietly and modestly" while lavishing their energy on flower gardens. Elder spinsters still told sad stories of heroics in the War Between the States. Younger women remembered the glory days of 1907 when the tercentennial prompted people "to cut the grass, paint the shutters and mend their paling fences."

Its central square become a midden of shacks and shanties, Williamsburg "retained somehow a charming quality with many of its houses and buildings quietly reminding one of a notable past," Perry believed. "The principal building on the College of William and Mary, much remodeled, stood as it had since the late 1690s. The Capitol building was represented only by its foundations. A school stood upon those of the Governor's Palace. But the general appearance of the town recalled quite simply the lines and areas of its original plan. It was an example of beneficent [or passive] architectural preservation, unaffected by progress and change. Its remaining buildings had patiently been designed in the vigorous and comely manner of the early 18th century."

Perry was especially intrigued by a stately brick wreck facing Palace Green. George Wythe's house "had been abandoned; its doors, front and rear, stood open and ajar; a window sash was missing. . . . Unfurnished and forlorn," it was coveted by the brother of a passerby who stopped to chat. "He'd like to remodel it into something useful, like a parish house," the lady said. Learning the stranger was an architect, she suggested he meet her brother, though Perry had to decline. Pressed for time the Bostonians continued northward by train, leaving the Marmon in front of their boardinghouse.

Months later when they returned for the car (less its dashboard clock and brass lamps), Perry's friend was stricken with appendicitis. While he recovered from surgery, Perry fell in with Dr. Goodwin who by now had acquired the Wythe House with the help of the Colonial Dames of America. Showing the Yankee around, the proud parson said "I have a decorator from Richmond, and he's come down and helped us on the restoration," a word that gave Perry pause.

"There are many definitions of restoration," he reminisced many years later, and Dr.

Goodwin's was one of the loosest though by no means the least popular in those days. He was bent on repairing the old building to suit new uses and embody "what he thought ought to have been." The definition Perry preferred was a return to "its original form through studied preservation and reconstruction." But Dr. Goodwin had been hard at work with his usual zeal. He'd installed paneling that had never been there before, no matter how closely it mimicked other period houses. This, in Perry's view, "was not 'restoration.'" The decorator had copied the front door motif from the Byrd family seat, Westover, though Wythe's house clearly never had "such an embellishment." As Goodwin led his graciously uncritical guest through the house, he said "We don't know how to terminate the cornice at this point." Though quite sure the front hall never had a cornice, Perry sketched a new one in a gesture typical of his charm and willingness to help.

Turning down his host's request for a donation in dollars, Perry offered something better. The original doors had lost their antique locks, so he measured the keyholes and marks that remained and promised to send down some old locks he'd collected. Delighted by the gift and astonished that the locks fit the doors, Goodwin had them installed. But a sorry admission dampened his effusive letter: "They were just in time for the dedication of the building. Let me thank you very much indeed, but let me also say, and I'm very sorry to have to report, that nine out of the ten keys were stolen that day." So far as Perry was concerned in the spring of 1926 "that was the end of that."

Partner in a firm that specialized in period architecture, he was unaware that Goodwin had already found the priceless key to building his dream when Rockefeller had passed through Williamsburg in March. After the philanthropist returned in November and authorized Goodwin to commission a few architectural drawings, the minister contacted an eminent Chicago architect who declined the job. Not missing a beat, Goodwin remembered Perry and wrote him directly if not succinctly:

"I find myself wondering whether you would be interested to join with me in trying to visualize, and then work out a plan which might be used to interest others in the work of preserving and restoring one or more" colonial shrines. As for the hope that anything would come of it, Goodwin was disarmingly vague. "If by any possibility, having visualized the effects desired, we could succeed in interesting others in the matter, it would be the most spectacular and interesting, and from the teaching point of view, the most valuable restoration ever attempted in America, and I should like above all things to have you associated with me in the preliminary study. We could have a jolly good time doing it together." Perry accepted without even settling on a fee.

Rockefeller had insisted on anonymity; Goodwin didn't even tell Perry he had a patron, let alone one who'd already bought an "antique...at eight." Nor was the preacher above some timely dissembling. As his faithful amanuensis Elizabeth Hayes would report, "Dr. Goodwin often said...the keeping of this secret would place a terrific strain upon his conscience as a clergyman, but that he was determined to keep the secret and that he hoped to save his conscience."

In fact Goodwin often misrepresented facts, as for instance when he later stated publicly that he was acquiring properties for the College or that his mysterious "associates" had definitely limited resources. Ingenuous as he might sometimes appear, he was an adept, even cunning solicitor of support for his many causes, a man who kept a looseleaf book of financiers' net worths and personal tastes for timely reference. His virtuosity comes clear in his letters: solicitous to people whose help he sought; businesslike to those whose services he was hiring; appreciative and even fawning to patrons, yet withal sincere. For all his prolixity, he could tell Rockefeller precisely what he was up to, and then share the intrigue. One 1927 postscript recounted the work of mapping the town with Perry in the dark of night:

"I wish you could be here and have some of the real fun that I am getting out of what we are doing. Last night the full moon joined in to help us. We found three College boys who wanted some exercise and with a long steel tape we measured the Duke of Gloucester Street... and plotted the houses.... Some of the colored folk whom we met must have taken us for maniacs or demon possessed men, and it was fun to see them jump off the sidewalk when they heard the long steel line rattle on the pavement and saw it move. When asked 'What are you doing?' the answer is that we are preparing a map to show people interested in history how to find the historic centers and the historic buildings."

These letters could be packed with information that proved he was moving ahead on several fronts. He dispatched Miss Hayes to the Library of Congress to peruse the *Virginia Gazette* for information about the colonial town. At the College he located the "Frenchman's Map" drawn by a French billeting officer during the Revolution, which he realized "will be invaluable to our study" for its house-by-house plan of Williamsburg. He found descriptions of the Capitol and pictures of the Raleigh Tavern. He persuaded the commander of a nearby air corps post to send a photographer aloft to shoot the town. Never one to miss a chance to drop a name, he took his own snapshots with "the fine camera" given him by "my friend Mr. R. T. H. Halsey (who is largely responsible for the American Wing at The Metropolitan Museum of Art)." For his own part, Rockefeller encouraged Goodwin with friendly notes and precise instructions.

In May 1927 Rockefeller returned to Williamsburg on the excuse (should public explanation be required) of showing his wife Memorial Hall. Receiving the couple in the newly furnished Wythe House study, Goodwin unveiled Perry's first architectural sketches, then walked them around town. Up to this point, Miss Hayes reported that Rockefeller "spoke always with an 'if.'" As was his habit, the millionaire asked scores of questions "about the future care of the property, about endowment, and what final dispositions could be made of the property. Again and again he cautioned him [Goodwin] not to let anyone know he was showing any interest."

The tale persists that upon returning to the study Dr. Goodwin reminded Rockefeller that they were sitting in the very room where Jefferson read law with George Wythe and then virtually summoned the patriots' spirits to join the colloquy. Whatever impressed him most, Miss Hayes recorded that at last "Mr. Rockefeller said, 'I am not interested in separate centers.'" He was taken by "the proposition as a whole, and a complete thing." Suggesting he'd have little time himself to give the project, "he called Dr. Goodwin 'the mother of the restoration—if a father can be a mother.' He asked if he would be willing to nurse the scheme along." Would a sinner like sainthood? Goodwin replied "he would love it above all things."

They decided that Perry should plat the entire town and Goodwin buy old houses one by one as they became available. Rockefeller was still not committed to anything more than providing the wherewithal; if the plan didn't pan out he might just put the properties back on the market. A few days later Rockefeller outlined the new phase of their arrangement in a letter which "authorizes my representatives to finance, on the general terms and conditions set forth, any or all of the projects enumerated therein." Another step was taken.

Like many homes, George Wythe's old house was often altered. Its plain facade of 1899 (above) received a porch early in this century (center), then a fancy pediment when Dr. Goodwin renovated it as his parish house (below). Finally, its original appearance would be restored (opposite above), but only after Bruton Parish's twenty-eighth rector and Mr. Rockefeller met in the room (opposite below)—now furnished as it might have been in colonial times—where Thomas Jefferson read law.

Miss Emma Louise Barlow planned to observe "the one hundred and tenth anniversary of Lafayette's visit to the city," a Williamsburg press agent revealed, when President Franklin D. Roosevelt came to town in 1934. Living in what became the Historic Area, she remained as one of the town's "life tenants." These citizens sold their homes to the Restoration with the proviso that they and their immediate descendants could stay on for their lifetimes. A few life tenants reside here still.

As he proceeded to buy houses, Goodwin was mindful that many were occupied by lifelong inhabitants. "It would be difficult, if not impossible, and I am inclined to think inadvisable" to force anyone out, he told Rockefeller. "If the thought and plan commends itself to you" he suggested a buy-now-take-later approach allowing residents "to continue to occupy their homes for the few remaining years of their lives, without rent, taxes or insurance." Such terms and $25,000 might induce septuagenarian Peyton Randolph Nelson and his wife to sell Tazewell Hall, the mansion built by Peyton Randolph's brother John "the Tory." All of $15,000 and life tenancy might wrest two properties from another "interesting character." Possessing one asset—an invitation to the banquet for the Marquis de Lafayette 103 years earlier—Miss Emma Louise Barlow feared burglars. Goodwin reported that the maiden lady "sleeps with six paper bags which she blows up and ties before going to sleep so that she can pop them in case she hears noises in the night which threaten disaster. She has not offered to sell the paper bags, nor is she much disposed to sell her house." But she might consider it if she could stay on.

Rockefeller seized upon the notion of a dollar-a-year rent and "life tenure," the device that enabled Goodwin to buy dozens of houses at reasonable prices. Some people criticized the Bruton Parish rector for pursuing an interest that so clearly conflicted with his pastoral responsibilities. While he was not accused of personally profiting from the transactions, his critics maintained (as a few still do) that he unfairly influenced many naive parishioners. No doubt the pastor enjoyed a unique advantage as a purchaser, and though he never made a clean sweep of old Williamsburg, antagonisms arose that clouded his ministry. Every Sunday one lady rose from her pew and walked out when he mounted the pulpit to preach; she did it regularly, you might even say religiously. Another woman would accost him on the street and ask "Are you going to preach the Gospel on Sunday? Or are you going to preach about wallpaper? I'm not coming to church if you're going to preach about wallpaper."

It was impossible to keep the campaign secret for long and soon the region was buzzing about the spendthrift parson. If prices didn't rise through the roof, two factors were responsible. For one thing, Williamsburgers knew all about the wages of speculation. Almost a decade earlier a Du Pont munitions plant at Penniman a few miles away had raised a boom-town of fifteen thousand people and house lots were hawked on Williamsburg's streetcorners. But when peace came and plans for plant expansion were canceled, Penniman became a ghost town of 3,778 souls. Judge Robert T. Armistead, who still inhabits one of the two Duke of Gloucester Street houses that Goodwin never got, remembers his father (also a judge) losing $30,000 the day the bubble burst. Notwithstanding people's reluctance to get burned by another boom, Goodwin used the press to spread his warning that inflated asking prices could smother the restoration project he was so rosily if vaguely forecasting.

No doubt, the intrigue was hard on his nerves as people tried to pry from him the secret of his backer's identity. Henry Ford was mentioned as was Harvey Firestone, George Eastman, J. P. Morgan (despite his death in 1913) and just about every other known millionaire. Vernon Geddy, who handled Goodwin's legal work, entered the rectory unannounced one day and heard a reference to "Mr. D." (Goodwin and Miss Hayes had taken to calling their benefactor "Mr. David," a code name adapted from *his* code name of "David's Father.") To no avail he goaded Goodwin with a bit of doggerel naming every rich man he could think of whose name began with D including "John D." When Goodwin took a short trip to escape the pressure, he wrote a codicil to his will that left the lawyer even deeper in the dark. Each time Rockefeller approved a purchase, his office sent an untraceable cashier's check which Goodwin deposited in his local bank before buying the property in his own name with his own check. The codicil stipulated that in the event of his death, houses that had been bought in this way were to be conveyed to "Colonel Arthur Woods" in New York. Colonel who? Geddy couldn't know Woods was executive officer to a captain of finance.

Goodwin's mysterious business was as much a boon to the young lawyer as it was to the town. "No one had any money in Williamsburg and no one needed any," Geddy would remember. "There was about fifteen dollars that would start out on Monday morning and everybody in town would get their hands on it" before the week was out. (That would change later, as, for example, when a family of shopkeepers pocketed $265,000 for their package of nine lots.)

As the preliminary buying continued, some owners started playing hard-to-get despite Goodwin's open letters to businessmen urging them to cooperate. One night a Chinese laundry burned to the ground; next morning three pillars of the Greek community announced they were ready to sell a movie theater, pool hall, "kandy kitchen" and several stores near the College. One of the sellers admitted the fire scared him: "Suppose my place had burned. I sell quick."

Meanwhile there was speculation in the local press, including a long account about the "Real Estate Boom" in the *Richmond News Leader*. Publisher John Stewart Bryan then wrote Rockefeller and tried to smoke him out: "I do not know whether you have had any role or part in this undertaking...as Dr. Goodwin has maintained an impenetrable silence." Bryan's suspicions were possibly not put to rest by Rockefeller's cagey reply. Expressing utter innocence, he wrote, "Let us hope, however, that [Dr. Goodwin's] hand will not be further forced until he is ready to show it, and that so long as he feels it best to withhold the names of his backers, his judgement in the matter will be respected."

By then Bryan's paper had carried an editorial applauding Goodwin and cautiously endorsing the restoration proposal. However, with vain prescience it cautioned against carrying the project too far: "No age can ever quite recapture the spirit of another....For its part the *News Leader* is confident that the restoration will not be carried too far—that its purpose will be to retain rather than to rebuild. Where attempts are made to reconstruct the more famous public buildings of the town, the unescapable limitations will be recognized and historical charlatanry will be avoided."

The acquisitive minister had told Geddy that the first time he earned money plowing as a boy, he saved up until he had enough to buy a book, *Buried Cities Uncovered*. Now he was preparing to live it. One day in November of 1927, Goodwin phoned Geddy from Washington and told him to meet his train at the station behind the school on the old Palace grounds. Thinking he wanted a briefing on the latest land titles he'd searched, Geddy was amazed when his client declared "Boy you haven't started....We're going to buy the town!"

Goodwin was returning from a carefully choreographed sojourn in New York's Vanderbilt Hotel. Though still in the dark, Perry had come down from Boston with his latest sketches for a restored town—one of them a nine-foot map—which they set up for display in a guest room. The country minister then asked the urbane architect to wait in his room all the next day in case he was needed. This was too much for even the obliging Perry, who would only agree to sit by the phone every hour on the hour.

Rockefeller arrived alone and marveled at both the map and letters from architectural

165

authorities whose endorsements Goodwin had solicited. He then offered Goodwin a salary to take on the coming work of pursuing the restoration, but the minister declined the offer saying he could only continue to buy houses if he could honestly report he had nothing to gain. Goodwin told his secretary that after his lieutenants arrived "Mr. Rockefeller took complete charge of the situation." He explained "every detail of the plan in a most masterful way, as though he had lived in Williamsburg for years.... He went through the town following the map, explaining the location of every prominent building, giving its history, and significance as it related to the plan, and the reasons why the Restoration appealed to his imagination and interest...Mr. Rockefeller intimated that he would be responsible for the development of the plans as they had been presented."

During the meeting they marked on Perry's map the status of properties purchased, optioned, etc. Meeting with Perry again, Goodwin showed him the map with its color-coded squares. "He was so astonished that he sat down *hard* on the bed. He had no idea that we had accomplished anything like that." And he still had no idea who he was working for.

Now the pace quickened. Rockefeller was no longer to be troubled with details, which would be handled by Colonel Woods, a gracious and able man militantly managerial enough to have been New York's police commissioner. Other Rockefeller aides would continue to review real estate and legal matters case by case. The restoration had become an enterprise of the Rockefeller empire however secret it remained. Soon after the new year, two corporations would be formed, the Williamsburg Holding Company to handle the physical work and Colonial Williamsburg, Inc., to consider impalpable programs.

In December 1927, Goodwin wrote Perry "At last I am able to...report that those associated with me in the Williamsburg Restoration development were most favorably impressed with the plans.... I am authorized to retain you and your firm for the further architectural work incident to the further development of the plans and projects under consideration." Goodwin insisted that the matter remain "*confidential*.... With this understanding you are hereby authorized to prepare the following full and complete plans," which he enumerated with price estimates: Wren Building, $409,000; Capitol, $188,000; Golden Horseshoe Inn (which was never built), $100,000; Palace, $200,000; plus unspecified amounts for town plans as needed. Perry replied with remarkable poise to the million-dollar letter: "We congratulate you upon your success. We are all agreed that the happy outcome is due to your extraordinary efforts.... We all thank you for your loyalty to us and thank you most sincerely."

In March 1928 the *New York Times Magazine* reported that "Historic Williamsburg, once the Capital of Virginia, will be rebuilt as nearly as possible in the preRevolutionary form, and stand as a living memorial of America's Colonial Days." It prompted a flood of mail that nearly swamped Goodwin. Heading home for lunch two blocks away, "I was stopped by three people, did not get home until a half hour after lunch was over, and found two men on the porch waiting for me when I reached my door." He then encountered a lady who wanted to start a tearoom, then a lawyer, and finally "a gentleman and his wife...wanting advice as to how to restore Carter's Grove." A letter from R. T. H. Halsey offered help locating furnishings, portraits and records in London.

Goodwin received permission to discuss the restoration with town officials—still without naming names—and start restoring the Wren Building (which always seemed to

One that got away: Neither old Judge Frank Armistead nor his son Judge Robert Armistead ever sold this handsome Greek Revival home beside Bruton Parish Church on Duke of Gloucester Street. At the other end of town near the Capitol, their cousins Misses Dora and Cara Armistead also stayed put while the town was restored around them. For many years they took in paying guests at their Victorian home, which the Association for the Preservation of Virginia Antiquities now rents as a museum.

have a life of its own). He'd also been authorized to contact the A.P.V.A., which owned the Capitol site and the Magazine. He admired the organization: "Those devoted ladies of Virginia bent like priestesses over the dying embers of ancient flames and breathed upon them and made them glow again. The fires, rekindled by them, lit the path which led to the fuller realization of the truth expressed by Ruskin when he wrote 'It is our duty to preserve what the past has had to say for itself.'"

But this band of far-flung gentlewomen hedged its bets. The executive committee expressed "its great interest in...the rebuilding of the House of Burgesses [sic] upon the original site." (The House of Burgesses was a corporate body of legislators; there was never a physical house.) But the ladies wanted the work done within five years or the agreement would expire. They asked for perpetual use of a meeting room in the Capitol, a tablet to commemorate their role and continuing oversight of the building's uses. All that agreed to, they had to poll their entire membership, which turned into a logistical nightmare.

The tangled conditions of this transaction were only a preview of the mammoth complexities to come, for while the Capitol site was owned by a private organization, the restoration plan involved public property as well. Thus a town meeting was called for June when the people of Williamsburg would vote on whether to transfer town acreage to unknown interests—but only after the "second Yankee invasion" became obvious. Strangers with sketch pads, surveyor's rods, slide rules and whatnot arrived on every train; one spinster said "Well I lived through one Reconstruction, I reckon I can live through another."

As the meeting date drew near, Dr. Goodwin requested an independent audit of Bruton's books, his personal accounts and city land records. The examination uncovered no fiddle-faddle, but it revealed the amount of Rockefeller money he'd spent thus far on properties: $2,225,189.87.

Work had already begun on Bracken Tenement, the first colonial building to be restored, when Williamsburg voters met in the auditorium of the high school on the old Palace site to consider two matters of signal importance to the restoration. Posters announced the mass meeting for 8:00 P.M., June 12, to discuss "a proposal to convey" the town's greens and jail to Goodwin and his nameless associates "in exchange for a new Court House and Jail." Goodwin and Geddy soon breathed easier because June 12 was also Election Day, and Mayor Henderson, who opposed the recent goings-on, was not reelected. The winner, Dr. John Garland Pollard, a politician on his way to becoming governor, was friendly to the restoration idea. He was elected to chair the mass meeting which attracted 450 people—only one-third of them voters. The proposed contract between the town and vaguely named corporations was read and explained. When a citizen asked what was wrong with the present jail, Judge Frank Armistead said it operated on the honor system; a prisoner serving a twenty-year hitch had recently absented himself, leaving a note that he'd be back later. As for the 150-year-old Courthouse, it lacked a jury room. Whenever a jury sat (which wasn't often) a clerk had to vacate her office "and she always fusses the next day about the cigars the jury smoke."

Goodwin rose to make his pitch. Pointing out that the town's attorney had endorsed the contract, he stressed "You may be sure that your legal rights will not be overlooked." Indeed, city land would be better protected than in the past when the town fathers had sold off lots around the Courthouse and Magazine. If his syndicate got these lands, "they shall never be sold off" but restored to states "which our ancestors planned. It is the purpose of

In 1928 Bracken Tenement became the first of the enterprise's houses to undergo restoration—even before the scope of the Restoration and the identity of its backers were publicly revealed.

our associates to make this favored city a national shrine," he declared. "Benefit will come in spiritual as well as material ways. Every business man will be benefitted. It should be a source of pride to you to feel that you will have here the most beautiful shrine dedicated to the lives of the nation builders. We will be the custodians of memorials to which the eyes of the world will be turned. We should return thanks that this place has been chosen as a shrine of history and of beauty. There will be windows built here through which men may look down the vistas of the past.... Williamsburg restored will transmit to the future an everlasting memorial of the events which were potent in the founding of the Federal republic and which inspired other nations of the world seeking to lay for themselves the foundations of popular government in liberty and justice."

The room was packed because people wanted to know not only what might transpire, but who was paying for what had already occurred. After further ado, which simply whetted his neighbors' razor-sharp curiosity, Goodwin declaimed "It is now my very great privilege and pleasure to announce that the donors of the money to restore Williamsburg are..."—here he paused, according to his secretary's record—"...Mr. and Mrs. John D. Rockefeller Jr. of New York." It brought the house down.

Still a few locals demurred. Major S. D. Freeman accepted "the unpleasant duty to voice the minority side.... If you give up your land it will no longer be your city. Will you feel the same pride in it that you now feel as you walk across the Greens or down the broad streets? Have you all been hypnotized by five million dollars dangled before your eyes?... What will happen when the matter passes out of the hands of Dr. Goodwin and Mr. Rockefeller, in both of whom we have perfect confidence?... We will reap dollars but will we own our own town? Will you not be in the position of a butterfly pinned in a glass cabinet, or like a mummy unearthed in the tomb of Tutankhamen?" Miss Hayes recalled "his talk was given in a clear, firm voice, with oratorical gestures. When he sat down there was perfect silence."

After short debate state roads commissioner George Coleman, who lived in the St. George Tucker House, asked for a standing vote. Some 150 citizens rose in the affirmative. According to one record, five voted no, one on the grounds that the ballot should be secret, four on the merits: Major Freeman, lame-duck Mayor Henderson and the sisters Dora and Cara Armistead, cousins of the judge who voted for the restoration but would thereafter be its frequent opponent.

Thus Palace Green and Market Square, along with some other plots, were transferred to Rockefeller's companies with the proviso that the public have perpetual access. In return, the town had the promise of a new jail and courthouse along with the prospect of improved streets, sidewalks, sewers, water mains, underground utilities, plantings and a state-of-the-art firehouse.

The story was reported in newspapers coast to coast. A Norfolk reporter was impressed that the Restoration (as it was now commonly referred to) might spend $15,000,000 to return "Williamsburg to her Colonial simplicity [sic]." Papers everywhere extolled Rockefeller and Goodwin for their vision. For the first time in America's history, a city had the promise of intentional resurrection for patriotic purposes. For the second time in living memory—the first since the town forgot about Election Day (until Geddy's father, the court clerk, belatedly remembered)—Williamsburg got national attention. Rockefeller's money and Goodwin's dream had put the vanished capital back on the map.

The First Restorers

Brick by brick, aged buildings were restored and vanished ones reconstructed—tasks easier to describe than to perform—as the Restoration sought to revive the town's eighteenth-century appearance. The restorers first had to discover such mundane things as the sizes and purposes of the very bricks: rubbed ones like these in a Palace arch (opposite), glazed ones, carved ones. Then they had to learn to make them by hand. They also discovered that many antique articles could be bought—entire houses for their molding and paneling, imported urns with allegorical figures to use as planters (left). In short, the task was a treasure hunt, an adventure in discovery and an exercise in invention, for no one had ever tried to restore a whole town before.

Often the first restorers learned by example; they studied surviving eighteenth-century buildings all over Virginia and beyond. Then they combined elements of "vernacular" architecture, like this beaded weatherboard on the side wall of the Pasteur & Galt Apothecary Shop and rusticated wood—cut to look like stone—on the side facing the street.

*A*s they rode around town in the borrowed limousine after the Phi Beta Kappa dedication, Dr. Goodwin and Mr. Rockefeller mused about "perpetual preservation." Then they walked the woods behind Bassett Hall where stands a huge tree that took root during George II's reign. The philanthropist asked "If I come back some day, can we bring our lunch down and eat it under the oak tree?" It seems such a naive request, almost a child's question by a fifty-three-year-old magnate who had nursed an interest in horticulture since his lonely boyhood on a sylvan estate. That evening the wistful patron made a tentative commitment to the minister's vague dream of restoring the town and weeks later Dr. Goodwin winningly sent him a Christmas box of holly, mistletoe and running cedar from the Williamsburg wilds. In his thank-you note Mr. Rockefeller wrote "I have thought many times of that marvelous oak tree which you took me to see and of the fall woods into which we looked. What a wonderful picture it was."

The question remained: Could they give their picture of resurrected Williamsburg a life of its own? That in turn could only be answered by the people they found to help them in the new work of creating a place that had been before. The raising of brick and mortar first depended on flesh and blood: employees, consultants, volunteers and friends; even some antagonists made a difference.

Bound simply by a gentlemen's agreement, Goodwin and Rockefeller had no idea what they were doing—namely inventing an interdisciplinary tradition. The genius of their plan lay in the fact that there was no plan and not much of a personnel roster to begin with. "Actually there were no people really prepared to administer an undertaking like the one at Williamsburg," Charles B. Hosmer Jr. would write a half century later in *Preservation Comes of Age*, his definitive history of the preservation movement. No one had tried this kind of thing before. "New professions, new organizational procedures, and a whole new philosophy of restoration would have to be created.... If a physical restoration was to follow, Goodwin had to find contractors, historians, archaeologists, furniture experts, draftsmen, landscape architects and engineers. These professions were available in 1928, but none of them had any experience in the re-creation of a colonial city."

Both Goodwin and Rockefeller had considerable experience in collective enterprise. The rector was a past master at marshaling support for Christian good works. The philanthropist was a devout believer in backing mostly temporal ventures with the soundest talent his impressive resources could hire. Thus, though they were blazing a trail through an interdisciplinary wilderness, by habit and experience they sought able help.

The Restoration required a host of disciplined talents and quickly set out to hire them. By the time the two-corporation enterprise went public, it had acquired an executive officer in Arthur Woods, had hired the firm Perry, Shaw and Hepburn as its architects and retained the contracting company that became Todd and Brown as its builders and engineers. Goodwin had long since instructed Perry to consult two respected architects, A. Lawrence Kocher and Fiske Kimball, who believed that the young discipline of historical architecture should rely on the purest "authenticity." Further, before offering Perry's first plans to Rockefeller, Goodwin showed them to five solons of the American Institute of Ar-

Some details of the Governor's Palace were presumed, some discovered by chance, still others learned through scholarship. The gate pillar (opposite) was mounted with the English lion carved in imported Portland stone. Brick floors (above left) were laid wherever brick might have been used in old Virginia. (It's worth noting that the reconstructed Palace is now about as old as the original was when Jefferson drew his plan of it.) The ballroom doorway (above right), surrounded by a bracket of carved bricks, was copied from a ruined Tidewater mansion, Rosewell. The wall surrounding the grounds (below) was based upon archaeological findings.

chitects who endorsed them in glowing terms, which impressed Rockefeller all the more. Strange as it seems, this kind of peer review hadn't occurred before, yet the Restoration would turn it into a virtual prerequisite for action. Within six months of the town meeting, the Advisory Committee of Architects was formed and began the work it would pursue for twenty years.

Appointment of the Advisory Committee gave Williamsburg a decidedly architectural emphasis, which seems in retrospect as inevitable as it was initially fortuitous. The complex reasons were happenstantial. For one thing, as Hosmer wrote, "The profession of architecture was already history-minded in the 1920s." Designers had been measuring old buildings throughout the country and borrowing details for office buildings and schools. But kindred professions "were not ready to assume roles of any consequence in a restoration program. Historians merely paid lip service to the idea that buildings could be classed as documents.... Landscape architects had restricted their activities mainly to developing city parks and planning gardens for the wealthy. Archaeologists had no experience in interpreting the foundations of buildings from the colonial period because their main interests lay in Grecian, Roman, Egyptian, Mayan and North American Indian antiquities.... No large contracting firms had done restoration up to 1928 because no projects had been started that would have needed them. In spite of these obstacles Goodwin and Woods began to assemble a remarkable organization that would help to transform the rector's dream into bricks and mortar."

In 1930 the Restoration's officers stood for a group portrait. Among them are (front row, second from left to right) *the Reverend W. A. R. Goodwin, roads commissioner George P. Coleman and President Arthur Woods;* (second row, left) *attorney Vernon Geddy;* (third row, left, center and right) *architect William G. Perry, landscape architect Arthur A. Shurcliff and executive Kenneth Chorley.*

Among the first to arrive was A. Edwin Kendrew, a junior man from Perry's Boston office. He left his bride, Melinda, at home in Massachusetts because his was to be a brief assignment after all—as he recalled six decades after fetching her to Virginia. He'd spend his life at Williamsburg, rising to the top of its architectural operations and winning many distinctions including an A.I.A. Gold Medal. Coming close on his heels in 1928 was Singleton P. Morehead, who rented a room in Judge Armistead's home. Finding life professionally challenging and socially inspiring, he also soon found a wife in Cynthia Beverly Tucker Coleman, daughter of the state roads commissioner.

"There wasn't a nice collection of architectural books as you would find for, say Connecticut or Massachusetts," said the Harvard-trained architect Morehead. The lack of published material "meant we had to go out in the field and measure and photograph." They made full-sized drawings of details "filling notebooks with sketched plans and elevations." They toured the countryside on weekends and wrote the book on Virginia's vernacular architecture. They examined old buildings, measured them in detail and made precise drawings. They were particularly interested in details: moldings, cornices, chair rails, paneling, staircases, outbuildings, building techniques evident in the "original fabric" of old structures.

"We discovered a very fortunate thing. I doubt if we could have done this job if it hadn't been so": Virginia colonial architecture had rather strict conventions. "There are only a few cornice types, interior or exterior. There were only a few window designs—sash and frames; the use of beaded weatherboard was almost universal. If it was not beaded weatherboards, then it was flush boarding, beaded or not. Shingling methods were all about the same. In chimney and fireplace construction there were seven or eight kinds.... Ceiling heights were very consistent.... So once you learned the words and phrases, once you learned your bag of tricks, you were in good shape to reconstruct and restore."

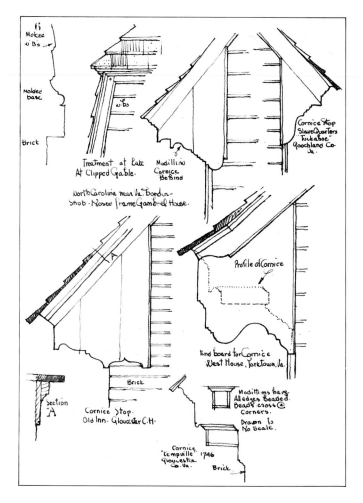

A host of talented people helped resurrect this town. Singleton Morehead, a junior architect with the firm of Perry, Shaw and Hepburn, recorded architectural details (left) from many Tidewater sources, thus providing a wealth of information about authentic elements to be used in the Historic Area. A plan and elevation of Duke of Gloucester Street's north side (below) exemplifies the precision that this architectural firm brought to bear as it drafted the entire town. The view runs from an "apothecary shop," now called Prentis Store, to a "store" occupied by one William Cowan, now Davidson Shop.

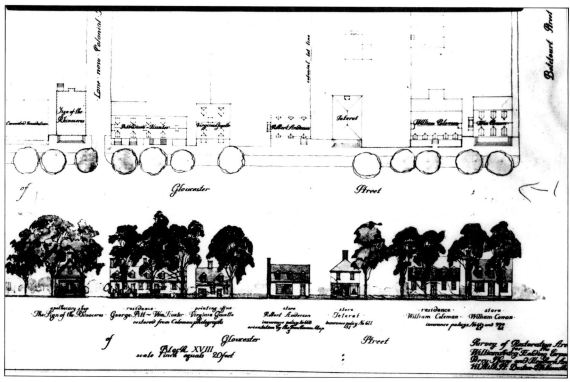

177

Splendid gardens became one of the "Six Appeals of Williamsburg" and the Palace formal grounds (left and above) won especially wide acclaim. Landscape architect Arthur A. Shurcliff paid closer attention to horticultural beauty than precise replication of colonial gardens—of which little was known in the 1930s. Thus, he often planted what he thought ought to have been and in so doing spectacularly adorned the town. Today, archaeologists seek to identify plants that colonists actually raised and horticulturists try to plan gardens as faithful to history as the buildings are.

The photographs they took and precise drawings they made became a source of details for reconstructions and restorations. They also sent the word out that they were interested in materials from eighteenth-century houses; the Restoration became a steady buyer of dismantled buildings. Many old buildings were bought and stored piecemeal, then used as architectural spare parts after experience proved that moving a house didn't always work; it caused "too much breakage." As they discovered these design elements, they often found that seemingly aesthetic details had practical implications: Shingles finished with rounded ends did not curl and split like those with square ends. Bricks rubbed flat for use around openings offered true surfaces when doors and windows were installed; thus they didn't leak.

As for living conditions, Williamsburg was a mixed bag. The local restaurants were "absolutely foul"; the old Pocahontas Tea Room was visited by rats as well as people. In self-defense Restoration House was opened, a place where the invaders suffered a steady diet of cold country ham and boiled potatoes until they learned they'd get fried chicken if they tipped the waitress. Drink was another matter: the best moonshine was $5 a gallon, and connoisseurs kept six months' supply on hand so it could "age."

Morehead found his southern hosts famously hospitable, sociable and cultured. The Restoration crowd attended oyster roasts and shad bakes in the country and marveled at visits by touring theatrical troupes that performed Shakespeare alfresco. (*Midsummer Night's Dream* was memorably canceled when an actor blew a few blasts on a conch horn which brought every mongrel cur and coon dog howling to the stage thinking a hunt was in the offing.) Alas, the Yankees' idea of a party shocked some locals. The 1930 New Year's Eve blast at the high school featured parody skits on stage, bizarre costumes among the audience and even more bizarre behavior that left some revelers stacked "like cordwood" in the basement. After the celebrants realized they'd almost burned the building down, parties became more private.

(Nonetheless, this must have been a caring community. When a young architect died after a sudden illness in 1931, his colleagues raised a small memorial to him beside the Bruton Parish Church walk. Now the bronze sundial shows the signs of reverent wear; its gnomon has been broken and welded on again; its corners are bright from the touch of passing fingers. "In remembrance of John A. Barrows 1906–1931 Architect Writer Antiquarian," it is graced by an inscription reading around its border: "The shadow fell for a moment upon the hour that marked his death then passed leaving his name and memory illuminated by the eternal sunshine.")

Iconography appealed to the first restorers. Witness the telling business of selecting a seal for Williamsburg. It shows how the Restoration went about its work: In one word, energetically; in another, deliberately; in a third, redundantly. If anything got lost in the shuffle it might only be efficiency, but better that than an unsatisfactory decision made in haste.

By Thanksgiving, 1931, it was decided to adopt an emblem: Colonial Williamsburg's own bit of heraldry complete with motto. Perry (in Boston) sent Chorley (in New York) a list of sentiments, each one loftier than the last, such as: For the perpetual remembrance of the thing; Honor and protection; To remember these things hereafter will be a pleasure; etc. Perry opined "To us the motto *Quae amissa Salva* seems the best of the lot," and kindly translated that: "What was lost is safe."

Minutes of a December meeting recorded that "Mr. Perry has presented the proposed seal for Colonial Williamsburg and it was accepted and approved, with the exception of the

Colonial Williamsburg's hard-won seal.

motto. Dr. Goodwin suggested that we use Ruskin's line 'It is our duty to preserve what the past has had to say for itself,' which was accepted and approved. Mr. Perry is to have this translated into Latin." While Goodwin dug up the rest of Ruskin's prolix homily for Woods to forward to Rockefeller, Perry waited upon his Boston scholars and Chorley demanded action. The next month a letter of accustomed formality went from the principal at 26 Broadway to his principal assistant at 61 Broadway: "Dear Colonel Woods: On the enclosed slip I have presented the various suggestions for a motto for Williamsburg which were discussed the other day. Either of the last two, preferably the last, seems to me the best, namely, 'That the future may learn from the past.' These I pass on to you simply for such further action as you think best. Very truly, John D. Rockefeller Jr."

The next day Woods instructed Chorley to send his employer's first two choices on to the architects for their opinion. But the day after that Perry sent Chorley translations of the original choice which one classicist rendered as *Vox Aevi Praeteriti Conservanda* and another as *Nos Oportet Praeterita Tradere.* A week later, Chorley asked Perry "Are you agreeable in deciding upon Mr. Rockefeller's first suggestion, . . . and, if so, would you recommend that it be put on the seal in English or Latin? Perhaps it is too long in Latin." Dr. Goodwin would yet offer something even longer, compliments of a Williamsburg scholar: *Ut Praeteritorum Gloria Posteritatis Memoriae Tradatur* ("In Order that the Glory of the Past May Be Handed Down to the Memory of Those Who Follow"). Deciding that Rockefeller's favorite was too long even in English, Perry redesigned the wavy ribbon to accommodate a few extra words.

Thus the motto evolved: a noble expression that caught the visionary's eye was boiled down by the committee that would make it all happen and selected by the patron. Rockefeller once told an aide: "All my life I have employed experts. I listen to what they say and then I exercise my own good judgement."

To plan the gardens, a project of considerable personal priority for Mr. Rockefeller, Perry's firm recommended a man of twenty-four-karat credentials and pinchbeck habits. Arthur A. Shurcliff (nee Shurtleff), a student of southern horticulture, had helped found Harvard's landscape architecture school with the son of Frederick Law Olmsted, designer of New York's Central Park and Washington's Rock Creek Park. As odd as he was able, Shurcliff habitually wore a black greatcoat and white socks. Whenever he stayed in a hotel he brought a rope and tied one end to a radiator in case of fire. When invited to dinner, he brought his own victuals in a brown bag. When World War II broke out he furnished his living room in Massachusetts with a carriage, stocking it with food and camping supplies in case an enemy invasion forced his family to evacuate.

However eccentric, he was an ambitious aesthete. Time would prove that he was more aggressive in pursuing his own ideas of beauty than in bringing colonial southern gardens into full flower. But if it would turn out that some of his designs were historically fanciful, it bears mention that scholars then knew precious little about colonial gardens. As happened in so many instances and specialties, Colonial Williamsburg itself would be responsible for making the great leaps backward in time. Further, the gardens he designed were soon numbered among the most beautiful in America. Indeed they earned premier status in what the Restoration later called the "Six Appeals of Williamsburg." (The others were architecture, furniture and furnishings, crafts, history and heritage, and preservation research.) Shurcliff designed the splendid formal gardens behind the Palace with its holly maze and ha-ha, which concealed railroad tracks. He planned the anachronistic but lovely El-

Tulips bloom in the garden of the Benjamin Powell House (left), home of the builder who repaired the Public Gaol, raised the Bruton Parish Church tower and constructed the Public Hospital. A paper mulberry—the tree planted in vain to feed silkworms—shades the Orlando Jones House garden (above). This home was named for the son of Bruton's first rector and grandfather of Martha Dandridge Custis, the widow who wed George Washington.

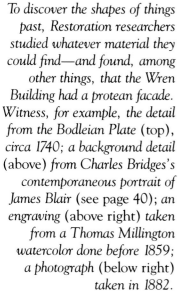

To discover the shapes of things past, Restoration researchers studied whatever material they could find—and found, among other things, that the Wren Building had a protean facade. Witness, for example, the detail from the Bodleian Plate (top), circa 1740; a background detail (above) from Charles Bridges's contemporaneous portrait of James Blair (see page 40); an engraving (above right) taken from a Thomas Millington watercolor done before 1859; a photograph (below right) taken in 1882.

kanah Deane House garden, fabulous topiaries and several planting beds in the shape of the Union Jack.

Shurcliff ignored practical considerations, like budgets, with such aplomb that even Rockefeller laughed in the end. When explaining one plan for the Palace gardens, he pretended not to hear the patron's repeated requests for a cost estimate until the normally diffident Rockefeller shouted for the first time in anyone's experience "What is the cost?!" Too aloof to have come up with the kind of solid figure the enterprise favored, the gardener said "between two and five hundred thousand" which left his usually sedate associates in stitches. Rockefeller answered "Oh well, let's just appropriate a million and go to lunch."

Shurcliff notwithstanding, the early restorers developed a dedication to historical accuracy. Dr. Goodwin had set an early if naive example with his investigations into what the town had been. When architects alone couldn't come up with the detailed information that soon appeared necessary, more conventional scholarship was called into play and made a substantial mark. Goodwin not only assigned his secretary to examine records, he lured his son Rutherfoord away from a Rochester newspaper job to handle many tasks, one of them historical research. Then the rector commissioned a cousin to search colonial records.

Following the trail back to England in 1929, Mary F. Goodwin haunted the British Museum, hoping (in vain) to prove that Sir Christopher Wren had indeed designed the College building that bore his name. Instead she came upon a catalogue of manuscripts elsewhere that led her to Oxford University's Bodleian Library in search of a copperplate engraving of "a village in Virginia." A few days before Christmas she fired off a message describing what came to be called the Bodleian Plate, a montage of the Capitol, Palace and College executed about 1740. Steel to restore the Wren Building had already been ordered,

Even old family photographs became useful sources of architectural information. These young people (above) posed in front of what had been colonial silversmith James Craig's house before its demolition in 1907. The enlarged detail (below) reveals not only a peeking boy but details of door placement, window arrangement and shingling. The building today (see pages 78–79), known as the Golden Ball and reconstructed to its original appearance, once again vends handmade silver objects.

but a crudely transmitted facsimile of the plate revealed different roof features than Perry and company had surmised. The rear roof of the main range wasn't straight; it featured an odd and totally unpredictable series of sawtooth gables. The Restoration was pleased to make it right.

Painstaking scholars proved their worth many times over. The State Art Commission had special oversight powers regarding the Wren Building, since it belonged to a state college. The commissioners rejected the restorers' plans because of the proposed location of staircases, saying that such a large building wouldn't have had a central stair. Kenneth Chorley mentioned the matter to Governor Harry F. Byrd, a descendant of the colonial patriarchs and as impulsive a politician as he was a faithful friend of the institution that brought national attention to his state. The governor offered to fire any commission members who stood in Williamsburg's way, but Chorley dissuaded him, thinking it would only make matters worse. In any event, the new Research Department found a letter which School Master Mungo Ingles wrote to Governor Nicholson in Annapolis after the 1705 fire. It referred to the stairs "(standing as your Exc[ellenc]y: well knowes) in the Middle of the Pile." This proved the theory advanced by Restoration designers; most important the building was *accurate*.

(Confrontations with state agencies changed Mr. Rockefeller's mind about the ultimate disposition of the Restoration. Initially, he'd thought to turn his project over to William and Mary when it was complete. He decided against that course because it appeared that political pressures could be brought to bear on any state institution and he disliked the notion that his legacy might be buffeted by the winds of faddish popularity and the whims of politicians. Beyond that, of course, it became evident that the Restoration would never be finally finished.)

As research efforts broadened, elementary archaeology was given its due. Though James Knight was trained as an architect, he was given the title of archaeologist and assigned the job of combing the entire 170-odd-acre Historic Area in search of building remains. Directing a gang of laborers, he dug trenches one shovel blade wide and a shovel handle apart. When he came to an old foundation, he uncovered it; when he found nothing he simply backfilled. Using the most heavy-handed techniques of the time, he thus traversed the town and found virtually every old foundation—though he ignored soil strata and artifacts, to the consternation of trained archaeologists later.

One who made as significant and far more graceful a contribution was Rutherfoord Goodwin. A man of keen intellect and winning personality, the youngest surviving child of the minister's first wife quickly took charge of education, training, public relations and publications. It was Rutherfoord who hit upon the idea of recruiting hostesses from among the region's gentlewomen and training them in matters of history and Restoration philosophy. He also had them dress in colonial clothes so that they could be identified by (and distinguished from) the visitors who started arriving in ever greater numbers once the Raleigh Tavern opened in 1932. His band of three ladies grew into something that wasn't considered at the outset, a corps of "interpreters" eventually numbering in the hundreds to make visitors' experiences "educational."

A skillful scholar and writer, Rutherfoord had both intelligence and imagination. Since Williamsburg started attracting visitors from the outset, he provided a Baedeker in

Declaration for Assurance. № 486.

THE undersigned *James Semple* — residing at *Williamsburg* — in the county of *James City* do hereby declare for Assurance in the Mutual Assurance Society against Fire on Buildings of the State of Virginia, established the 26th December, 1795, agreeable to the several acts of the General Assembly of this state, to wit:

My *four* buildings on a *back street south of the old capitol at Williamsburg* now occupied by *myself* situated between the *House* of *Robert H. Waller* and that of *Benj. Bucktrout* in the county of *James City* in the *City of Williamsburg* their dimensions, situation, and contiguity to other buildings or wharves what the walls are built of, and what the buildings are covered with, are specified in the hereunto annexed description of the said buildings on the plat, signed by me and the appraisers, and each valued by them as appears by their certificate hereunder, to wit:

The *Dwelling house* marked	A	at	1700	Dollars, say *Seventeen hundred* — — —	Dollars
The *Kitchen & Smoke ho* do	B	at	100	do — *One hundred* — — —	do
The *Stable & Carriage* do	C	at	100	do — *One hundred* — — —	do
The *Office* — — do	D	at }	100	do — *One hundred* — — —	do
The *Office* } do	E	at		do	do
The — — — do	F	at — —	do		do
The — — — do	G	at — —	do		do
The — — — do	H	at — —	do		do

$$\underline{2000}$$

by Two thousand   **Dollars in all.**

I do hereby declare and affirm that I hold the above mentioned buildings with the land on which they stand, in fee-simple, and that they are not, nor shall be insured elsewhere, without giving notice thereof, agreeable to the policy that may issue in my name, upon the filing of this declaration, and provided the whole sum does not exceed four-fifths of the verified value; and that I will abide by, observe, and adhere to the Constitution, Rules and Regulations as are already established, or may hereafter be established by a majority of the insured, present in person, or by representatives, or by the majority of the property insured represented, either by the persons themselves, or their proxy duly authorised, or their deputy so established by law, at any general meeting, to be held by the said Assurance Society. Witness my hand and seal at *Williamsburg* this *twentieth* — day of *July 1801*

Teste   *James Semple*
Lewis Rivalain

WE the underwritten, being each of us house-owners, declare and affirm that we have examined the above mentioned property of *James Semple Esquire* — and that we are of opinion that it would cost in cash *four thousand* Dollars to build the same, and is now (after the deduction of *two thousand* Dollars for decay or bad repair) actually worth *Two Thousand* Dollars in ready money, as above specified to the best of our knowledge and belief, and be the said subscriber has acknowledged before us his above signature.

Geo: Jackson —   } Residing in *the City of*
Champion Travis   } *Williamsburg*
Wm Russell

Documents as mundane as insurance policies could provide a wealth of information. This one (opposite) includes a list of dependencies and sketches of the house James Semple owned in 1801. Now called the William Finnie House for an eighteenth-century occupant, it may have been designed by Jefferson and anticipates the Federal style of the early nineteenth century. The painstaking act of restoration (above) required removal of rotten wood and made the place look a wreck before its resurrected beauty emerged (below and detail opposite).

the sort of book once called a "conceit." The choice volume contained his entertaining and accurate narrative written in the style of the eighteenth century along with appendices of historical documents. Printed and bound in engaging mimicry of colonial books, *A Brief & True Report Concerning* Williamsburg *in Virginia* first appeared in 1935 and still sells steadily more than fifty years later. Intended as the Restoration's first guidebook, albeit unlike any other, it opens with the telling salutation:

> GOOD FRIEND, what Matter how or whence you come
> To walk these Streets which are the Nation's Home;
> Rest for a Time and—resting—read herein,
> Seek from the Past and—seeking—Wisdom win:
> For if the Things you see give you no Gain,
> The LIVES of many MEN were lived in vain.

Sad to tell, Rutherfoord's career at Williamsburg was not an unalloyed success. This despite such random duties as standing in for his father in a movie about the Restoration (opposite Rockefeller who played himself). Without credit, he also wrote a conventional guidebook that sold over three million copies until finally retired in 1985 after thirty-four years in print. Rutherfoord was a "creative" and sensitive person, one among many bound to fall out with the aggressive Kenneth Chorley. It seems to have been a matter of clashing personalities, dissonant purposes, differing opinions and—on Chorley's part—perhaps too much devotion to duty. Hosmer wrote "The restoration needed a 'conscience' and Rutherfoord ably filled that role," but Chorley didn't welcome many players on Mr. Rockefeller's stage.

From the beginning of the Restoration, Chorley was the man from New York who visited Williamsburg most often and most forcefully. His ability, energy and loyalty to his superior were as imposing as his 6'5" frame. "KC" seems to have suffered no inferiors very gladly. Born in England, the son of an Episcopal clergyman, he was raised in a chic New York suburb and turned down an appointment to West Point; instead he sought his fortune in the southwest as a railroad man. He boasted of once working 397 straight days—at 12 hours a day—before becoming the youngest railyard superintendent in the land. After working briefly for the spectral Henry Ford, he returned east and met Arthur Woods through one of his aristocratic father's friends. Soon he became his right-hand man. Earning Mr. Rockefeller's confidence and affection, he succeeded Woods as president of Williamsburg in 1935 and held the post until 1958; he then acted as a consultant until 1963 when he was elected trustee emeritus, a capacity in which he served until his death in 1974.

Two decades after his retirement and one after his death, Chorley was still remembered variously with admiration, awe, affection and fear. His faithful secretary says "no executive ever knew how to get so much" from his subordinates. Others say he demanded too much. A Williamsburg physician found himself overworked before Chorley's periodic visits, which invariably prompted epidemics of gastrointestinal distress among Restoration supervisors. Called "a brute, a boor and a bully" by one bitter survivor, he was a taskmaster. On at least one occasion, he summoned one administrator to his office simply to witness him dress down another. And he required executives to keep letters of resignation typed and ready for signature. Many who knew him would remember him as an ambitious man who coveted power and access to powerful people; a member of the Rockefeller family who saw him operate would remember him as an able and loyal family retainer, indeed "a lackey." (One of the things that irritated several Rockefellers was Chorley's cheek; he loved playing host to visiting dignitaries and when there wasn't a Rockefeller in town he got to monopolize the show. Sometimes he even forgot himself when the family was present. On one ceremonial occasion Mrs. Rockefeller urged her firstborn son—then chairman of Williamsburg's board—"Now John, don't let Mr. Chorley push you out of the carriage.")

Some of Chorley's minions thought him so dedicated to fault-finding that they made certain he'd see something wrong lest he keep them up all night looking for a gaffe. At least once they hung Queen Anne's flag upside down so he could order it righted. Yet he could also be famously generous. He was perfectly capable of rewarding a job well done with a week's stay at a resort with all expenses paid. After Vernon Geddy's unexpected death, Chorley summoned young Vernon Jr. and ordered: "I want you to do something for me"— serve as Mr. Rockefeller's personal attorney for Virginia matters. It was a bit of business that helped the fledgling lawyer launch a distinguished career. And while whatever quiet credit went to Mr. Rockefeller, it was Chorley who established secret trust funds for several genteel paupers living in the Historic Area.

Chorley was also a very able administrator. As Hosmer wrote, "When one takes Boston architects, New York contractors, and northern money into a Virginia town, it requires great organizational skill and tact to achieve success." Chorley applied the skill within the organization; the tact he reserved for townspeople when it suited him, playing poker, for example, with influential local cronies whom he cultivated and genuinely liked.

Hindsight suggests it was Chorley who made Williamsburg work, albeit at some cost to the people who worked for him, including the talented, if eccentric, Rutherfoord Goodwin. Mr. Rockefeller's eldest grandchild, longtime trustee Abby O'Neill summed him up as adroitly as anyone, calling him "a very powerful and energetic man stubborn enough to get things done." Kendrew, and several others, credit him with a larger, more nebulous achievement. It was Chorley who kept Rockefeller interested in what was going on in Williamsburg, and when his interest lagged apparently got the ball rolling again, sometimes by starting a new project that would intrigue his employer. One of the ironies is that this fearsome man adored his gentle-mannered boss.

The Restoration could not have thrived without the aid of devoted outsiders like Horace M. Albright who'd been Yellowstone National Park Superintendent when Rockefeller toured the West in 1924. Later, as director of the National Park Service, Albright found he shared a new interest with the philanthropist, namely the creation of a colonial national monument. Subsequently named the Colonial National Historical Park, this project would physically link three sites that were bound by history in Dr. Goodwin's estimation since "Williamsburg is the continuation of Jamestown and Yorktown is the vindication of Williamsburg."

The idea for a park emerged after Michigan Congressman Louis C. Cramton visited the Wythe House. Connecting the site of the first successful colony, the colonial capital and the battlefield where independence was won, it would feature one of the nation's first scenic highways, but its creation involved a political tangle. In 1929 Albright escorted Cramton's appropriations committee to Williamsburg and found his mettle sorely tested. For example, he was asked to organize a party at Chorley's house after a formal banquet hosted by the governor. Since Prohibition was still the much-flouted law of the land, it would not do to invite a "dry" like Cramton to a "wet" social event. Not knowing which congressmen drank and which didn't—and believing a mistake could be fatal to the cause—Albright showed

Mr. and Mrs. Archibald M. McCrea at Carter's Grove. The house they renovated as their home later became an annex of Colonial Williamsburg.

up at Chorley's party alone. The next day the group was invited to Carter's Grove by Mr. and Mrs. Archibald M. McCrea who were renovating the 1750 plantation house built by Robert "King" Carter's grandson Carter Burwell. For refreshments, the McCrea's "didn't *offer*" anything but had a bar set up. "The Congressmen pretty nearly broke the antique furniture rushing over."

Back in Washington, Albright began plotting to get the highway approved. Here the problem lay in the proposed route—through an ammunition depot along a stretch of the York, which navy brass enjoyed to the limit. In addition to officers' homes overlooking the river, the installation had boat docks, bathing beaches, duck blinds and other amenities of military life. "It was just a little paradise in there, and they were not going to let anybody invade." Even the Park Service director wasn't allowed on the property without special permission. If the parkway-through-paradise proposal went through normal channels, the navy would block it by one ruse or another. Instead Albright drafted a presidential proclamation and Secretary of the Interior Ray Lyman Wilbur persuaded President Hoover to sign it before the Secretary of the Navy even saw it.

Politicians proved eager to support the plan for a colonial park comprising much of struggling Yorktown, all of Jamestown (moribund save for its ruins) and a right-of-way through Williamsburg. The colonial capital had been considered as a potential part of the park, but a group of townspeople led by Judge Frank Armistead opposed that. As his son remembers it, he opposed placing any part of Williamsburg under the aegis of a federal agency that might override local authority. Armistead had spoken in support of Goodwin's proposition at the town meeting that launched the Restoration. After that he came to be regarded as anti-outsider in general, anti-Restoration in particular and anti-Rockefeller in person.

His Classical Revival brick house hard by the Church on Duke of Gloucester Street was one of a handful of properties never acquired by Goodwin or Colonial Williamsburg. (The judge offered to sell this handsome home much later, but at the astronomical figure of $80,000 or twice the going price at the time. Chorley said turning him down was his worst mistake.) The Victorian home by the Capitol, which Armistead's maiden cousins kept as a guesthouse, was another. When Miss Cara Armistead died in 1984, the house was leased to the A.P.V.A. The last notable holdouts were a scattering of properties acquired by a lady who left them all to a foundation established just to receive them.

Virginia Braithwaite Haughwout "caught on in the beginning" to the local importance of Mr. Rockefeller's historical adventure, according to Colonial Williamsburg's longtime legal and financial manager Roger Leclere. A descendant of the Bucktrout clan of cabinetmakers and builders, she lived on Duke of Gloucester Street in the "Bull's Head," a substantial building that dated back to colonial times. For reasons long since buried "she came to despise Kenneth Chorley and all the Rockefellers," Leclere remembers, but that did not blind her to the opportunities created by their presence. By the late 1940s she came to possess several parcels in or adjoining the Historic Area, lots that had been owned in generations past by various relatives or ancestors. Town lore has it that she further acquired a certain fourteen-acre tract which she bought at auction on the Courthouse steps back when Vernon Geddy Sr. was handling the Restoration's business affairs. He'd gone to the tax sale with instructions to bid as much as $25,000. Every time he bid Miss Ginny raised him a few hundred dollars. When he reached his limit, Mrs. Haughwout won the prize. The story, which has acquired the vague aura of myth, though no archival documents illuminate it, goes on: A few days later, the landed lady called Geddy to admit she really didn't want the property; she just believed that the Restoration shouldn't get it for such a poor price as his original bid. She would gladly let Geddy buy her out, in fact she hoped he would—for $1,000 more than she paid. Geddy refused to be gulled in such a manner. It was dishonorable. Besides, they didn't need the property even if it did front on Francis Street and what became Bucktrout Lane.

Mrs. Haughwout then decided to build on another property, a ravine called Ginny's Bottom that ran from Duke of Gloucester Street to Nicholson Street. Already possessing a home in town, she didn't want another; she wanted a rental property, an in-town motel, but her plans fell somewhat short of meeting zoning regulations. She appealed, Colonial Williamsburg opposed her and the matter became a court contest joined by attorneys whose names would echo around town one way or another. The lady's lawyer was Robert Armistead, the judge's son (and later a judge himself who would become involved in a dispute with Colonial Williamsburg over an abandoned family cemetery at Greenhill, the land behind the Robert Carter House). The Restoration was represented by Lewis F. Powell Jr., later associate justice of the Supreme Court and for a short period chairman of Colonial Williamsburg's board of trustees. When she did not prevail, Mrs. Haughwout abandoned her plans and instead leased the ravine to Colonial Williamsburg for ninety-nine years. Ginny's Bottom became the site of the Printing Office, Bindery and Paper Mill, that lovely colonial industrial park. But Miss Ginny would never see it; she died soon after signing the lease.

She left the use of her properties to four children during their lifetimes and thereafter to the Bucktrout-Braithwaite Memorial Foundation. One heir leased the property known as the Redwood Ordinary to Colonial Williamsburg for a century. Another heir lived on the deep Francis Street lot that Geddy had refused to buy for more than the tax sale price. It had been improved after a fashion by an eighteenth-century building that had stood in the way of a new highway in Providence Forge, Virginia, until it was bought for a song and towed to Williamsburg. The land's value had been further enhanced by the success of the adjacent Williamsburg Inn, which kept growing and needing new amenities like a belle needs balls.

Mrs. Haughwout's daughter let it be known that she wanted to improve the property further, perhaps by renting it all to a major hotel chain. Rather than see that, Colonial Williamsburg agreed to restore the relocated building, now known as Providence Hall, stopping place for heads of state. Colonial Williamsburg built the Inn's Providence Hall wings on the rented land and added a few other embellishments like tennis courts. Living in her own house on the property, the heiress receives rent that reflects the property's increased value, Leclere says, or about four times as much a year as her mother paid for it.

Another daughter continued living in the Bull's Head. She finally found her rambling digs too much to handle and proposed leasing them to Colonial Williamsburg. Of course she had a condition. This had been her home, woman and girl, and she wanted Williamsburg's promise to restore it—the word sticks in Leclere's memory—"sympathetically." It wasn't an unreasonable request. In short order a long lease on the property was arranged and the building was treated with more sympathy than the lady could have hoped for. It became the site of a major dig by historical archaeologist Ivor Noël Hume, who examined it with extravagant care before it reopened under its historical name, Wetherburn's Tavern.

The Growing Years

The Restoration quickly became a sort of time machine as it set out to accomplish nothing less than the preincarnation of Williamsburg. The goal was two-fold: to discover what the city had been and to re-create it as it appeared in the third quarter of the eighteenth century. Often this meant building from the ground up, though wonders could sometimes be wrought just by removing "improvements" like chimneys and false fronts. For example, W. T. Kinnamon's garage (left) reappeared as milliner Margaret Hunter's store (opposite).

Removing modern "intrusions" proved a major part of restoring the antique scene, and one ubiquitous eyesore proved surprisingly easy to hide. Utility lines were simply buried and the poles removed from the offending median strip along Duke of Gloucester Street. It took longer to eliminate another sign of modern times: cars were finally banned in daytime on this street in 1974.

*T*wo years after Mr. Rockefeller was so taken by the "wonderful picture" of the Bassett Hall woods (and by Dr. Goodwin's vision) the new Restoration got its first real picture, Charles Willson Peale's portrait of George Washington. Yet however systematically Mr. Rockefeller worked, he had no clear image of what his new endeavor would create. Among other things, a superb collection of art and furnishings would evolve, because the restored village's buildings would otherwise remain empty shells. An educational institution would arise too though the patron opposed an "education" program per se until it was dubbed "interpretation." However grand Dr. Goodwin's vision, neither did he imagine the magnitude of his and Mr. Rockefeller's common cause. In restoring the colonial capital for posterity, they would rebuild a town of some five hundred structures comprising eighty-eight renewed originals or "restorations" and five times that number of "reconstructions."

They moved modern intrusions such as a railroad station and the line that served it. They would bury utility lines and reunite the divided Duke of Gloucester Street. They would remove modern stores from its length and relocate them in the new business district called Merchants Square, one of the first planned shopping areas in the land. They would raze almost all the postcolonial buildings, from hovels and shanties around Courthouse Green to the splendid Greek Revival church beside the Magazine. They'd embark on a program to relocate displaced downtowners, most of them black tenants who found new homes in specially funded low-rent neighborhoods. They would renovate and equip the homes of "life tenants," a process that required the residents to move out for a year or more while the house was taken apart down to the scantlings and put back together better than new.

Predictably the town fathers had something to say about all this. According to City Council minutes, Goodwin explained "in a general way" what he had in mind to do around town in 1927. In response, "Whereas the Council has contemplated [drafting a new building code]...for some time," it would not do to act hastily. The council decided to address such matters on a case-by-case basis until they got around to writing new codes—in 1947!

The early Restoration's approach was reflected in—and ratified by—the eventual zoning ordinance. It authorized the "restoration or reconstruction and use" of pre-1800 buildings in the Historic Area. "In the event the original foundations have been obliterated" reconstructions were allowed "where there is documentary evidence of the existence of such buildings prior to the year 1800." However, they must be "designed so as to present substantially their original appearance and dimensions" and be put to "a use that existed in this area in the 18th century."

Ably served by the Advisory Architects and a growing staff, the Restoration settled on a goal that can be stated simply enough: to restore the town to its eighteenth-century appearance. Wisely they decided against choosing a specific date—1770, say—because it was obvious that their blueprint must be a composite based variously on spottily preserved legislative and land records, old letters and diaries, the occasional published picture or amateur's watercolor and on foundations that could be absolutely dated by architectural or historical means. Further, picking a precise date would mean removing original buildings erected even a year later. It would also have dictated reconstruction of the second Capitol (built after the first burned in 1747), for which no detailed descriptions have ever been found and which was almost certainly less architecturally distinguished than the first.

The chosen goal—tempered by the determination to avoid speculative answers to historical puzzles whenever possible—predicated two basic rules: Buildings present in the colonial era would be restored or rebuilt; later buildings (with some exceptions) would be torn down or moved away. These tenets were enumerated in the "Decalogue," a set of commandments as sacrosanct around Williamsburg as Mosaic Law in Palestine and observed about as imperfectly. In some respects a model set of standards for historical restorers everywhere, it provided that:

＊ All Williamsburg's buildings of the colonial period should be saved.

＊ "Great discretion should be exercised" before destroying any buildings of the postcolonial classical period.

＊ All later buildings should be razed or removed from the Restored Area.

＊ Other old buildings in Williamsburg should be preserved on their sites, not moved to what became the "Historic Area."

＊ "If any reasonable additional trouble and expense" would enable it, an old building should be restored, not razed.

＊ Architects must distinguish between the "scrupulous retention" and repair of old structures and "the recovery of the old form by new work."

＊ While such work goes slower than ordinary construction, "a superior result should be preferred to more rapid progress."

＊ Use of old materials and period details "is commendable."

＊ Demolition is not an acceptable way to secure old materials, if an old building might be saved on its original site.

＊ Necessary new materials should resemble old ones in character without attempts to "antique" them by phony means.

Of course there were slipups. The eighteenth-century Jackson House, located outside the original Restoration boundaries on Francis Street, was pulled down prematurely and had to be reconstructed from photos when the Historic Area was enlarged. The Restoration also worked too fast on occasion. As many as three houses at a time might be moved simultaneously, thus blocking three streets. The dust was so thick that once a bulldozer went to the wrong address and knocked down half an original house before the error was discovered. The Greek Revival church on Duke of Gloucester Street was demolished, an event that the next generation of historical architects would call shameful.

Within the Restored Area the desired end would be historical fidelity as determined with the help of scholarship, architectural research and archaeology. As luck would have it, the Restoration benefited from the Tidewater's geology. Its clay preserved the details of vanished buildings with telling clarity. Here were signs of two-century-old postholes and foundations that would have long since vanished in other soil.

As for restorations, one of the first was also the most difficult, in part because it was the largest. Huge, fragile and hogged by various fires, the Wren Building had meandering lines. The engineers developed a delicate method of reinforcing the building so that the old walls supported only their own weight; floor and roof loads were supported by a new and hidden steel framework. Thus the antique footings, which were not disturbed, now carried only the weight of the original exterior. When it came to replacing the cornice beneath the roof, it had to be made with undulations to fit the curves of the warped structure. "The Wren Building was almost a course in restoration," Singleton Morehead would remember, while the Capitol was a course in reconstruction and the Palace one in the surprises of archaeology.

Reconstructing the latter two offered a variety of textbook problems; the first of them being to learn what they looked like. Buried foundations provided considerable evidence, but written material offered even more. The original act that chartered the city and ordered the building of the Capitol survived to serve the Restoration's designers and draftsmen. A sketch of the Palace drawn by Thomas Jefferson—who contemplated improving it—was found among his papers. This provided an accurate, measured floor plan by a premier designer of the era.

But these major structures couldn't be built until the problem of the bricks had been solved; modern suppliers couldn't provide brick that looked authentic, so the Restoration set out to make its own. Experimenting with obsolete methods and importing brickmakers from the Carolinas, they mixed native clay with water, then packed it into wooden molds. After a day the wet bricks were set out to dry, then stacked—thousands at a time—into a "kiln," a hollow pile as big as many outbuildings. After the structure was sealed with mud, the bricks were "burned" by filling the kiln with firewood and tending the blaze for a week. All these manual techniques were refined by trial and error, though the special glazing found on many original buildings remained elusive. These bricks lacked the characteristic blue-gray glaze on sides and ends exposed to the flames until pinelog fuel was replaced with hardwood. This produced the right color glazing for the decorative patterns favored in the early eighteenth century. Thus the Restoration replicated the colors of the early colonial period.

As for the distinctive bond of the Palace walls, the restorers found examples in the original building's ruins. When the building burned in 1781 it had collapsed into its cellars, which meant that excavators in the 1930s found countless "documents" in the buried artifacts: utensils, crockery, tiles, a hart carved in marble to adorn a fireplace (as it would again!)—and sections of wall still bound with lime mortar. Of course, many modern techniques were employed: the Capitol's roof was supported by steel framing and fireproof panels, since they'd be hidden from view. When the few sources of handblown crown glass were exhausted, the 1930s restorers found that the cheapest varieties of new window glass had similar bubbles and imperfections. (Decades later, manufacturing techniques made even cheap windowpanes flawless, and Colonial Williamsburg would have to rely on salvage companies for antique glass.)

Exploratory digging behind the Palace uncovered an alarming surprise: a graveyard containing more skeletons than the diggers bothered to count. This prompted action with notable dispatch. Construction crews were pulled off other jobs and ordered to erect a six-foot solid fence at once. (Fiscal niceties, which often took weeks to iron out, went by the boards; they'd decide which account to charge it to later.) The governor was notified and the Smithsonian Institution dispatched the preeminent physical anthropologist Aleš Hrdlička to appraise the boneyard. It was known that the Palace site had been used as a hospital, first by Washington's troops, then by both sides during the Civil War. The question remained: Who buried their dead in the back garden? Examining almost half the 137 skeletons, Hrdlička decided they came from a homogeneous group of white males (and two females)

When the Governor's Palace burned to the ground in three hours in 1781, it collapsed into its cellars, which became a time capsule of charred debris. In the wreckage, Restoration excavators found a shattered marble panel (top), the carving of a hart, which was then repaired and returned to the front parlor mantel (above).

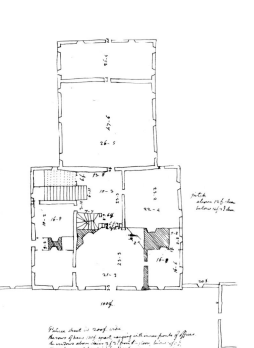

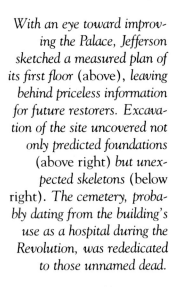

With an eye toward improving the Palace, Jefferson sketched a measured plan of its first floor (above), leaving behind priceless information for future restorers. Excavation of the site uncovered not only predicted foundations (above right) but unexpected skeletons (below right). The cemetery, probably dating from the building's use as a hospital during the Revolution, was rededicated to those unnamed dead.

between the ages of twenty-five and thirty-five. Since few showed signs of trauma, most must have died of disease rather than battle wounds. The few buttons and nails found could not be identified, but seemed to have been made in the eighteenth century. In the end the bodies were reinterred and the place dedicated as a cemetery of Revolutionary War dead. But despite the fence it was discovered that one skeleton now lacked its skull. This caused waves of anxiety among Restoration executives until they learned that Hrdlička had taken it for his collection at the National Museum of Natural History.

In the 1930s Colonial Williamsburg was quite simply the most famous destination in Virginia if not in the entire Old South. It received the requisite coverage in *National Geographic,* while *Architectural Record* and *Antiques* magazine devoted entire issues to the newly fabled place. President Roosevelt came down from Washington in 1934 for the opening, or reopening, of Duke of Gloucester Street, which he declared was "the most historic avenue in America." When the Capitol opened, the Virginia General Assembly repaired from Richmond to the earlier capital for the first of its commemorative sessions in the reconstructed edifice. When the Raleigh Tavern opened as the first exhibition building, the preacher who offered the benediction was sufficiently carried away to ask a blessing "in the name of the Father, and of the Son and of the Williamsburg Holding Company."

If the restoration movement had been about to happen anyway, the Restoration was its model and its most celebrated exponent, by consensus the single most influential font of inspiration in the realm of domestic architecture and decor. "Williamsburg style" houses began appearing wherever houses were being built; reproduction furniture and tableware became the rage among people who were buying amenities at all. The announcement of Rockefeller's participation in the project had shared newspaper space with the news that Herbert "Hoover's Nomination Now Seems Assured." When the Capitol opened Hoover was out and bread lines were in. The Depression was on. People hungered for something to cheer about, and they found it here.

The opening of the Capitol, Palace and Raleigh Tavern marked a conclusion and a commencement. All the work called for in the initial design and building contracts was finished. The firm of Todd and Brown was dismissed; locals could handle any building work under Restoration supervisors as the need arose. Perry, Shaw and Hepburn was offered a retainer to continue advising the Restoration on architectural matters; the firm's protégé Ed Kendrew, assisted by Sing Morehead, would handle further design chores as Restoration employees. In later years, the work completed thus far—by 1934—would be called Phase One, though Phase Two had no real beginning. Kendrew would remember that Chorley issued instructions to plan activities one year at a time, with no clear long-term agenda. The decision to make the Restoration a perpetual organization just sort of happened naturally—as inevitably as Mr. and Mrs. Rockefeller returned each spring and fall to their new retreat at Bassett Hall.

To the beholder, the young Restoration looked romantic and conservative in the original sense; it brightened the eye of architectural expert and historical innocent alike, and it stirred every patriotic heart during the most disheartening of times. There were many problems to be solved and unexpected issues to address as the institution grew, and even the New Deal would become involved. The old road from Williamsburg to Yorktown had been paved to serve local military bases during World War I. But once it reached Williamsburg it be-

Speaking on the Wren Building's back porch in 1934, President Franklin D. Roosevelt dedicates Duke of Gloucester Street, calling it "the most historic avenue in America."

Not all scholarship and finesse, the Restoration often used brute strength. When through-traffic proved a problem, a tunnel was carved through the Historic Area (above) to dispatch intrusive cars underground. When Travis House proved improperly sited, it was hauled back (below) to its original location.

came Duke of Gloucester Street, a main artery, nay the aorta, through town. Now that an antique *mise-en-scène* had been created, the question arose how to divert the modern automobile traffic so markedly increased by this new attraction. Several alternative routes were proposed—such as cutting through the woods behind Bassett Hall—but none seemed satisfactory.

Dr. Goodwin came to the rescue again, or so he thought when he proposed a tunnel under the Restored Area! This would carry the Colonial Parkway, the road Herbert Hoover's administration had cagily approved, but Goodwin was "practically thrown out of the Rockefeller office" in New York, said Horace Albright who received him next. Having left government for private industry and a seat on the Restoration's board of directors, the former Park Service director thought the tunnel idea "just seemed like a desecration that couldn't be tolerated." That didn't deter Goodwin, who made his pitch to every trustee and official he could reach. After FDR's flamboyant Secretary of the Interior Harold Ickes heard of it, and feasibility studies were made, the seemingly absurd notion of burrowing beneath the Historic Area proved to be the easiest and cheapest solution. Thus the tunnel, by now endorsed by the Williamsburg establishment, was undertaken as one of the New Deal's recovery projects. A curving route was found that skirted the Peyton Randolph House and the tunnel was built by the old "cut and cover" technique of digging a trench and laying the roadway within it, then restoring the surface. The Ludwell Tenement, which had been destroyed during the Civil War, was reconstructed with the help of an elderly resident's recollection, atop the tunnel.

Tazewell Hall, John "the Tory" Randolph's mansion, did not have such a happy fate. It was sold off and towed away in a move as controversial as it was drawn out. As early as 1928 when a Randolph descendant made inquiries, Dr. Goodwin's secretary wrote that the recently acquired home was "one of the handsomest of the colonial homes in Williamsburg and its historical connections make it even more interesting." It was then scheduled to be restored after its occupants' life tenancy expired, though Peyton Randolph Nelson, a crusty old man, wasn't going to budge before he had to. When he got a form letter warning occupants to guard against frozen water pipes, he replied in this vein: "Yours recd &c. I enclose it and mail it back to you for you to stuff it in the waste basket &c. You dont seem to know your and my status—as related to each other.... I am the land-lord of these premesis...and no tenant of yours &c. & you needn't trouble yourself about what I do here as all my Rights I ever had were reserved to the letter in the Bargain—with W. A. R. Goodwin until I die— & you do nothing here but what I choose for you to do and you have thus far failed very materially..." etc. etc. Relations between the life tenant and the well-meaning Restoration agents declined from there, as did the property.

By 1936, Nelson was sending his water bills to Goodwin, claiming he hadn't used any water anyway because the pipes had broken or somesuch. Goodwin forwarded a bill to Vernon Geddy with the acknowledgment that "Mr. Nelson seems to hold me responsible for all of his troubles." By now everybody was fed up with Nelson who was evidently infirm in years, and insisting that the house be allowed to go to rack and ruin. When the old man finally moved to a nursing home, Chorley decided to give up on the building while others argued for its restoration.

The handsome and important mansion at the end of South England Street had been built before 1732 as a showcase, the centerpiece of a "vista." In 1836 it had been massively renovated by Littleton Tazewell, who removed one wing and added a second floor. In 1909 it had been moved aside to allow the straight extension of the street (which passed between the eventual sites of the Inn and Lodge). Bill Perry believed "the picture of Williamsburg will never be complete until the South England Street vista is closed." As late as 1944 he proposed that the home's restoration to its first location be given first priority—even at the expense of all other projects in the Restored Area and even though it was outside the boundary. By war's end the house was vacant, filled with trash and frequented by kids who crawled in through broken windows. In 1948 Chorley wrote Ed Kendrew, "When Mr. Rockefeller and I were in Williamsburg last... he asked me why we were holding off taking down that building." The opinions of Kendrew, the Advisory Committee of Architects and Perry, Shaw and Hepburn notwithstanding, "I think we might as well face the facts: It is not within the realm of possibility that it would ever be moved back or restored on its present site... saved from further deterioration. If the above premises are correct, does it not mean that eventually the building will have to come down? If that is so, why not now?"

Kendrew argued manfully that he wanted to study the building's fabric, adding that a "very disastrous blow might be dealt to our good public relationship with the people of Virginia if the greatest tact is not employed in reaching a decision." There were many Randolph descendants to think of, in addition to the apparent violation of the Decalogue. But the writing was on the wall. A member of the House of Delegates bought the house and carted it away for reconstruction on a James River site in Newport News, paying half the price it would have cost to tear it down.

Despite Mr. Rockefeller's misgivings, the Restoration addressed the inevitability of actively welcoming visitors. First the Travis House was restored as a restaurant with a few guest rooms at the foot of Palace Green on Duke of Gloucester Street. Originally the home of the Public Hospital's superintendent, and once the scene of a fatal fire, the house would be moved three times before it was finally returned to its original site and dedicated to office space. (This despite the inexplicable sound of footsteps in the night and the faint smell of woodsmoke. A director of research, a scholar who started work before dawn, reported often hearing the sound of someone overhead. No one can offer a rational explanation; but then many original buildings are said to be haunted.)

Some thirty-one thousand people visited the three exhibition buildings in 1934 and the number tripled in two years. It was becoming clear that the old and misnamed Colonial Inn (a Victorian wreck) would have to come down to make way for the reconstruction of Chowning's Tavern. The idea of a new hotel called the Golden Horseshoe had been proposed for the Historic Area, but cooler heads prevailed after much debate. A large building was needed and it was finally decided to build the antebellum style Inn *outside* the area so as not to impose an anachronism within it. Opened in 1937, it had a restaurant seating 250 diners and 61 rooms for well-heeled guests who could afford the deluxe price of $9.50 a night. It did a busy trade but people of ordinary means were left out in the cold and the staff proposed to build cheaper accommodations, though Mr. Rockefeller thought the idea nonsense.

The trustees endorsed the proposal to build a lodge at a summer meeting that took place while Mr. Rockefeller was vacationing in Maine. His son, John 3d, then chairman of the board, agreed to take the news to Bar Harbor with his brother Laurance. The next week

Returning the town's old look required many transformations. The store that colonial entrepreneur William Prentis bought was one of many with a harlequin history. A barbershop in the early 1920s (above), by 1928 it had become another of the garages that blighted Williamsburg (below). Then it was restored to its original form and charm (see page 95).

Built in 1770, the Courthouse was probably intended to have pillars of English stone. But the Revolution blocked imports and the pediment stood unsupported for generations, as in this 1891 watercolor by Dwight Williams (above right). A fire caused heavy damage and in 1911, while repairs were under way, town fathers ordered the addition of columns (above). In 1932 they vanished again when the building was restored to its original state (below right).

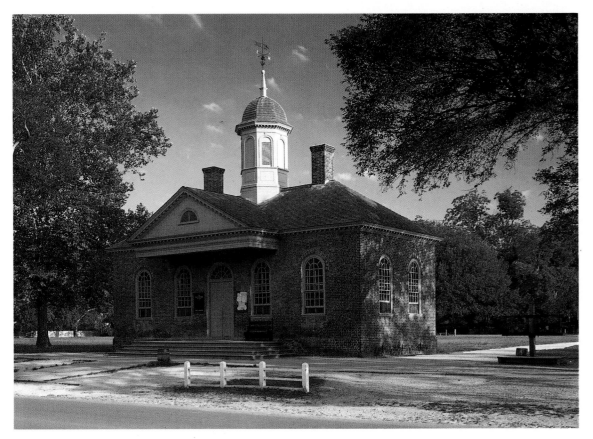

An antebellum artist rendered this bucolic view of the Magazine (above left), which had become a private dwelling. Thirty years later it was a livery stable (above) beside a grand new church of Classical Revival style. Still later a casual museum called the "Powder Horn," it now appears (below left) much as it did when Governor Spotswood designed and built it in 1715.

board member Horace Albright received a summary invitation to lunch in New York with the pater familias who was not his usually cordial self. He wanted an explanation; another hotel would just be a fiscal millstone around his heirs' necks and the Restoration shouldn't be in the hotel business anyway. Albright explained under duress what his own sons hadn't been able to sell him.

After studying the matter, Rockefeller called a board meeting for the next day and had each member of the board explain in detail why he felt a modestly priced hotel was necessary. There were not enough economical accommodations, they said, even in boardinghouses like the one the Armistead sisters maintained next to the Capitol; the Restoration would soon be attracting more people than anyone imagined; Williamsburg should accommodate the common man as well as the wealthy, etc. As the meeting progressed, it was clear that Mr. Rockefeller had already changed his mind. John 3d whispered to Albright "I don't think we could stop him from building the Lodge" now. Notwithstanding his new opinion, it was a decision that Mr. Rockefeller might regret. Kendrew remembers later that when annual attendance approached the five hundred thousand mark, the patron suggested closing the doors lest wear and tear destroy painstakingly restored buildings.

Colonial Williamsburg came of age in many ways during the 1930s, a decade that saw many changes. Its fabled collections of formal art and the decorative arts, of furniture and furnishings were begun. Some fifty "major" buildings were restored or reconstructed, among them the Capitol, Palace and Raleigh Tavern, the Magazine, Public Records Office and Market Square Tavern. Many houses bearing eighteenth-century names were renewed and opened as exhibition buildings (the Wythe House, for example—no longer a parish house) while others were occupied as homes. The central town was inhabited again, now by modern families inhabiting a museum. Since the goal had been to restore and reconstruct a living city, what purpose would hundreds of uninhabited buildings serve? Encouraging life tenants to stay on (the unlamented Mr. Nelson notwithstanding) and leasing other houses to Restoration employees would give the town a new life. That had been part of Dr. Goodwin's original dream, to make the hallowed precinct vital again.

Thus a new generation of Williamsburgers grew up in the antique place, among them Goodwin's own "second family." His three youngest boys were rambunctious enough; one is remembered for having baked a cat. (They matured nonetheless. The eldest, William Jr., a fighter pilot in World War II, would not return from a sortie over Salerno. The able and energetic Howard would join Bethlehem Steel, picking up after a fashion where his grandfather left off in Richmond, and become sales manager for New York. Jack, the youngest, would stay in Williamsburg, a slender pillar of his father's church.) Ed Kendrew raised a brood of girls here. Vernon Geddy Jr., who would become Rockefeller's attorney in Virginia and later a board member of Colonial Williamsburg, remembers his boyish delight at watching trucks pull down whole buildings and the eerie spectacle of the Palace cemetery digs. Then, as for decades after, children of this town would discover artifacts in the stream running past the Armistead sisters' guesthouse, learn to play fife and harpsichord in the Music Teacher's Room wearing clothes of another era, even to fish in the pond in Bassett Hall woods which "officially" has no fish.

Dr. Goodwin himself did not see the end of the decade. While his influence slowly declined as the Restoration became ever more professional, his health waned as well, though

In marked contrast to the colonial buildings, the Williamsburg Inn displays the Regency style of architecture popular in antebellum Virginia. Opened in 1937, it provided luxurious modern accommodations where there had been none for the millions of travelers who began seeking this antique and rustic place.

he was active to the end. He urged the creation of a crafts program to display eighteenth-century trades. He advocated the realistic representation of the entire spectrum of colonial society: slave, artisan, indentured servant, gentry. From his sickbed he still managed to raise six-figure donations for William and Mary.

He is remembered for that remarkable gift; as Chorley told him "You can raise more money from an oxygen tent than most men can at a desk." He was also remembered for his tenacious persuasion. One now elderly lady recalls he once sat beside her on the train to Richmond and seemed intent on hypnotizing her into selling her home to the Restoration. His former curate John Bentley remembers his conviction and thoughtfulness. His own remembrances make his will an interesting, touching document. After his principal heir, his wife, he made bequests to every child and a number of colleagues: To Bishop Bentley the choice of theology books from his library, to his faithful secretary Elizabeth Hayes $2,000, to his sexton $5, to Bruton Church $25. To Mr. Rockefeller he left "the old silver spoon which I dug up between Jamestown and Williamsburg as a token of my heart's deepest gratitude for his friendship, his example and for his generous and gracious consummation of the dream of the restoration of Colonial Williamsburg."

He saw the second restoration of Bruton Parish Church nearly completed; his funeral was the first service held there and he was buried in a crypt beneath the nave, his head toward the altar in the hallowed position accorded ministers. The stone reads simply "Here rests the Rev. Dr. William Archer Rutherfoord Goodwin, a native of Virginia, late rector of this parish. Born June 18, 1869. Died September 7, 1939."

A more eloquent inscription graces a wall not far away:

Dr. Goodwin stands in Bruton Parish Church with foreman William Holland near what would soon become his burial crypt beneath the aisle. Though he lived to see the city largely restored to an image of its former self, the rector died before the second (and more complete) restoration of his sanctuary.

To the GLORY of God
and in MEMORY of
William Archer Rutherfoord Goodwin
Minister, Teacher, Man of Vision
in whose Heart and Mind
was conceived the Thought of restoring the Beauty
of this ANCIENT CITY and who was himself
the Inspiration of its Fulfillment
THIS TABLET
is erected by his Friend and Fellow Worker
JOHN DAVISON ROCKEFELLER JR.
ANNO DOMINI 1941

PART THREE

The Modern Era:
A Once and Future Williamsburg

A Family Place,
An American
Enterprise

Year after modern year, people of every ilk seek out this colonial capital incarnate in order to see, to imagine, to learn or just to test the tenor of another time. Each autumn Williamsburg welcomes a small army in antique dress (opposite)—women and children included (left)—to celebrate the Colonial Fair and pretend for a brace of days that two centuries have not passed.

A visiting blacksmith works his portable forge during the Colonial Fair.

212

When Dr. Goodwin greeted the first visiting millionaire to Williamsburg, J. P. Morgan rode through town in a wagon. Seventy-six years later when Colonial Williamsburg welcomed the president of the United States and seven foreign heads of state at once, they came in helicopters that shook the old foundations. Between those two events a late train stranded a hapless traveler in Richmond. Times were bad, the weather foul, the night cold. Finding a phone booth on the empty platform, the man was relieved to have one nickel in his pocket, the price of reaching the operator who became impatient when he couldn't come up with the change to call Williamsburg. "May I reverse the charges please?" he asked, his spirits falling lest something else go wrong. Before Ma Bell's minion would place the call, she demanded: "Your name?" "Never mind, you wouldn't believe it anyway" said John D. Rockefeller Jr.

Truth be told, even as the founder himself had his bad days, the one-horse town was not transformed as easily as the pumpkin into Cinderella's coach. Herein lies one secret of Colonial Williamsburg. For all the "perfection" some critics see in the well-groomed town, it remains an institution built by mortals possessed of all the genius and foibles that flesh is heir to. Further, as a corporate organism it has undergone metamorphosis more than once. The question remains: Why did the founder choose Williamsburg to receive his munificent indulgence in the first place? Then later, how did it achieve its own independence?

The answer to the first question no longer lies in Williamsburg but in family lore, that body of shared experience and insight that members of any clan know and often take for granted. The fact that Colonial Williamsburg was founded by a certain pater familias has much to do with the ways in which it grew. Its evolved character is the product of the human folk who made it, starting with the founding father.

Laurance Rockefeller, the oldest surviving son, sees no mystery in Williamsburg's attraction for both his parents. Unlike their other haunts, here "they could be just like everybody else." In New York City "Father" was compelled to be on guard against beggars, thieves and fortune hunters alike. By the same token, the Rockefellers lived "behind a wall" at the 2,200-acre Hudson River estate Pocantico Hills, while their traditional summer home in Maine was another gentrified community possessed equally by every generation of Rockefellers.

Williamsburg was different; Mr. and Mrs. Rockefeller could claim it uniquely as their own. Their parents had not known it and once this couple found their haven it would not become a playground for the gathering clan. "They went there for the self-renewal and serenity, not to bring the family and make a rodeo of it," says Laurance. He remembers with a hint of gratitude that Williamsburg's townfolk embraced them and "they mingled with everybody." If many were awed at having a millionaire in their midst, they soon overcame it in light of this middle-aged couple's modest way of living. Edward Spencer, a native and career employee of Colonial Williamsburg, remembers Mr. Rockefeller accepting his older sister's girlish invitation to take tea at ramshackle Palace Farm behind the ruin of the governor's residence. Others still speak of the Rockefellers as old-shoe neighbors two months out of every year.

John D. Rockefeller Jr. ("Mr. Junior") and all his sons in 1937 (from left): David, who as a boy enchanted Dr. Goodwin, would head Chase Manhattan Bank; Nelson, a champion of his mother's folk art collection, would become vice-president of the United States; Winthrop, who chaired Williamsburg's governing board, would serve two terms as governor of Arkansas; Laurance, who sat on the board, would become an avid conservationist and philanthropist; John 3d would win distinction in international affairs after directing Colonial Williamsburg.

Typically each spring and fall they set up housekeeping in Bassett Hall which they bought and restored to their liking after a fire damaged it in 1930. Once ensconced, they settled into the life of the town like cousins. Mr. Rockefeller walked the woods, identifying plants, planning paths with rustic benches on which to rest, hanging a camper's tin cup on a tree beside a stream so that he could drink its pure water whenever he happened by.

His wife had the neighbors in for tea and together they hosted supper parties. Abstemious themselves, they never served liquor but once tried to show their liberality by having the butler offer cigarettes after dessert. (Matching their hosts' consideration, not one of the tobacco-fond guests lit up.) The typical evening's entertainment was the seven-o'clock movie in the theater Rockefeller built at Merchants Square. By day, he relished his presumed anonymity, quartering the town and checking up on every project armed with a tape measure carried in his pocket. He studied the dimensions of old buildings and reconstructions alike. Laurance remembers that Restoration executives encouraged this and "went out of their way to make him feel at home."

Mrs. Rockefeller took special interest in community projects. Segregation was the rule in the Old South, and when the Restoration prompted the relocation of a Negro school, she paid to equip it so well that some grumbled it was the best in the Tidewater. They supported their own Baptist church, but because the Restoration placed special demands on restored Bruton, they endowed a special fund dedicated largely to its music program. When the nation went to war, the flood of tourists ebbed to a trickle—except for servicemen from nearby bases whose admission fees were paid by the Rockefellers, who established the town's USO center. These relatively small efforts were the community benefactions of two newcomers to town who happened to have a little more to give than their neighbors.

Of course, because rank hath its privileges, they were able to do certain things that might have been prohibited to others. On arising, Mr. Rockefeller liked to see the flag flying above the Capitol from his bedroom window. The first morning of one autumn visit he couldn't see it because a tree had grown too tall; it was pruned back before nightfall. Later he notified Chorley that Mrs. Rockefeller was awakened at night by the screams of patients in what was by then named Eastern State Hospital. Correcting that took longer to arrange than a tree-trimming, because it required a decision by the state to replace and relocate the hospital complex that had become woefully obsolete. But in due course, and after negotiations involving the Rockefellers, the College and the state government, the hospital moved across town and Colonial Williamsburg was able to acquire the original site.

Bassett Hall's renovation did not conform to the strict standards applied elsewhere in town. The acknowledged reason was not that the eighteenth-century house belonged to Rockefeller, but that it stood outside the Historic Area—which he had paled, with the town's endorsement. The boundary of the Restored Area originally ran down Francis Street, but to prevent commercial eyesores from encroaching on the antique *mise-en-scène*, the line was then nudged two hundred feet beyond the curb. Since Bassett Hall happened to be four hundred feet from the street, it remained outside the sacrosanct zone. Thus the Rockefellers had greater license; they changed Bassett Hall by enlarging the rear wing and added outbuildings as they saw fit, not only upon ancient foundations. In this the donor was playing by the same rules as everyone else; only he had a hand in defining the boundaries of the playing field. And if he ever found himself losing, he could sometimes change the players.

When Colonel Woods retired as chairman of the board in 1939, the oldest of Mr.

Rockefeller's five sons succeeded him. John 3d served ably through the war years and into the troubled times of the Cold War and McCarthy Era. But by the early 1950s, it is remembered, he started setting new goals for the Restoration. His widow, Blanchette, says "John had very strong feelings about it as an educational institution as well as a museum." So deep was his interest that the couple spent one week a month there—somewhat more time even than President Chorley, who tended to run things from New York. Thus Williamsburg began hosting frankly educational programs. Foreign visitors and groups of promising young people were invited to debate great political issues. Emissaries were dispatched to distant places to learn about life abroad—even in Socialist countries. Conventional wisdom around town holds that in promoting these intellectual adventures John 3d clashed with Chorley who found such projects suspect. Thus, the story continues, Williamsburg became too small for both of them, and Mr. Rockefeller reluctantly decided that Chorley was not as expendable as his son. As senior staffers tell the tale, Mr. Rockefeller played the role of Solomon arbitrating a dispute between rivals.

The family tell a different story, a simpler one: John 3d was chairman of the board but his father was still boss. As the son became increasingly interested in education and international projects, the older conservative simply dug in his heels. John 3d was entitled and even expected to pursue his interests; having inculcated a sense of public service in all his boys, the senior Rockefeller hadn't meant to raise any slouches. But he believed his firstborn son could walk to his own drummer on his own turf and that Williamsburg should stick to its steady course. According to relatives it wasn't Chorley who clashed finally with young John but Mr. Rockefeller himself. He had opposed efforts to make Williamsburg "educational" in the first place, and only let the staff pursue de facto educational projects when they were thinly disguised as "interpretation." This was not a matter of a wise judge settling a dispute, it was a contretemps between father and son that ended in the son's resignation.

Intentionally good neighbors in their part-time hometown, Mr. and Mrs. Rockefeller supported many local causes. During World War II they funded a USO canteen and at its opening in 1943 cheerfully posed with three enlisted men.

In any event there was nothing very final about John 3d's departure in 1953. Becoming chairman of the Rockefeller Foundation and turning to international matters, he remained a devoted Williamsburg visitor for twenty-five years. His mother had died in 1948 and his stepmother, Martha Baird Rockefeller, refurnished Bassett Hall to her liking. After Mr. Rockefeller's death in 1960—and a memorial service under the old oak—John 3d inherited the house. Blanchette remembers that "All the boys wanted it kept as their mother had it." So with the help of a Williamsburg maid who'd served the first Mrs. Rockefeller for decades, they put every hooked rug, ladderback chair, mourning picture and porcelain figurine back in its original place. The house, then bequeathed to Colonial Williamsburg after John 3d's death in 1978, became a popular exhibition building that reveals the elder Rockefellers' personal tastes.

Brother Winthrop succeeded John 3d as chairman and held the post for twenty years. Perhaps because his home was distant Arkansas, where he served two terms as governor, he is remembered as an almost model chairman. He didn't hover. "Win" came often enough to chair board meetings and oversee general policy. One of his notable accomplishments, was to acquire Carter's Grove, the downriver plantation owned by the McCrea's who decades earlier had sought Dr. Goodwin's advice on restoration and then entertained the thirsty congressmen sent to study the idea for a colonial park. The Restoration was "incomplete" without an associated plantation. For all its greatness, the old city had depended for sustenance and economic lifeblood upon country plantations. Thus, there was a need for a restorable plantation to act as a modern adjunct to the Historic Area.

Shirley Plantation was actively sought in vain and some closer-in estates were ruled out because they had been subdivided and developed. Laurance, who was then a member of the board, remembers that when Carter's Grove became available Mr. Rockefeller, his new wife and Chorley all thought it "inappropriate"—especially Chorley, who felt it would be a financial millstone around the Restoration's neck. Others on the staff and the interested brothers thought they'd best not let it slip through their hands. Thus, at Winthrop's behest it was acquired by one of the family trusts, which retained title until Colonial Williamsburg demonstrated it could be operated as an exhibition annex without running up deficits.

The change in chairmen in 1953—and the nearly simultaneous arrival of a new administration—had been a kind of omen. Colonial Williamsburg was about to experience an identity crisis regardless of who wielded the gavel at board meetings. It now seemed soundly established; but then so the dinosaurs had been. Colonial Williamsburg's future—whether or not it had a future—really depended on its continued appeal, its meaning to people outside its pale. Mr. Rockefeller would doubtless continue to support his creation. But if it became simply his expensive recreation and semiannual retreat it could be as perverse a place as Citizen Kane's reconstructed castle, an oddity, a theme park with roller coasters only in the mind. The benefactor would die eventually and his heirs turn to other interests (as indeed they did). Then Williamsburg might simply go the way of Ozymandias's city of stone. Quite obviously that didn't happen.

Instead the restored colonial capital continued to grow internally and to diversify. Broadening its appeal to the American public, it became an international spa of sorts and embarked on courses potentially as "radical" as those John 3d suggested, albeit with the sympathy and consent of new directors—including members of the family. In a word, Colonial Williamsburg changed to meet changing circumstances. Perhaps the pervasive reason was the arrival of an ebullient printer's son from the unlikely burg of Hagerstown, Maryland, via a most circuitous course that began on the eve of World War II.

Carlisle H. Humelsine, an ambitious young man, had been a junior university administrator and a free-lance reporter when the war began and he joined the army. For many people the national emergency offered stepping stones to the stars; he took them two at a time. Through a chance encounter at a football game, he found himself assigned to Chief of Staff Gen. George C. Marshall's communications center and was soon night duty officer, the man in overall charge. It was a demanding business—to oversee the receipt and distribution of messages from every military theater. It was a delicate business, too, especially on the night shift, since the duty officer was responsible for deciding which few cables warranted waking up the chief of staff.

One night early in the war, when young Humelsine was still decidedly in awe of authority, he was ordered to fetch Marshall's deputy from his hotel suite, whence he'd escort the reputedly forbidding soldier to an emergency conference. Maj. Gen. Joseph McNarny had a cold, and when he came out of the bedroom a voice followed him, summoning him back. It was his wife calling "Joe, do you have your handkerchief? Take your handkerchief." For some men on the way up, the key lesson is learning that those already on top still put their pants on one leg at a time. For Humelsine, it was realizing that even McNarny's nose ran and wife nagged. As he would remember it, "From then on generals were just like everyone else." So too presidents and princesses.

Humelsine was a genius at handling details, a necessity when setting up Gen. Dwight D. Eisenhower's communications center in London. He also had a way of finding things, like a typewriter in Newfoundland during a refueling stop and a colonel who could type General Marshall's upcoming speech. In Potsdam for the historic conference, he could impress the secretary of state by providing bourbon and branch water before being asked. A colonel himself before he was thirty, Humelsine was smart before he became a soldier.

By war's end he'd been twice decorated and crossed Kenneth Chorley's path when the Joint Chiefs of Staff met at the Williamsburg Inn, which was specially opened for the occasion. Valuing attention to detail, Chorley had been impressed by Marshall's young officers who planned for every eventuality and handled problems with efficient dispatch. When Humelsine mustered out, Chorley lured him into becoming his personnel director, a persona he adopted for barely a few months before deciding "I made a mistake." Unable to see his own future in the reconstructed past, he resigned and retreated back to Washington. At the State Department he served variously as assistant secretary and deputy undersecretary for operations under secretaries Byrnes, Marshall, Acheson and Dulles.

With President Eisenhower's new team coming aboard, Humelsine prepared to leave government. He had several "opportunities" to join giants like ITT and Pan Am but a glimpse inside them revealed forests of ladders, each one crowded with executives answering to those on the next rung up while treading on the fingers of those below. When Rockefeller's general counsel invited him to a meeting in New York, Humelsine assumed he might be asked to assist in one of Mr. Rockefeller's many corporate interests. Instead he was astonished to be offered the top job in Williamsburg. Chorley wanted him back as his on-site executive officer and heir apparent. Hardly needing time to consider, he told his Virginia-born wife the news and returned to the Old Dominion in 1953 as executive vice president and resident governor of Colonial Williamsburg. Five years later he succeeded to the presidency.

A matter requiring early attention was pure business—how to attract more of it. Humelsine left Washington knowing that the State Department had a chronic problem: what to do with visiting dignitaries. His old friend and associate, Deputy Chief of Protocol Clement Conger was sick to death of holding foreign visitors' hands while leading them around places like Detroit automobile plants which resembled factories everywhere. The visitors were neither markedly impressed nor put in a receptive mood for whatever official business awaited them in Washington. The former deputy undersecretary realized that he had a superb alternative, one that would help the institution he now headed and serve his old employers as well.

Williamsburg was different, indeed unique and uniquely American, a place unlike anywhere abroad. It offered comfortable guest facilities, rides in carriages, and glimpses of the national genesis. Once the State Department discovered it—with Humelsine beckoning like a Siren—it became a virtually mandatory stop for every visiting head of state bound for an Oval Office meeting. It was appealing, entertaining, diverting, interesting—and its cuisine didn't disturb foreign stomachs. The Inn could handle a state visit on short notice, the bellmen didn't lose luggage and, Conger remembers, it offered him bargain rates. Relatively removed from cities and hotbeds of dissidents, it also offered good security, while enabling the visitor to recover from jet lag less than 150 miles from the White House. Almost every administration from Eisenhower's time onward happily made use of it by scheduling a stop en route to Washington for reigning dignitaries. And as one hand washes the other,

Williamsburg profited from the business which enhanced its image in the eyes of American travelers and attracted more civilian visitors.

The tradition of the state visit had begun in 1934 when President Roosevelt reopened Duke of Gloucester Street, though the comings and goings of foreign heads of state could often be less solemn. Marshal Tito of Yugoslavia visited several times. When demonstrations threatened to disrupt his scheduled trip to San Francisco, he got "sick" between Washington meetings and "recuperated" here. (Tito spoke idiomatic English in private, such as when the mayor escorted him around Williamsburg. Astonished to learn their carriage cost $35,000 to build, the independent Communist retorted "I can buy five Cadillacs for that.") When the king of Morocco checked in, an attending satrap demanded to see a floor plan of the Inn. Though Eisenhower's old room was reserved for the king, only the suite where Queen Elizabeth had slept would do. It was reserved for a couple who came every year, but the Moroccans simply commandeered it anyway. Then a bodyguard lay down across the doorsill where he remained for the duration of the visit to the astonishment of passing guests. Certain of the smaller Arab and African state visitors nearly tested Williamsburg's capacity. It became axiomatic for planners that the less stable a government the larger its delegation since the man in charge brought with him every potential rival who might get ambitious if left at home.

Managing the state visit required little more than an exquisite attention to detail; to ensure this Humelsine's administration developed the "Operations Plan," a step-by-step, person-by-person program, which is still routinely prepared for every special event. (Often two inches thick, these directories assign chores down to the delivery of kindling wood for cressets and the locking of the milliner's shop door after a Lanthorn Tour.) Sometimes overly meticulous planning backfired—as when a team of horses was tranquilized before being hitched to a carriage; they fell asleep while awaiting their royal passengers at the Wythe House so Queen Elizabeth II and Prince Philip had to finish their tour on foot. More often the systematically exhaustive planning paid off. Touring the town, the president of Hungary mentioned a passion for volleyball, so while the party toured the Palace Humelsine dropped a word to an aide, and a volleyball net was erected beside the official guesthouse before the party returned. After one near disaster in the culinary department, they began to check dignitaries' dietary preferences in advance. A memorable Chorley memo said that doing this earlier would have "saved the embarrassment at finding that neither the Lord Mayor [of London] or the Lady Mayoress had ever eaten an oyster and had no intention of doing so."

Some years only one head of state might visit, other years one came every other month as Williamsburg welcomed the presidents of an alphabet of nations from Argentina to Zambia. In addition there were some seventeen prime ministers as well as reigning monarchs, dictators, heirs apparent, cabinet ministers and the like: Queen Elizabeth II and Prince Philip; King Hussein I of Jordan; King Baudouin I of Belgium; King Bhumibol and Queen Sirikit of Thailand; the vice president of the People's Republic of China; the crown prince of Libya; King Zahir and Queen Homaira of Afghanistan; Burma's Revolutionary Council chairman; from Nepal King Mahendra Bir Bikram Shah Deva and Queen Ratna Rajya Lakshmi Devi Shah; Norway's King Olav V; King Faisal of Saudi Arabia; Queen Rambhai Barni of Thailand; Poland's first secretary; the duke of Gloucester; Canada's governor general; the earl of Dunmore; the shah of Iran; Prince Gyanendra and Princess Komal of Nepal;

Two exhibition buildings reflect both their eighteenth-century origins and twentieth-century owners. At Bassett Hall, furnished as it was when Mr. and Mrs. Rockefeller lived there, antique corner cupboards and folk art adorn the morning room (above). Most of the folk art that Abby Aldrich Rockefeller championed is housed in the collection that bears her name. The house at Carter's Grove (opposite), site of the early settlement at Wolstenholme Towne, was built in 1755 by Robert "King" Carter's grandson. In the late 1920s it was massively renovated to suit affluent new owners, whose decorating tastes have been preserved. Now this James River plantation provides Colonial Williamsburg with a rural annex, a locale for exhibitions dealing with colonial life outside the antique city.

the emperor and empress of Japan; Dame Te Atairangikaahu, Queen of the Maori; Charles, Prince of Wales; Queen Beatrix and Prince Claus of the Netherlands and so on.

In addition a parade of American presidents followed Roosevelt's example: Harry S Truman, Lyndon Johnson, Richard Nixon, Gerald Ford, Jimmy Carter (as a candidate), and Ronald Reagan. Plain old Ike came, wearing his famous Eisenhower jacket and escorting his old ally Winston Churchill, who uttered a memorable bon mot en route. Introduced to Board Chairman John 3d, he noted that the English "number our Georges; here you number your Rockefellers."

While Rockefeller lived, there was no need to solicit major financial support on the open market so to speak. But Humelsine was swift to accept gifts of art and antiques from serious collectors, many of whom visited regularly and attended the annual Antiques Forum (an event adroitly held in late winter when attendance was otherwise slow and hotel rooms empty). He cultivated *Reader's Digest* founder DeWitt Wallace (of whom more later) and Philadelphia publisher Walter Annenberg, who visited Williamsburg serendipitously and became a benefactor with an unsolicited check for $50. Humelsine's personal letter of thanks for that prompted a six-digit donation by return mail and a substantial annual pledge from the man who later served as ambassador to Great Britain. Humelsine also made special friends with an engaging man/wife team of collectors; in this he not only increased Colonial Williamsburg's collections but splendidly augmented the population of the Historic Area as well.

Elizabeth and Miodrag Blagojevich had missed the first annual Antiques Forum but came to all the rest. Their home in St. Mary's, Maryland, was celebrated not only for its seventeenth-century origin, but for their inspired restoration and splendidly ancient furnishings into the bargain. Getting on in years, they decided to sell the farm overlooking St. Mary's River, a tributary of the Potomac, and find a less removed place to live. Chief curator Graham Hood and Humelsine got wind of their predicament and came up with a plan that profited everyone. Colonial Williamsburg immediately acquired the choice Maryland real estate and, piecemeal over a period of years, the couple's fabulous collection of antiques. In return, the elderly pair received an annuity and life tenancy on Duke of Gloucester Street where they became lively fixtures of the town. While the arrangement was designed to have tax advantages for the sellers, it eventually served Williamsburg better than anyone expected. The state of Maryland declined to buy the historic land, but eventually agreed to buy a scenic easement for a six-figure sum; Humelsine then sold the property to a private party for even more.

Humelsine also paid close attention to building a notable board of directors, a slowly changing group of men and women who enhanced the institution with their often eminent names, their connections and their expertise. (If he was especially sensitive to the importance of trustee boards it might be because he served on so many himself, including those of the National Geographic Society, Smithsonian Institution, National Gallery of Art and National Trust for Historic Preservation.) During Humelsine's years as president and later chairman of the board, the roster included such distinguished Virginians as Richmond attorney Lewis F. Powell Jr., who became a Supreme Court justice and served briefly as chairman after Winthrop's death. At one time or another it also included former Secretary of State Dean Rusk, cabinet member and federal judge Shirley M. Hufstedler, author and

Foreign leaders flock to Williamsburg as if it were a Mecca of democracy: (Top left) Winston Churchill drinks with Dwight D. Eisenhower at the Raleigh Tavern in 1946; unlike their respective predecessors 170 years earlier, this English prime minister and American general willingly visited Williamsburg together. (Center left) Queen Elizabeth II and Prince Philip ride in a blue phaeton with board chairman Winthrop Rockefeller in 1957. (Top right) Emperor Hirohito and his consort see the Capitol with Colonial Williamsburg president Carlisle H. Humelsine, seated second from right, in 1975. (Center right) Prince Charles meets Mr. Humelsine's successor, Charles Longsworth, second from left, and chief curator Graham Hood, far left, in the newly restored Governor's Palace in 1981. (Below) President Ronald Reagan hosts the ninth Economic Summit of Industrialized Nations in 1983, welcoming six other heads of state to Williamsburg; standing left to right are Prime Minister Pierre Trudeau of Canada, Gaston Thorn, president of the European Economic Community, Federal Chancellor Helmut Kohl of the Federal Republic of Germany, President François Mitterand of France, Reagan, Prime Minister Yasuhiro Nakasone of Japan, Prime Minister Margaret Thatcher of the United Kingdom and Prime Minister Amintore Fanfani of the Republic of Italy.

teacher Ralph Ellison, television journalist David Brinkley, Librarian of Congress Daniel J. Boorstin and AT&T Chairman Charles L. Brown, who would be chosen to succeed Humelsine as Williamsburg's chairman in 1985. It was also Humelsine's inspiration to bring new Rockefeller blood to the board. In 1966 Abby Milton O'Neill, eldest daughter of the founder's only daughter, began an association with Williamsburg that hasn't ended yet.

During all these years Williamsburg honored its legacy of free speech—but not aloud or boisterously. For example, one pillar of the community remembers a traditional cortege at William and Mary by sons of the Confederacy who mustered around the solemn effigy of Dixie's coffin. Bearing the Stars and Bars, they would march down Duke of Gloucester Street to the Wren Building, go in the front door and then disperse out the back. In the 1960s, a time of civil rights activism in the land, a group of black students decided to protest this atavistic rite and lined up before the hallowed steps. The Confederates marched, and reaching the edifice sang "Dixie." The protestors stood their ground, responded with "We Shall Overcome," then parted ranks and let the marchers pass—fitting accommodation in a place famous for honoring the right of free speech.

Far more spectacular was the row that followed a sermon in Bruton Parish Church. The thirty-first rector, Rev. Cotesworth Pinkney Lewis delivered the address in which he most respectfully asked for "some answers" to explain American foreign policy in Southeast Asia. "The political complexities of our involvement in an undeclared war in Vietnam are so baffling that I feel presumptuous even in asking questions. But since there is a rather general consensus that what we are doing in Vietnam is wrong... we wonder if some logical, straightforward explanation might be given without endangering whatever military or political advantage we hold.... While pledging our loyalty—we ask respectfully, why?"

The sermon was a model of dignity and restraint, but it was delivered before what instantly became a national audience, because the entire White House press corps was in church that Sunday and not much else was going on in the world. President Lyndon B. Johnson was sitting in the first pew, the one with George Washington's name on it. He was winding down a whirlwind national tour: seven speeches since Thursday, albeit all of them at military bases where he urged the Asia-bound troops onward. The last stop had been Williamsburg for a Saturday-night banquet and LBJ "roast" hosted by a Washington insiders club. Next morning as the commander in chief listened to the sermon, he seemed the soul of composure to Carl Humelsine, who was sitting beside him, except for one thing—he was gripping the pew rail tight enough to splinter it. At the door as the first family was leaving, Lady Byrd managed to compliment the rector on the choir and it first appeared to reporters that Johnson would not shake the parson's hand. But he did and said "Thank you."

Colonial Williamsburg hastily announced that Bruton was not the institution's "official church" (whatever that meant); Humelsine called the sermon in "exquisite bad taste." After the gist of it echoed from coast to coast—it was on the front page of the *New York Times*, just about every paper in the land, and on the networks too—Lewis responded that he had not intended to be critical and regretted if the president had taken offense. He'd only meant to make a point as ancient as Isaiah's timeless prophesy "They shall beat their swords into plowshares and their spears into pruning hooks."

If Colonial Williamsburg could not have survived the early years without Chorley, it would not have matured without Humelsine. After Mr. Rockefeller's death in 1960, Colonial Williamsburg was on its own in a way it had never been before. The challenge facing Humelsine was to direct its metamorphosis from one man's favorite philanthropy and consuming hobby to an independent institution that could hold its own in the competitive nonprofit world. Now he would have to begin soliciting major financial gifts both to augment the endowment fund and support special projects of several sorts. In time he hired a development officer, made him a vice president and took his advice on several fronts—including the chartering of the Raleigh Tavern Society. (Its members, proven friends of the institution, pledge substantial gifts in objects or money. By way of thanks they receive the finest hospitality Colonial Williamsburg has to offer one weekend a year.) One index of Humelsine's success is that the endowment stood at roughly $50 million when Rockefeller died; when Humelsine retired as chairman of the board in 1985, it was $130 million.

But he did more than oversee the financial development of the institution. He addressed such political problems as persuading a governor to provide easy access to Williamsburg from new highways and such aesthetic ones as augmenting Mrs. Rockefeller's personal collection so that it became a major national repository of American folk art. Humelsine counts among his major achievements the acquisition of buffer properties around the Historic Area; the purchase of the Public Hospital site; development of the original Information Center; the closing of Duke of Gloucester Street to daytime traffic. A most visible acquisition during his administration, of course, was Carter's Grove, but equally important was a complex sequence of transactions involving King's Mill, an adjacent estate. This was bought, then sold for development after a right-of-way was retained through it for the Country Road, a uniquely charming lane leading to the plantation annex. (Anheuser-Busch then bought a large part of King's Mill, which became the site of a brewery, theme park and subdivision to substantially increase struggling James City County's tax base.)

Humelsine's years as executive officer and board chairman simultaneously saw the growth of both collections and programs, and the taking of significant steps for the future. Importantly, in 1977 he named a committee of "junior faculty" members to review Williamsburg's "educational missions" over the first half century and answer the salient question: "What should its future mission be?" The committee report laid the groundwork for significant changes in philosophy and direction by Colonial Williamsburg under its next president. Finally, Humelsine sees as one of his finest works the progressive transfer of power to his eventual successor. Announcing his intention to step aside as president three years before the mandatory retirement age, he urged the trustees to find an able executive with proven skills in a singular combination of fields: education, business and development.

Colonial Williamsburg's next president, Charles Longsworth, came aboard as chief operating officer, then two years later in 1979 succeeded Humelsine as chief executive officer. Armed with impressive academic and administrative credentials (as well as a pilot's license), Longsworth had the varied kinds of experience Humelsine had called prerequisites. Elected to Phi Beta Kappa at Amherst College, he took a graduate degree at Harvard Business School, then worked for Campbell's Soup and a major advertising agency before returning to Amherst as development officer and assistant to the president. He then became a founder of Hampshire College and its second president. Putting his own stamp on Colonial Williamsburg he would lead it even higher in the competitive world of nonprofit institutions.

Adapting many state-of-the-art business practices, Longsworth established "management goals," then delegated responsibility to his executives, many of them new recruits from a variety of outstanding museums and business corporations. Key department heads have come not only from the National Portrait Gallery and Boston Museum of Fine Arts, but from Lever Brothers, Gillette, Harvard and Citibank to address the challenges that Williamsburg and Longsworth have offered.

In his first years he oversaw completion of many projects begun by his predecessor. The Visitor Center was completely remodeled, the Public Hospital built, the DeWitt Wallace Decorative Arts Gallery opened. In addition, the Williamsburg corporations were reorganized, the institution's financial posture strengthened and hotel management restructured. The new administration has also successfully expanded its efforts in the Balkan realm of "grantsmanship," the solicitation of support for specific research projects. At the same time, new managers have updated everything from Personnel to accounting practices in the craft shops with notable results.

Another of Longsworth's strengths has been his willingness to take risks. It was his decision, for instance, to host the 1983 Economic Summit of Industrialized Nations which brought President Reagan, French President Mitterand, British Prime Minister Thatcher and five other heads of state to town along with three thousand reporters. The event required closing Williamsburg to the public for several days, which cost some ticket revenue. The event further cost some two hundred panes of eighteenth-century window glass, which cracked when howitzers boomed salutes and helicopters landed behind the Courthouse of 1770, over the objections of the Resident Architect. It also raised morale in unexpected ways, by showing some of Colonial Williamsburg's employees just how good they really were. (The U.S. Army provided its crack "colonial" marching band; said a knowing employee "their uniforms were *wrong* and they played nineteenth-century tunes.") Preparing for it all nearly cost some Indians and chiefs alike their sanity—as when the contract with the State Department arrived by Trailways bus only the night before the conference began. But the marathon event reasserted Williamsburg's status as an international way station and conference center of major repute.

Also during Longsworth's tenure, Senior Vice President Robert C. Birney spearheaded a campaign to integrate Williamsburg's diverse activities for the educational benefit of the visitor. Thus, the Research Department's scholarly studies of colonial economics have been shared with craftsmen who endeavor to present a more accurate picture of work and commerce in the eighteenth century to all who pass through their shops. The interpreters' training involves more rigorous classroom study, while a new costumed troupe has been deployed on Duke of Gloucester Street. Each of these "actors" takes on the persona of a known (or composite) eighteenth-century Williamsburg inhabitant. Their job is to encounter visitors as if they were neighbors and improvise conversations that illuminate the lives and times of yore.

In general, under Birney's guidance Williamsburg has explored new territory in scholarly research, Historic Area activities, educational programs and restoration projects. The archaeology program, which has gone through several metamorphoses, is a case in point. The most physically ambitious work was supervised by James Knight, who was instructed in 1938 to start excavating the entire Historic Area by digging his innumerable trenches. His method was crude by contemporary standards, his assigned purpose shortsighted: simply to locate the remains of every building. When he struck brickwork he uncovered and mapped it. When he found nothing but potsherds and bits of corroded metal, his men shoveled them

Ivor Noël Hume, the English antiquary who brought systematic archaeology to Colonial Williamsburg, digs for the past. His excavations unearthed a wealth of physical evidence about colonial life.

back in the ground with the fill, and in so doing destroyed whatever meaning they might have for later archaeologists. If there was substantial error here, it was a matter of nomenclature. This was a hunt for old building foundations, not true archaeology, which is grounded in scientific method, systematic discipline and a sense of objective inquiry.

In the 1950s, Williamsburg looked to the Old World to see if rigorous investigation could accomplish something more, and Ivor Noël Hume proved it could. Born in London, where he learned the particular discipline of classical archaeology by excavating Roman sites, he transplanted its proven techniques to the erstwhile colony. Setting out to learn from the ground whatever it could teach him of the past—not just about building sizes and locations, but about the habits of passing generations of people who raised them—he expanded our view of old Virginia.

Until he began work here, many American historians grandly assumed that the recent past spoke for itself only through written materials, while archaeologists proudly confined their efforts to prehistory, the uncovering of natives' relics from periods before Columbus and the tides of European invasion. Practicing the distinct discipline of *historical* archaeology, Noël Hume broke new ground, much to the chagrin of members of both groups who resented his intruding on their academic territories. (Hell hath no contempt like a scholar challenged.)

The truth of the matter is that neither conventional historical study or archaeology alone could have done the job required. The historical record has too many gaps and voids; official papers and the diaries of statesmen may record great events but often tell too little about commonplace things and everyday life, matters of growing interest to many scholars and laymen and of growing importance to Colonial Williamsburg. So too the archaeological record without the written one may be able to yield clues to the past but cannot reveal the full story. Almost single-handedly (at first) Noël Hume proved the worth of historical archaeology as a hybrid discipline with roots in two fields. The history fraternity came to recognize that archaeology unearths objects containing information that was never recorded and thus eluded conventional scholarship—like what sorts of implements people actually used, even what diseases carried them away under the rubric of "natural causes." The archaeology community begrudgingly learned that excavating historical sites could provide the means to test techniques and theories relating to prehistoric investigation.

Recovered from datable layers of earth around Wetherburn's Tavern, broken glassware (top) and fragments of Chinese export porcelain (above) reveal that innkeeper Henry Wetherburn provided utensils of notable quality for the time. The ceramic cup and saucer could well be part of a set of six listed in the 1760 room-by-room inventory of Wetherburn's estate.

In his search for the artifacts of colonial Williamsburg, Noël Hume used the time-honored techniques of classical archaeology—stratigraphy for instance. Soils build up in layers through natural processes and humanly induced ones. The archaeologist who depends on common sense as well as a rigorously systematic approach spends much of his energy plotting distinguishable layers before assessing everything found in each one: artifacts, chemicals, seeds, etc. Find a dated coin—or more likely a bit of glazed porcelain known to have been designed in say 1740—and it follows that the layer in which it lies could not have been deposited before that year. Thus every layer below the find antedates 1740, and every layer above it postdates it. Needless to say, there is little room for poor technique because the process of even careful excavation destroys the ground along with any original evidence.

Assisted by his wife, Audrey, Noël Hume painstakingly excavated countless Williamsburg sites and revealed special particulars about the city's past. In the ravine by the Anthony Hay Shop he found clay tiles, which provided the prototype for that building's restored roof. In the shafts of short-lived wells, which were typically abandoned and filled with trash, he

Today's gardens run the gamut from a tobacco patch guarded by a scarecrow in colonial garb (above) to a most formal arrangement of brick walk and topiary (right) beside the house once owned by Benjamin Waller, the gentleman and scholar who taught George Wythe law.

Gardener's tools stand in the potting shed (left) behind the Brush-Everard House. The fossilized scallops (above) may someday mark the borders of restored gardens.

227

found extensive inventories of well-worn household goods. (A corner cupboard in the Middle Room at Wetherburn's Tavern now contains serving wares of the exact types used there in colonial days; shards found by excavators enabled curators to identify specific china patterns.) Artifacts found in the cellar brickwork of Wetherburn's dated the additions to the building so that it could be accurately restored to the eighteenth century. Corroded implements discovered in the old Public Hospital site proved the methods used to treat the insane.

Most spectacularly, an exploratory dig on the grounds of Carter's Grove led to the excavation of Wolstenholme Towne, one of the James River outposts overrun by Indians in 1622. Among Noël Hume's most prized artifacts are the only closed helmets found *in situ* in North America, pieces of armor previously thought to have been obsolete by this era of settlement. All these objects and more provided new knowledge about colonial life. Further, they enabled Noël Hume to write widely (and popularly) about the discipline he championed and his chosen corner of the historical period, thus contributing to knowledge of colonial America generally. Specifically, his *Guide to Artifacts of Colonial America* is the standard reference, a work of inestimable value to academics and amateurs alike. An honorary research associate at the Smithsonian, Noël Hume augmented and amended the historical record through the discovery and analysis of physical artifacts.

In 1980, Noël Hume stepped aside as boss of day-to-day operations in order to devote his time to writing and planning a new archaeological museum for Carter's Grove (while remaining a member of the Colonial Williamsburg hierarchy). He was succeeded by Marley Brown III, a young archaeologist who brought even newer techniques to bear. For example, his crews have excavated the yard behind Peyton Randolph's house and catalogued every artifact using a system that can be manipulated by computer to answer any future question phrased in statistical terms. In time, and if funds are ever forthcoming, he hopes to excavate the Custis site, where Martha Washington's first father-in-law tended his famous gardens. Using sophisticated archaeobotanical and biochemical techniques, this dig could provide unprecedented information about colonial horticulture—not just as the gardeners said they practiced it, but as it actually happened.

(Alas, while the microscopic study of buried pollen and other space-age technology can add chapters to the Longsworth administration's achievements, the ways of bureaucratic communications remain a mystery. At the same time that the Department of Archaeology and Conservation was applying for a National Science Foundation grant to date old brick via radioactive means, Buildings and Maintenance bulldozed a new parking lot just outside the Historic Area. A dismayed archaeologist looked out his window just in time to see an earthmover scrape away the last of the archaeologically virgin ground, destroying its stratigraphy, artifacts and all.)

Conventional scholarship has been performed here since the early 1930s when Kenneth Chorley insisted on it to save Rockefeller possible embarrassment lest the Restoration err in its building (and rebuilding) programs. Early efforts, reflecting historical disciplines of the time, depended on conventional archives and the unearthing of written documents. The "great man theory of history" was popular then—the notion that events turn on personalities who thrust themselves to the forefront of their time. In recent years, the emphasis has been more on "social history," which offers the hypothesis that conditions of any era push individuals to the fore. To overstate for the sake of example: If a Patrick Henry didn't rise to champion a cause that led to insurrection then a Patrick Doe would.

Social historians examine the past with special reference to ordinary people in a manner that reflects another shift in emphasis around Williamsburg. The first restorers set out to commemorate the founding of the Republic and the great events leading to the Revolution. By contrast, the Longsworth group has chosen "Becoming Americans" as the long-term theme and centerpiece for its research and interpretation. The focus is on the evolution of American society and the life of all its people. (This shift had its roots in the report written in 1977 by Humelsine's committee of young historians, curators and administrators.)

Thus the celebrated York County Project, brainchild of research director, historian Cary Carson. This investigation would have been practically impossible a generation ago, since it involves the analysis and correlation of all surviving court, land and church records in the county from which half of Williamsburg was originally carved. (Records for the other half, annexed from James City County, were removed to Richmond for safekeeping during the Civil War. But Williamsburg proved safer when the capital of the Confederacy was torched, and the records perished.)

The first step was to compose a baseline profile of the county in 1705. The task involved compiling a file on index cards that eventually filled three hundred boxes, each with a capacity of one thousand cards. A card was made out for every name, whether recorded as a plaintiff, witness, juror, dependent, defendant, landowner, tenant, bride, communicant, convict, voter or whatever. Then the corps of researchers tentatively assigned people to families, households and hamlets. Using land records, they even programmed a computer to map homesteads on the basis of recorded acreages and known stretches of common boundaries. Cybernetic graphics aside, Carson's project promises to reveal so much about a representative eighteenth-century community that it has received major funding from the National Endowment for the Humanities.

One segment of the community noticeably absent from the early Restoration's interpretation was the black population. In its first several decades Colonial Williamsburg was clearly remiss in overlooking the diverse roles of eighteenth-century blacks, both slaves and freemen. The only blacks in colonial dress punched admission tickets and, with few exceptions, demonstrated "domestic" crafts, though in the colonial era many blacks were employed in highly skilled professions. The oversight was not exclusively the fault of management. The civil rights movement itself may have delayed the emergence of a "black presence" in the Historic Area.

By the 1960s, many blacks who worked for Colonial Williamsburg were solidly middle class, proper and conservative. Tentatively invited to interpret black life in the eighteenth century for the visitors, they declined out of a reluctance to be associated with either slavery or the civil rights movement, which some of them thought rabble-rousing. Simultaneously, young blacks were uninterested in Williamsburg. Several locals who were recruited to work there in the 1980s remember that the Historic Area was simply not a place they visited as children growing up nearby. It wasn't that they were barred—to the contrary, the Restoration quietly flouted Virginia's segregation laws and welcomed all comers. Rather, as one program director recalled in 1984, "There just wasn't anything here for us." In large part the onus for this lay in the fact that the institution stressed Williamsburg's role as a seat of government and hotbed of dissidence. Since government and revolution were the business of gentlemen, blacks simply didn't have featured roles. It was more a case of historical emphasis than discrimination.

"Soldiers' wives" (above) pass the time of day during the Colonial Fair while their menfolk (right), members of a costumed infantry company, step out in front of the Capitol.

A figure around town for decades, carter James Sampson (above left) rests in his oxcart. A pretty maid (above right) hawks pastries. Youngsters (below) dance a reel during the Fair.

The new generation of Colonial Williamsburg executives would address this imbalance out of their desire for historical accuracy and a commitment to eschew discriminatory practices. Dennis A. O'Toole, an experienced museum education director who became Longsworth's vice president for Historic Area Programs and Operations, took the lead. As part of his intention to accurately represent eighteenth-century life in its intriguing and instructive diversity, he recruited blacks as interpreters, supervisors, craftsmen and program presenters. Similarly, he realized that women were only seen practicing gentle occupations, when, in fact, colonial women did every sort of work. Thus, just as more blacks appeared in real eighteenth-century roles, lectured on black history and performed Afro-American music, women began to appear as shepherdesses, coachmen and apprentices—even in the blacksmith's shop. (Yes, female smiths were known in the eighteenth century.)

Physically as well as programmatically, the town is becoming an apparently more faithful image of its eighteenth-century self. The continuing work of historical architects, directed by another Longsworth recruit, includes such arcane subjects as the study of pigment formulae and dendrochronology. The latter involves the study of tree rings found in the timber of old buildings to determine when they were constructed—or at least when the lumber was cut. The principle is simple enough: Trees grow more in wet years than dry years and their annular rings reflect this. A sample of living trees provides characteristic sequences of wide and narrow rings back to, say, 1900. Dendrochronology labs contain sections of mature trees that died early in this century; the pattern of their last (or outer) rings matches the oldest (inner) rings of living trees. By matching up sequences of rings in even older trees, dendrochronologists can now read the years all the way back into colonial times and make a probable estimate of when a tree was cut.

Thus, when conventional scholarship failed to pinpoint the construction date of the Ludwell-Paradise House, Resident Architect Nicholas A. Pappas had the first-floor timbers examined by an expert who judged the trees to have been felled in 1752. Pappas, who came to Williamsburg after restoring the Washington headquarters of the National Trust for Historic Preservation, is also a stickler for correct colors. Quite early on, Colonial Williamsburg developed a somewhat pastel palette, possibly because researchers assumed the early coats of paint they found in old buildings fairly represented their original shades. But over time paints fade and change. To determine their original shades, chemists analyze the components of old paints, mix them afresh and see what colors emerge. By and large, this has demonstrated that the colonists and Founding Fathers had chromatic tastes we might consider garish.

Less arcane research suggests a "hierarchy" of exterior decor. A residence facing Duke of Gloucester Street would have been adorned to the nines with fine brickwork, careful molding details and the like. The kitchen behind it would display less aesthetic embellishments, a smokehouse even less and a lumber shed at the rear of the lot perhaps none at all. ("Lumber" was a catchall term encompassing a range of miscellany. When Robert Carter's daughters dressed up in grown-up gowns, tutor Philip Fithian recorded that they stuffed the bodices with "lumber.") Similarly, paint was applied with discrimination. The early Restoration was fond of a pleasant and varied color scheme even among the outbuildings. The new look tends more toward the ubiquitous and cheaper "Spanish brown," barn red and whitewash. It may not be as pleasing to our eyes, but it is more accurate.

For Williamsburg, moving forward has always meant looking more closely into the past, and under Longsworth's administration this tradition continues. Research proceeds; in some respects it broadens as resident investigators and visiting scholars pose new questions, many of them purely practical ones, such as how to grow and process wool according to a manual published by a Williamsburg planter in the 1770s. Rarely, however, do searches for verisimilitude in crafts and agriculture create the kind of uproar that followed on the heels of one seemingly innocuous experiment. It happened this way:

Europe saw the boundless New World as a trove of botanical and mineral treasure. When newly named Virginia was discovered to lack cities paved with gold, English adventurers settled for baser riches, like ships spars and tobacco. Briefly they tried glassblowing and iron mining in this colony, Williamsburg historians learned, and even tried to start a silk industry though, alas, the worms didn't cotton to paper mulberry trees (to mix fibers if not a metaphor). Yet hemp, the source of an important naval staple, rope, did better in Virginia and a Colonial Williamsburg weaver proposed reviving the historical business of ropemaking. It seemed a natural addition to the exhibition repertoire: They'd grow hemp, harvest it, process the natural fiber and turn it into cordage as colonists had done—all right before the visitors' eyes. Scholarly research uncovered the historical facts of hemp growing. More research of a practical nature would discover techniques.

The weaver was a Scotsman remembered as so nimble-fingered that he could spin woolen thread one-handed from a ball of fluff cradled in his palm; he didn't need a spinning wheel to make yarn while discoursing on all kinds of lore in a brogue thick as old tweed. A kind of manual genius with a sense of history and the gift of gab, he asked Purchasing to get him the seeds he needed to plant, and they were duly ordered from a seed catalogue in the Midwest. The seeds thrived in Virginia's famous soil. Come harvest time the weaver and his crew brought in a surprising crop. Using antique tools, they extracted fibers to spin into thread to twist into rope. The first year they let the plants grow to full height, and learned it would be best to cut them sooner because mature plants branched, which meant tangled fibers. At any rate, when they cut the plants they stored them in a barn to dry and paid no mind when birds swooped in to snatch the seeds, and then swooped out again with less agility. The birds seemed more flighty, more gay; they flew a little higher, to borrow a phrase. This delighted certain visitors who giggled at the idea of growing this plant for rope.

Years later one who helped grow the hemp said they *really didn't know* that a rope by any other name could cause such heat. They learned otherwise when detectives descended in high dudgeon. "Hemp?" they frowned. "That's marijuana, pot, herb, Mary Jane and you all are under arrest." The charge, which threatened to become a federal case with international implications, was possession of an illegal drug. The Scottish weaver, a guest in the Commonwealth, was alarmed, and threatened to call his embassy before things got out of hand. Needless to say the colonial precinct's overseers were concerned as well.

Eventually all was put right. One erstwhile suspect's scrapbook contains, among many nobler mementos of a life spent ably plying colonial crafts, a yellowed clipping from the local press. It reports a grand jury, that honored panel born of English common law, weighed the evidence and instructed the prosecution to drop its case. There was no malicious intent on the several craftsmen's part; they had simply planted what had been ordered from a reputable catalogue and were growing hemp for rope not dope. That was simply that. (It was understood by all, however, that the stuff that filled the barn was contraband and should not be grown again.) A panel of peers set the tradesmen free, their names and records as clean as Colonial Williamsburg's abiding reputation in the world at large.

A Manifold Museum (I): The Galleries

An institution of parts, Colonial Williamsburg became a repository of splendid objects, a museum first of Virginiana, then of Americana, then of folk art and the decorative arts as a whole. Many possessions that didn't suit the Historic Area in terms of geography or time are now displayed in two special galleries. The gilded Indian-on-horseback weathervane (opposite), a unique piece made of pine and sheet iron late in the nineteenth century, stands in the Abby Aldrich Rockefeller Folk Art Center. At the other end of the artistic spectrum, the crewel stag (left) in the DeWitt Wallace Decorative Arts Gallery represents the epitome of sewn elegance. The detail comes from an eighteenth-century English bedcover that formerly graced a Governor's Palace bedchamber.

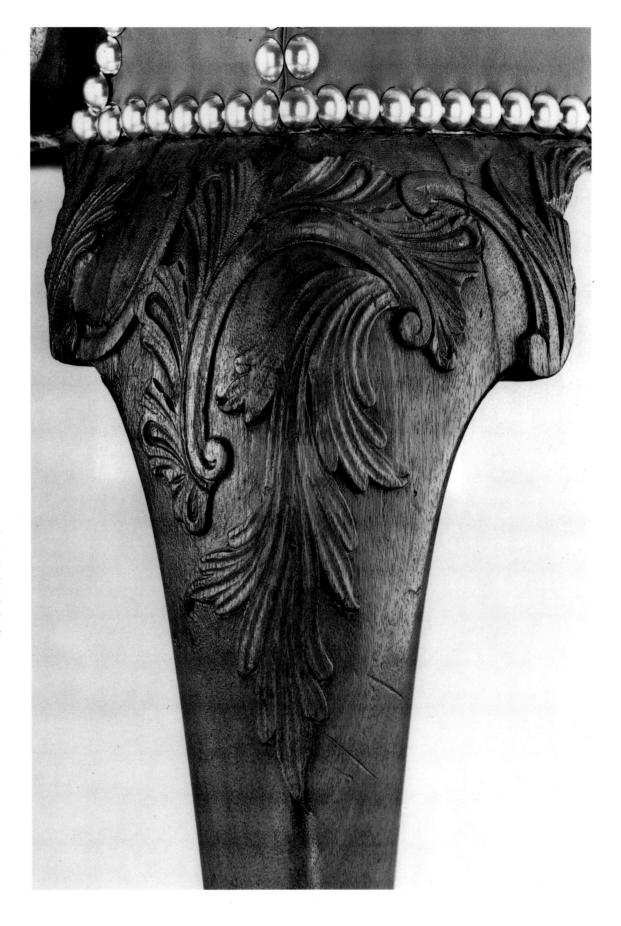

The Capitol, or Governor's, Chair (opposite above), *a ceremonial seat that probably served the presiding officer in the General Court, displays virtuoso carving. Probably constructed in Anthony Hay's shop about 1755, it is made of mahogany with beech as a secondary wood. Acanthus leaves adorn the legs (right) while the arms end in regal lion heads (opposite below). Taken to Richmond with the rest of the government's furniture in 1779, it was consigned to an attic in this century and given to a janitor who sold it to an antiques dealer. Dr. Goodwin bought it for Colonial Williamsburg in 1928 and it now stands in the Masterworks Gallery at the DeWitt Wallace museum.*

Colonial Williamsburg [is] America's most cherished testament to its past.
—Robert McCormack Adams
Secretary of the Smithsonian Institution (1985)

*T*oday Colonial Williamsburg is a complex, an amalgam of institutions. It is certainly a "destination" in the lexicon of travel agentry, a place that attracts as many as seven thousand visitors on a good day and upwards of one million in a typical year. It is also a conference and convention center for groups as distinct as trade associations, the Southern Governors Conference and the American Horse Show Association. In another of its guises, this is a patriot's mecca, a shrine dedicated to the nation's founding that grizzled veterans seek out on commemorative occasions. At Christmas it is a holiday spa, one weekend every fall a colonial fairgrounds, on Independence Day the place where local folk converge for fireworks. Williamsburg is a perennial garden club, a crafts bazaar, an old-fashioned hideaway for honeymooners and other lovers. But more than any of these, it is a museum, indeed a complex of museums.

Since the great library in ancient Alexandria first used the term, "museum" has meant a multitude of things. In eighteenth-century London a museum was typically an aristocrat's private collection of objects. Charles Willson Peale opened America's first successful public museum, which displayed his passion for collecting curiosities: paintings, dinosaur bones and whatnot. In living memory, museums have usually been dusty places, each one a kind of mausoleum featuring ranks of vitrines filled with insects impaled on pins tagged with their names in dead Latin. But in recent decades museums have come into their own as places that amuse adults and instruct children, or vice versa.

What are they today? A modern museum is an institution that collects a chosen body of material things because they are valuable—whether intrinsically as in a trophy cup weighing two hundred ounces of gilt silver or impalpably as in a common eighteenth-century man's private diary or the apothecary's ledger that suggests which Virginia gentleman suffered "the French disease." It is a sanctuary for objects, a place whose mission is to hold them in safekeeping for posterity. A museum is also properly a place of exhibition that mounts shows of this or that for public enlightenment and pleasure alike. Finally, a museum is a center for the study of its own objects and collections and, by extension, a nexus for the study of all the arts and sciences relating to those objects. In sum, a museum is an institution that collects, protects, displays and reveals its chosen ken.

For modern Williamsburg that sphere comprises the historic town that was capital of both colony and newly independent Commonwealth, then by extension all Virginia and eighteenth-century America. Almost inevitably its curators concerned themselves with everything they found within the boundaries defined by time and place: with antiques, art and ideas, with historic guns and historical theories, with artifacts as base as leg irons and notions as lofty as St. George Tucker's belief in emancipation four score years before Lincoln. Wisely, Colonial Williamsburg's stewards never decided to make it a "political museum" (whatever that might be). Neither is it just a museum of pots, art, furniture or folklore. It grew into all these things in one because it is a history museum.

The deep grain and bright brasses of this chest-on-chest (above and opposite) gleam as on the day it left Thomas Affleck's Philadelphia workshop on the eve of Independence. For 209 years it was handed down through the descendants of the first owner until Colonial Williamsburg acquired it. Standing in the Wallace Gallery, it ranks among the most important American antiques anywhere because of its superiority in several respects: grace that belies its large size, elegance of design, superb workmanship, immaculate condition and ironclad provenance.

The museum's de facto purpose is to reveal its chosen site and era according to lights that vary from generation to generation. For decades the emphasis was on the town as the best preserved of the Revolution's many "cradles" (and arsenals). Colonial Williamsburg saw itself as the Shrine of Freedom, a place of political genesis in a world threatened (ironically) by proselytes of new revolutionary ideas. Lately the emphasis has shifted toward the lives of our ordinary forebears and how it was that they *became* American—in their folkways, science, philosophy, economics, jurisprudence, aesthetics, social behavior, politics, business, agriculture and in their very minds. In a way twentieth-century Williamsburg is as dynamic and protean as Jefferson hoped his Republic would become.

Colonial Williamsburg qualifies as a museum on many grounds, first as a historic and historical town of 173 acres and 500 period buildings from privies to Palace including shops, stores, a Courthouse and Capitol. (Nearly a hundred are painstaking restorations, the rest careful reconstructions of lost originals. More than forty major structures—the number varies from year to year—are exhibition buildings. Nearly a hundred dwellings and larger outbuildings such as kitchens are the homes of life tenants and Colonial Williamsburg employees; another dozen are guesthouses while most of the rest provide offices, storage and "break rooms," i.e. places where costumed staff take coffee breaks.) Here the structures themselves are the first objects on display.

The entire town is an exhibit—its gravel streets, its greens and ravines, even its human activities from the smith's casting of brass candlesticks in the Geddy Foundry to the harpsichordist's playing of Handel concerti upon a baroque instrument in the intimacy of the Palace ballroom. As a museum, the whole displays a priceless collection of artisans' rediscovered skills, resources as special as the rare objects which were created by similar workers lifetimes ago. And of course, Williamsburg is a museum in the intellectual work that goes on here, for this is a place of research, study, convocation and scholarship.

It is also a cluster of museums in the conventional sense. Its larger possessions—the buildings themselves—contain myriad smaller objects of very special quality and importance: Antique silver hollowware and pitchers, like those James Craig raised from scrap sterling, are now displayed in the Golden Ball; the Speaker's Chair built for the first Capitol has been loaned indefinitely by the Commonwealth for display in the reconstructed Capitol; the imposing but imperfect portrait of Rev. James Blair that hangs in the Great Hall of the Wren Building; the Chelsea porcelain figures that grace the mantel in the Palace dining room. From the copper saucepans in his kitchen to the coverlet in Lord Botetourt's bedchamber, all of these are "museum pieces" as the saying goes. Yet many of them are not grand *objets d'art*. Many are as common as chamber pots since the historic buildings have slowly—and controversially—evolved to reflect forgotten commonplaces of the eighteenth century, as we shall see.

Two special exhibition buildings are traditional museums as well, structures built for and dedicated to the display of prized antique objects. One of these, the Abby Aldrich Rockefeller Folk Art Center, came to be by virtue of the founder's fiat; the other, which nearly didn't get built at all, arose out of ingenious design. (A third, the James Anderson House, is a reconstructed building that was adapted to house an archaeological exhibit in 1975.)

The latest addition to Williamsburg's complex of museums is a complex in itself: the

Public Hospital and DeWitt Wallace Decorative Arts Gallery. It comprises both the largest reconstruction in fifty years and a purely contemporary gallery. It came to be through a series of small miracles; that it did is both function and proof of Colonial Williamsburg's growing up as an independent institution.

Having been the ward of one benefactor, the historical hamlet did not have much experience in fully managing its own affairs when Mr. Rockefeller's heirs set it loose in the world. Never having had to support itself, Colonial Williamsburg hadn't ventured far into the competitive world of nonprofit institutions. When the first professional development officer was lured away from Duke University—like any college, an aggressive solicitor of gifts—he was bemused. Looking at a list of regular guests who returned repeatedly and had clearly demonstrated their interest in one way or another, he asked how much money they'd been invited to give. "None," was the answer. That would be set right.

One frequent visitor stood tall among those known for generous support of their favorite charities. His name was high on every fund-raiser's wish list. DeWitt Wallace and his wife, Lila, founded the *Reader's Digest*, arguably the most successful periodical on earth.

The Tompion Clock (above) stands alone as a horological masterpiece that combines inspired design, superior materials, royal provenance and exceptional workmanship. The works (opposite right) are by London clockmaker Thomas Tompion. Made for King William III about 1699, the clock bears his monogram. A small dial counts seconds; two calendar apertures show the current month, its number of days and the current date. Standing just over ten feet tall—that's Minerva on top (opposite left), goddess of arts and trades—it is too elegant to ever have been seen in the colonies.

Their little magazine grew into a publishing empire that hardly knew national boundaries, and their fortune was of the same magnitude. DeWitt Wallace was very wealthy and very patriotic. (He started the 1960s craze of putting little American flag decals and patches on everything.) He also loved Williamsburg. He not only visited several times a year, but he sent a small planeload of employees down from New York about once a month for their recreation and inspiration, all expenses paid.

Eight *Reader's Digest* hands, typically maiden ladies, would arrive on a Friday night, each with a little dividend in her purse for spending money. When they got back to work on Monday, at least one would be interviewed by the boss who liked to hear about goings-on in the colonial capital. It was always good news, until one year a lady reported that she had not seen *The Story of a Patriot.* Her employer was incredulous. *Not seen 'The Patriot'!?* The idea was shocking. She'd tried, she said, but they weren't screening it anymore.

This film is something of a museum piece itself, a fine example of Technicolor filmcraft (if not the masterpiece that scenarist James Agee was contemplating at the time of his early death). Directed by George Seaton, famous for *The Country Girl,* and starring Jack Lord, later a private eye on television, *The Patriot* relates the history of Williamsburg on the eve of the Revolution with a kind of dated charm and sentimentality. Projected continuously at the old Information Center, it prepared visitors for what they would see around town. Made in 1957, the subtly jingoistic film reflected the national mood; it was "dedicated to the principles of liberty wherever and whenever they may be threatened." Withal, it was made with great historical care; Thad Tate, then a member of the Research Department and later director of the Institute for Early American History and Culture, spent two years assuring the accuracy of its content. (Still, there were some inside jokes. "Thaddeus Tate" appears as a burgess-elect because an instant change in the script required a fictitious name that "sounded colonial." Executive Roger Leclere turns up as a bewigged extra; a barrel of goods imported from England bears the name of chief architect Ed Kendrew.) Almost every visitor has seen it, and none more delightedly than Wallace and his favored employees.

But that year Williamsburg was gearing up for the Bicentennial and had come to believe that thirteen million patriots would be making the pilgrimage to its hallowed halls. A shorter film had been made in order to better accommodate the throngs, and *The Patriot* had been shelved pro tem. In a flash Wallace was on the phone offering to build a new and enlarged Visitor Center with three theaters capable of screening his favorite movie for each and every arrival. In a manner of speaking he offered to endow *The Patriot* in perpetuity.

Williamsburg was loath to look this gift horse in the mouth and nearly took the offer without a second glance. Fortunately cooler heads prevailed. Early plans called for Wallace's building to handle several million people a year, even though few more than one million have ever showed up. The donor offered a gift of $4 million, but the price tag would have been more. When Bicentennial Year attendance fell short of the grandiose expectations, and rising gasoline prices caused several lean years, Colonial Williamsburg seriously reconsidered. Wallace was told in effect, we don't want that gift—or rather we don't want it for the purposes you had in mind. In 1975 the board of trustees had endorsed a new gallery in principle, but had not yet found the money to fund it. Furthermore, a major reconstruction project had been postponed for decades: the last major public building, the mental hospital. Having demonstrated his willingness to help Williamsburg, Wallace was invited to consider funding

The orrery (below), *made in London about 1800, represents the kind of instrument that the College brought to Williamsburg for students' edification. The first orrery, named for the peer who commissioned it from Tompion and George Graham, traced the circuits of known planets. This advanced model, the work of William and Samuel Jones of London, shows the rotation and revolution of both earth and moon and also includes Uranus—the outermost planet shown—which was discovered in 1781.*

King George III, displaying hauteur and extravagance suitable for a monarch, wears his coronation robes in 1762. Allan Ramsay painted many copies of the state portrait and by 1768 one hung in the Governor's Palace. This original copy adorned Knole, the duke of Dorset's home, until it came to the decorative arts gallery at Colonial Williamsburg.

General George Washington strikes a pose similar to that of the king he opposed. Charles Willson Peale painted this monumental picture, complete with the pivotal 1777 Battle of Princeton in the background, on bedticking in Philadelphia in 1780. The painting hung at nearby Shirley Plantation until Mr. Rockefeller bought it in 1928, making it the first of many pictures to be acquired by the Restoration. While Peale probably saw King George's portrait either in Williamsburg or London, where he studied with Benjamin West, it's unlikely that he meant his portrait to be a parody; rather, he intended to show the commander in chief in a heroic pose. In any case, the two paintings hang in resonant juxtaposition in Colonial Williamsburg's newest museum.

A silver-gilt horse-racing trophy, the Richmond Cup was commissioned by an English profiteer who made a fortune provisioning royal armies for the Seven Years War and then dedicated himself to achieving social prominence. One of a series wrought annually for several consecutive years by Britain's finest silversmith, the cup represents monumental silverwork of the highest order—a paradigm against which all other pieces may be judged. It is also a most dramatic expression of early neoclassical design. Though this one did not reach Virginia until 1980, commemorative cups were cherished by colonial aristocrats about the time it was made, namely 1776.

a decorative arts gallery and the Public Hospital. Would he be willing to complete work that Mr. John D. Rockefeller Jr. hadn't been able to finish? Yes, he would consider it.

Thus the reconstruction of the Public Hospital became conceptually and financially linked to the DeWitt Wallace Decorative Arts Gallery, which opened in 1985. Indeed the benefactor contributed $14 million to the project and established a fund to defray the gallery's annual expenses.

Kevin Roche, the celebrated architect who designed it, says the complex evolved in this wise. The first notion was straightforward enough: to reconstruct the old Public Hospital facade on its original site with a couple of underground levels for exhibition galleries. But as the Collections Department spelled out its space requirements, it soon appeared that the whole building must resemble a huge submarine sunk in earth with the old Hospital rising above the sod like a puny conning tower. Impractically expensive, it was, in a word, ludicrous as well.

The more Roche visited the site the more he was troubled by the city's present courthouse and jail building. Located outside the Restored Area, this modern brick building lay behind the Hospital site like a sleeping ogre. It was an eyesore in brick and concrete. People wandering through the old town often found themselves pleasantly lost in time, transported back two centuries—until this sorry sight jolted them back into modernity. A self-styled "unreconstructed modernist," Roche was more offended than an antiquarian architect. This courthouse not only clashed with its carefully restored surroundings, but in his opinion was a shoddy modern design to boot.

After pondering for many months and visiting the site several times, the architect pressed a new specification on his client: The project must somehow screen the courthouse from view. Plantings or landscaping seemed a likely answer. But no one could come up with a plan that would serve year-round short of an earthworks mightier than Yorktown's battlefield, which clearly would have violated the notion of restoring the town as it had been. Roche found a solution in one of the causes of the two-fold dilemma, namely the Historic Area's invisible boundary. The line lay sixty feet beyond the Hospital's rear foundation.

Roche suggested reconstructing the little Hospital on its old site and building a modern gallery sixty-five feet away, just over the Historic Area boundary. He'd make its exterior serve more purposes than simply containing the museum: It would conceal the offending lockup and resemble a structure often encountered in the eighteenth century, a blind brick garden wall laid up in a variation of the familiar Flemish bond not surprisingly called garden wall bond. (Alas, the thin wall, built on a cement block core, required expansion joints which break up the brickwork's serene visual rhythms.) The Hospital building, detached and insular as of yore, would provide access to the gallery building by way of an underground tunnel.

This complex of reconstructed asylum and modern gallery is unique in its combination of elements, a singular mix of old and new. The rebuilt Hospital's exterior appears to be as faithful a copy of the original building as scholarship and technology could make it, while all that appears of the sixty-two-thousand-square-foot gallery building is the brick wall. Though magnified, it looks as modest as the brick fences that surround the little family cemeteries and some gardens hereabouts. If it lacked imposing granite columns to announce itself as a museum, that was fine with Roche who intended it as an unobtrusive "frame for

The cup's details—handles, gadrooning (ornamental bands), surmounting Angel of Victory and swags—were cast, then heightened with punch and hammer. The whole piece was painted with powdered gold mixed in mercury and then heated; the mercury vaporized, leaving the gold in place and the gilders reeling from toxic fumes.

The Wallace Gallery houses diverse treasures: Spectacularly decorated, the enameled and gilt brass urn (above left) must resemble the "tea machine" listed among Palace amenities in the 1770 inventory of the penultimate royal governor, Lord Botetourt. The elegant body was painted in Staffordshire just about then; the source of the superbly wrought ormolu mounts remains unknown. A brocaded Spitalfields silk gown and petticoat with separate stomacher (above right) represents the height of rococo fashion. Made in England in the 1760s, it might only have been worn in court circles. A detail from a rare sampler (below) shows Britain's heraldic beasts, the Scottish unicorn and English lion, romping in the Garden of Eden. An English girl named Mary Best stitched the raised embroidery in 1693.

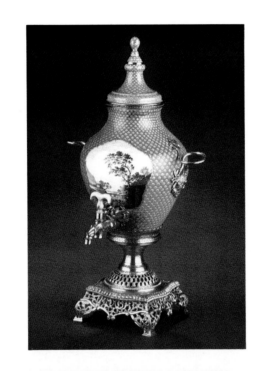

Published in 1755 as Britain girded for the French and Indian War, this six-foot map (above) played a major role in history: diplomats used it when writing the Treaty of Paris, which formalized American Independence. It was drawn from surveys by John Mitchell, a native-born physician and botanist who fled Virginia's climate for London's scientific circles and who sponsored Mark Catesby's membership in the Royal Society. America's first artist-naturalist, Catesby drew the "Mock-bird" on a dogwood branch (below) and spent much of the 1710s and 1720s studying New World wildlife from a base in Williamsburg. (He gave John Custis, the town's most famous gardener, the cutting for his rare pink dogwood.) He devoted twelve years to engraving the plates for his magnum opus on natural history, all of which, like the Mitchell map, were tinted by hand. These superb specimens are now in the Wallace Gallery's Prints and Maps collection.

objects which mirror history."

The Hospital's facade was fairly easy to ascertain because several pictures of the original building survived, including nineteenth-century photographs showing it with an added story and several wings shortly before it burned in 1885. The elements used to create the new facade were hard to find. In the 1930s the Restoration could afford the luxury of making its own brick; clearly it would use so much that fashioning it by hand—after arduously learning how by trial and error—made a certain kind of fiscal sense. But no longer, and indeed, the art form of making usable brick had been lost again. Colonial Williamsburg's architectural historians combed the East for a supplier who would make bricks that looked like, well, "Williamsburg brick," their color that rare rich salmon hue, their shapes showing slight variations, their composition spiced with inclusions of lighter material added to the wet clay before firing, like raisins in rice pudding. Then every brick destined to lie exposed was selected by two architectural historians who picked over seven railroad cars of bricks by hand.

Next on the agenda was the roof, known to have been cypress-shingled in the original building. While it wasn't impossible to buy cypress logs, it was harder to turn them into sixty thousand shingles. After several false starts, a Yankee woodsman was found who could do the work by hand. Douglas Wilson hadn't made shingles before, but he'd done every other sort of work with wood including live off the pine forests of his native Maine, and he was willing to have a go at it. Taking eighteen-inch-long sections of log, he split them with a froe and carved each section into scores of shingles with a drawknife. Each shingle was then shaved to a slight taper toward the top and rounded at its lower end. The operation might almost have been a craft demonstration, except that Wilson worked in a garage off the beaten track and wore modern clothes. His Down East accent might have jarred aurally sensitive visitors; more important, a Colonial Williamsburg tradesman who must explain what he's doing while he works gets less actual work done and, as it was, Wilson spent nearly a year at the task.

The weathervane atop the cupola also took considerable work and an odd compromise before it was installed. Silversmiths James Curtis and George Cloyed raised flat disks of copper into two halves of a sphere as big as a medicine ball, which was then gilded. Blacksmith Peter Ross made the armature and the vane itself, discovering tricks of construction as he worked. (In order to turn in the wind the slender arrow must be almost perfectly balanced. Thus antique weathervanes often have a bit of extra metal welded to one end.) For visual accuracy, Ross also forged a lightning rod, a single bar of three-quarter-inch iron that rose four stories to the top of the cupola. This is where one of the compromises came in, because modern building codes require a "lightning arrestor" in the form of an oddly shaped disk fixed at the very top of the armature. (From the ground the disk resembles a squashed version of the coronet atop the Capitol's cupola.)

As for the building's interior, the second floor is devoted to offices while the first floor has two patient's cells furnished as they would have been in the eighteenth and nineteenth centuries respectively, along with an explanatory exhibit. The rest of the first floor provides access to the basement level "tunnel"—actually an introductory exhibit hall—leading to the DeWitt Wallace Decorative Arts Gallery. What are the decorative arts? One of the Gallery's purposes is to answer that question and to educate an interested but often daunted public. The decorative arts include painting and sculpture but go far beyond these two

Even antique weapons are beautiful enough to be displayed in the decorative arts museum—in its Masterworks Gallery. The long rifle (left) was made in Staunton, Virginia, about 1800 by John Shetz. Curators believe that it is unique for America in its silver wire veining and that "the carving, inlaid silver sheet and wire, and engraved brass mountings combine to create a balanced and tasteful masterpiece of American art." The flintlock pistol (center) displays many French traits, though it was made in London about 1710—at a time when the best English gunsmiths were immigrants from the Continent. The fowling piece (right) also shows influences of French design, though it too was made in London, about 1725, by a gunsmith named Hutchinson, who was probably trained in Scotland.

Graphic arts in the Abby Aldrich Rockefeller Folk Art Center include the works of unschooled, yet naturally gifted artists, who often commemorated benchmark events in the lives of rural Americans. Sentimental "mourning pictures" were so popular in the nineteenth century that Mark Twain has Huckleberry Finn remark on them at satiric length. Polly Botsford and Her Children (above), a watercolor in this genre from about 1815 that Mrs. Rockefeller acquired personally, anticipates modern design in its stark reduction of forms to their most basic elements and its dramatic composition. The fraktur (below), certifying the birth and baptism of Alexander Danner, was inscribed on handmade paper about 1804 by a schoolmaster known only by his initials. Enough examples of his multimedia work survive to suggest that "C. M." accepted commissions on a semiprofessional basis.

250

To judge from sales of reproductions, Baby in Red Chair *is one of the most popular* objets d'art *in Mrs. Rockefeller's collection. Possessing an ineffably naive charm, it remains a mystery. Despite curatorial sleuthing, nothing has been learned about its origins, though the best educated guesses assign it "possibly" to Pennsylvania between 1810 and 1830.*

disciplines. They also embrace furniture, textiles, ceramics, silver, tableware et al.: homely objects and useful amenities that people chose to embellish for the simple sake of beauty. The term can be widely encompassing, as broad a concept as "interior design" in its many manifestations today.

Roche expected the visitor to lose his bearings underground; thus he had the tunnel lead to a bright two-story atrium with plantings and a forest of concrete pillars that serves as the Gallery's entrance court. Ideally, art galleries have only artificial light which lacks ultraviolet rays (the part of the spectrum that bleaches natural colors), but Colonial Williamsburg's curators wanted some natural light. Roche, too, who also designed the new American Wing at the Metropolitan, insists that his galleries serve human visitors as well as objects "and people need natural light." He provided it in this entrance space which features a split staircase curving up to the Masterworks Gallery on the upper floor and its centerpiece: a royal governor's chair (made in Williamsburg) flanked by portraits of "the two Georges," the American general who won the Revolution and the English king who lost his colonies. In Allan Ramsay's celebrated portrait, George III, standing in his coronation robes with one leg cocked, is the epitome of regal and somewhat pompous grandeur. Charles Willson Peale's heroic rendering of General Washington after the Battle of Princeton mimics the king's posture and reveals a victorious man.

The real heroes of the Wallace Gallery are the exhibition spaces and the collections they contain. Here some eight thousand objects represent the spectrum of English and American furniture, paintings, arms, ceramics, silver and pewter, prints, textiles, clothing and more. Many were acquired decades ago during the Restoration's acquisitive heyday, but languished in storage because they didn't suit the Historic Area in terms of date or style. One of the pieces on display, for example, is an English tall case clock of such unique splendor that it would never have found its way to any colony and could not even be legally exported from Britain today; the works were built by Thomas Tompion of London about 1699 for the newly crowned King William III. Here is Peale's remarkable portrait of Benjamin Harrison, there Lord Dunmore's suite of hunting arms. Furniture in the Miodrag and Elizabeth Ridgely Blagojevich Gallery—much of it from the donors' collection—displays the relationships between English and American regional designs. The ceramics gallery and metals gallery present definitive arrays of serving wares in stunning diversity. These exhibits in particular are works of art themselves.

In addition there are examining rooms and study alcoves, for this museum is designed to serve both casual visitors and serious students of several disciplines. Colonial Williamsburg's three thousand prints, for example, are stored so that all may be examined. Collectively and separately, the galleries within the Wallace serve as "libraries" of English and American objects. The place also contains storage ranges, laboratories, a café and 240-seat auditorium with state-of-the-art audio and video systems donated by Joseph H. and June S. Hennage.

Since the Gallery must preserve the objects it displays, the heating and air-conditioning systems are so finely tuned that the interior temperature may not vary more than five degrees throughout the year. And it bears mention that the passing seasons don't present the worst problems; people do. In any gallery the patron is as destructive an organism as foxing on an old print; we constantly exude moisture by the simple act of breathing and radiate heat just by being warm-blooded. Surprisingly, perhaps, even in winter the central air-conditioning will do more work than the steam boilers to counteract the thousand-odd lightbulbs and people emitting 450 BTUs of heat an hour.

Williamsburg's older museum building is the Abby Aldrich Rockefeller Folk Art Center. When Mr. Rockefeller was walking near the Inn after Abby's death in 1948, he pointed to a spot and said "I want it here!" That was that. In this rare instance he did not seek the staff's advice, nor carefully weigh their recommendations. He knew what he wanted and where he wanted it. Having found the site, he made a special gift—above and beyond his others—and separately endowed the memorial to his first wife. Though the little Georgian Revival building turned out to be awkwardly located between the Inn, swimming pool and Lodge, it has become a mecca in its own right, a destination for devotees of folk art, a panoply of painting, sculpture, metalwork and textiles created by unschooled artists of memorable skill.

During Williamsburg's eclipse in the nineteenth century, American folk art flourished; early in this century Abby Rockefeller became one of the rare individuals to recognize its aesthetic and educational value. She was a tastemaker and began collecting this intriguing material—by definition the oeuvre of artists who lacked only academic training or technique. In the end, her collection was a nonpareil.

Its undeniable merits aside, however, the question was discussed at length as to whether Colonial Williamsburg should pursue the lady's passion. No less a light than Kenneth Chorley broached the matter with Mr. Rockefeller when the collection was on display in the Ludwell-Paradise House. It seemed clearly anachronistic within the Historic Area and Chorley suggested that if the works had been bequeathed by a "Mrs. Smith" they would find a repository elsewhere. Troubled by the soundness of that position, Mr. Rockefeller agreed that something would have to be done eventually. If the situation were left unresolved until he left the scene, the collection would inevitably be jettisoned one way or another. So it was up to him to devise a better solution. He seized on the idea of locating the collection outside the colonial enclave and with that established the Abby Aldrich Rockefeller Folk Art Center in its own handsome quarters. The building and its collection are no more anachronistic here than the Regency-style Inn or the modern-functional Lodge.

Mr. Rockefeller's solution turns out to have been a reasonable one, since expertise in the decorative arts generally has become a forte of Colonial Williamsburg. One might even argue that to exclude folk art here would be contrary to good sense. In any event, the folk art museum has become a perennial favorite, especially at Christmastime when its collection of nineteenth-century toys goes on display. Perhaps more significant, folk art gained recognition, even respectability, by virtue of its having received the Williamsburg imprimatur. (Published reports that the museum purchased a fruit vendor's charming advertisement, a watermelon rustically carved from a log and adorned with house paint, made wooden melons the rage in some circles.) Since 1939, more than two thousand objects have been added to the collection, and special exhibitions are mounted each year. In the last analysis, Colonial Williamsburg owns a folk art collection of the first magnitude and has made substantial contributions to the serious appreciation of a great native tradition—even though it doesn't suit Colonial Williamsburg's chosen period. The institution and the town proved big enough to accommodate nineteenth-century art as well.

A Manifold Museum (II): Collections and Collectors

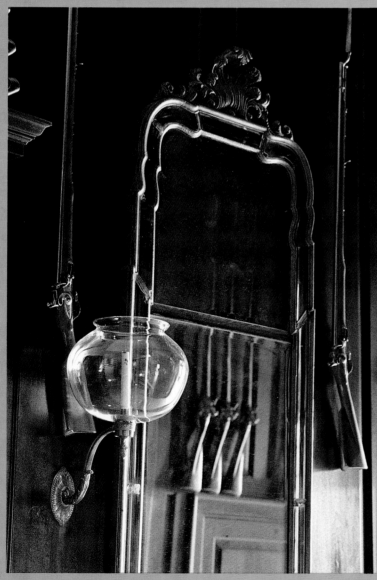

Formal galleries aside, this
dynamic museum displays
antique objects in period rooms,
both in restored buildings and
reconstructed ones. Furnished
as closely to original styles as
scholarship allows, these rooms
are occasionally refurnished to
reflect newly gained knowledge.
Thus, the Governor's Palace,
reconstructed and furnished in
the 1930s, was "reinterpreted"
a half century later in light of
newer information. Boasting
elegant glass and a veritable
arsenal—governors stored some
actual arms here—the
"new" entrance hall (opposite
and left) has a look that
impressed visitors with the
power and influence of the
king's representative.

Lord Botetourt ordered three stoves from London ironmonger Abraham Buzaglio: two for the Palace and one for the Capitol. This reproduction "warming machine" heats the Palace supper room. It represents one of the first examples of the coming neoclassical style to reach Williamsburg. "Antick" design then began to replace the earlier rococo style.

The heart of any museum lies in its collections, the objects which it has come to possess. In Williamsburg that means roughly six thousand pieces of furniture, ten thousand ceramic and glass objects, fifteen hundred firearms, five thousand machines and tools, three hundred paintings, five thousand prints and maps, fifty-five hundred examples of textiles, seven thousand rare books, fifty-five musical instruments, four thousand pieces of metalware, three thousand costumes, a dozen period vehicles from handcarts to a blue landau and much more. In short Williamsburg's collections represent the entirety—the chaos or the microcosm if you will—of an eighteenth-century town and then some.

During the early years the Restoration acquired art and furnishings in a manner that was prodigal. Mr. Rockefeller himself was a masterly acquisitor, corralling such masterworks as Gilbert Stuart's portraits of Washington, Jefferson and Madison with typical dispatch. He bought the first, then saw the second over a friend's mantel and asked her to bequeath it to his patriotic cause where it would be cared for and appreciated in perpetuity. The third was in the Metropolitan Museum, one of his family's annual beneficiaries. In a letter to the director, he wrote that the portrait could be displayed in the Capitol, adding simply that Mrs. Rockefeller joined him in hoping they could support the Metropolitan as generously in the future as they had in the past. The hint was effective.

Along with Dr. Goodwin two people, more than any others, were responsible for laying the foundation of today's collection: William Perry, who acquired the first furnishings, and Susan Nash, who supervised their use in the exhibition buildings. Together they traveled to England where they scouted out great antiques. Rockefeller and his wife then joined them to assay the best pieces of art, furniture and furnishings that could be had in London. Collecting according to criteria that would have made a pack rat proud, they came back with enough to furnish a Governor's Palace and more (albeit not in a fashion that would stand the test of time, as we shall see).

When James L. Cogar came aboard as the first curator in 1931, the motive for collecting was simple enough. Once the first phase of restoration and reconstruction had begun, Colonial Williamsburg was compelled to furnish the buildings or settle for a village of empty shells. The early method was understandable too: They bought eighteenth-century objects of English, French and American origins, delighting in acquiring especially fine pieces regardless of whether these might ever have found their way to colonial Virginia. The result was a fabulous, if somewhat diffuse, selection, according to later generations of collectors and curators who refined the Restoration's purposes. Advances in scholarship and a clearer sense of what Williamsburg should be eventually led Colonial Williamsburg to cull both out-of-place and out-of-time furnishings from the exhibition buildings. Only those objects that could have been made in Williamsburg or brought there sometime during the eighteenth century would remain in period buildings by the last quarter of the twentieth.

Thus over the years much of what had formerly been in various period rooms became consigned to storage. The result was an embarrassment of warehoused riches and Williamsburg faced a choice: Either it could dispose of myriad objects or find a rationale for keeping them without violating the integrity of the Historic Area buildings. The dilemma was finally

Rare objects reflect the exotic tastes of an era when chinoiserie was in highest fashion. This intricately carved gilt mirror bears fabulous cranes and a pagoda of Chinese inspiration.

By intent the fire screen would shield a sitter from the fire's direct heat. Yet the mores of colonial gentry called for practical things to be beautiful as well. Thus, the device's elegant embroidery contrasts with the neat fluting of the fireplace's marble surround and the plainly molded woodwork in this room of the Peyton Randolph House.

In a time when constant labor was the norm, privilege meant affluence and ornament to enhance the luxury of leisure. The corner of the Wythe House dining room is graced with a built-in "Bowfat," or buffet (above left). Among other porcelain, it holds creamware decorated with early transfer prints. The mantel in the Palace front parlor (above right) holds Chelsea birds like the set of "11 Chelsea china Figures" mentioned in the 1770 inventory of Governor Botetourt's possessions. The Brush-Everard House parlor table (below) holds an earthenware tea set with a Whieldon-type salt glaze called "tortoise." The enameled kettle was made in England in the 1760s.

resolved with the decision to build an exhibition building that wasn't confined to one time or style, namely the DeWitt Wallace Decorative Arts Gallery.

But in the meantime, Williamsburg had amassed diverse and superb holdings and become celebrated for them, thanks in large part to John Graham II, curatorial mastermind for two decades starting in 1950. Working in broad strokes (and sometimes buying in large lots), he is remembered for building the collections to their present dimensions and excellence. Graham also enhanced this institution's standing by augmenting the staff and hiring the first of its curators to specialize in given areas—metalworks expert John Davis and John C. Austin, who found himself charged with the enviable task of refining the broad-ranging ceramics collection. For the most part this meant filling in the gaps, occasionally paying the freight by "deaccessioning" redundant material. To accomplish this required an encyclopedic knowledge of the field and a certain eminence in the eyes of private collectors, dealers and competitors. By the time Colonial Williamsburg published a catalogue of its Chelsea material, it had only one rival in this type of porcelain in the world, the British Museum. Further, Williamsburg could boast of possessing "one of the finest collections of English 17th and 18th century pottery and porcelain ever assembled."

What makes a collection great? Dollar values aside, the worth of a group of objects derives from its status as a collection per se. To be simpleminded about it, an art or history museum's collection can be said to resemble a mechanic's tool box: If it lacks sufficient breadth it will be as limited as a tool box that contains only wrenches of one size. But the collection that includes the full spectrum of a chosen medium can reveal the history of an entire form of human endeavor. In the context of a museum it becomes a resource for the serious student, for the historian investigating an ancillary question and for the layman curious enough to be moved by the variety of utilitarian and creative expressions found within that medium.

At Williamsburg, *all* the various collections contribute to an understanding of what this place was like in colonial times. Take, for example, the ceramics collection and the way in which it helps Williamsburg fulfill its evolved function as a comprehensive history museum. First it provides objects for the period buildings, thus supplying the specific means to furnish the Palace bedchambers and reception halls as they would have appeared during Lord Botetourt's years here. Similarly, the breadth of the collection allows for the display of seasonal settings at different times of year. It also permits the representative furnishing of lesser houses from gentleman and scholar George Wythe's to entrepreneur Benjamin Powell's and artisan James Geddy's. Decorated accessories and serving ware were part and parcel of eighteenth-century life among the gentry. The posset pot, china basket, three-tiered centerpiece, animal-shaped soup tureen and decorative figurine graced aristocratic houses while every middling family aspired to such amenities. Further, surviving examples of these fragile objects reflect their owners' taste and the period's aesthetic sense. These porcelain objects reveal aspects of their time.

(Conversely, other disciplines often clarify matters for curators working with collections and exhibits. When the homes of the slaves and freemen in the Carter's Grove "Quarter" are furnished, they'll contain little porcelain or pewter. This reflects one of the ironies revealed by the intellectual symbiosis that occurs in a community like Colonial Williamsburg. Physical anthropologists have learned that blacks often lived longer than whites by virtue of being poorer in material goods! Comparative biochemical studies of human re-

Artisans at the world-famous Chelsea Porcelain Manufactory made figures, representing innumerable subjects, in soft-paste porcelain. This piece is one of a series of masqueraders that grace the mantel in the Governor's Palace dining room.

mains elsewhere reveal that colonists who ate off pewter and many glazed ceramics were poisoned by lead absorbed from the vessels; people at the bottom of the economic ladder typically ate off wooden vessels and lived longer.)

"Material culturalists," scholars who study the past through objects, fondly speak of corroded tools, chipped pots and even shards as "documents" which may be "read" as precisely as handwritten drafts of the Constitution. For example, the varied plates and bowls known as "Chinese export" prove the stages of cross-fertilization that occurred between the Orient and Occident over the course of centuries. Wares first imported to Europe in any quantity were exotic and popular; English potters, predictably, copied them to provide the growing market with cheaper items in the same style. As trade continued and grew, Oriental potters then invented their own methods of serving a larger clientele. They adorned platters and dinnerware with images of European country scenes; their hunters riding to hounds had Oriental features since that's how the Chinese porcelain painters knew to make faces. Artisans in England's Chelsea and Holland's Delft districts in turn copied these stylized decorations, variously in porcelain and earthenware, sometimes with a counterfeiter's intent, sometimes just to offer a cheaper line of goods to less affluent buyers.

For the collector today the subtle difference between Oriental export porcelain and a contemporary English copy of this Chinese ware is difficult to learn unless the objects can be seen simultaneously, in other words, in a collection. Thus some people visit museums to increase their discrimination, understanding and appreciation. To the economic historian studying commerce in the 1750s, discovering where a given Chinese style was copied can indicate the direction and extent of trade routes. To test a thesis, the scholar examines a good collection and consults a curator like John Austin, a specialist with perhaps only a dozen peers in his field who can pinpoint the origin of specific objects by virtue of his experience and on the basis of objects in his museum.

This fiddler is another masquerader from Colonial Williamsburg's superb collection of Chelsea porcelain.

To the schoolchild or undergraduate, experiencing objects from far away in space or time is a fundamental part of education. To the visitor who is not a serious student of history or artifacts but who just likes beautiful things, examining an array of like objects is an aesthetic experience, a worthwhile expenditure of time and money. To understand the value of a collection to laymen, consider a parallel between the figurines made in the factories of eighteenth-century Chelsea and modern athletes across the Thames at Wimbledon. To watch the goings-on in center court is to see tennis perfected beyond the realm of simple exercise; it is to experience a *ne plus ultra*. So be it with these finest examples of soft-paste porcelain, perhaps the most advanced plastic medium of its time. Chelsea figures were molded, then painted with certain glazes and fired. They were then glazed and fired again and again with colors that cured at even lower temperatures so as not to disturb the previous ones. These objects possess special beauty and a kind of intrigue. To examine at leisure Colonial Williamsburg's array of masquerade figures is to see the acme of a whimsical and antique art form at its most expressive.

By a similar token, to use a vacuum pump that George Wythe might have owned lets the scholar of science replicate the old investigator's work. To view spittle under an eighteenth-century microscope is to see the "animacules" that electrified members of the Royal Society and marked the beginning of a whole new realm of investigation. Some collections exist to serve a specific intellectual, scientific or quasipractical purpose; others to delight the mind. Some collections have several *raisons d'être*.

This notion cuts several surprising ways, and could eventually be responsible for lopping off some possessions as celebrated as the Gilbert Stuart portraits that Rockefeller so adroitly acquired. Were Colonial Williamsburg solely a museum of early American art, these paintings of three early presidents might be sacrosanct. Were it simply a museum of the eighteenth century, it might proudly display them along with chamber pots from Maine, artifacts from recently salvaged Spanish treasure galleons and whatnot. But this is a very special museum. Its specialty came to be defined in two dimensions, space and time. It was interested first in Virginia's capital before 1780; then by extension in American art and history at large. For decades those of its possessions that did not suit the primary locus were consigned to storage and rarely seen by visitors. The recent opening of the DeWitt Wallace Decorative Arts Gallery allowed the display of these wider interests and foretold the broadening of Colonial Williamsburg's purview.

Nonetheless one day, hypothetically, Williamsburg might consider selling the Stuarts, which were painted long after the town's late eighteenth-century eclipse and thus relate to the post-Revolutionary period. Remaining very valuable, under foreseeable circumstances they could be sold to pay for some as yet undiscovered treasures that might suit this museum even more perfectly: a portrait of Jefferson the law student in George Wythe's study, say, or a group of burgesses that includes Henry and Washington.

What are the chances of such a discovery? Put it this way: Stranger things have happened, and the possibility that they will again is part of the lure of this business. Building collections is a byzantine affair requiring the eye of a connoisseur, the scent of a bloodhound and the sweatless glands of a horse trader. Graham Hood, who succeeded John Graham as chief curator and vice president in charge of the collections in 1971, approaches it all with a certain calm: "I'm not one of the Grand Acquistors." Nonetheless, he has made some grand acquisitions of singular importance to this specialized museum. He's found these prizes variously by strokes of luck, inspired sleuthing and plain old "coppering"—working the turf like a bobby his beat in Hood's native England. Some of these feats happened quickly and simply; others took ages. While some acquisitions have been outright purchases and others gifts, almost all the transactions have been made with an eye to the Internal Revenue Code.

Long before Colonial Williamsburg was founded virtually every substantial gift to nonprofit institutions in America has meant a tax break for the donor. The framers of the Internal Revenue Act intended this back in 1913. They encouraged people to support bona fide educational and charitable institutions by defining the value of their gifts (in cash or property) as deductible from gross income. Thus the donor reduces his taxable receipts, and perhaps finding himself in a lower bracket, may even be taxed at a lower percentage rate. Churches, colleges, charity groups and performing arts companies as well as museums have received many gifts in part because donors saved money overall through the deduction device. The many extraordinary art collections to which the public has access—not the least of them here—owe their existence in large part to what some tax reformers periodically (and shortsightedly) call a loophole. As of this writing, the Internal Revenue Act has achieved its legislative purpose in this regard; starting with Mr. Rockefeller himself, Williamsburg's benefactors have taken advantage of write-offs.

Some donors have had a one-of-a-kind antique appraised, then sold it to Colonial Williamsburg, for, say, half its appraised value. They were then entitled to deduct the balance as a charitable gift since in fact and effect they gave away that much of its value (or its

Gilbert Stuart, painter of several presidents, limned Thomas Jefferson's life portrait in 1805. He made several copies of the famous picture and this one, which was owned by President Madison before Colonial Williamsburg acquired it, may be the original. The Foundation also owns Stuart portraits of Washington and Madison.

likely sale price at auction). The mechanics of the deduction are understood by all: donors, institutional recipients, the IRS, even dealers. Witness Colonial Williamsburg's acquisition of a small treasure trove which a dealer felt ought to come here. This array of objects included one of two known copies of an antique map and an almost equally rare print. The center-piece was the curious portrait of Mary Sabina, a South American girl of mixed ancestry painted in Cartagena in 1740, the year Governor Gooch led a military expedition to that Spanish stronghold. The painting, by an unknown Englishman, is a lovely primitive with a crude cartouche framing a caption for the edification of Enlightenment men interested in human genetics, a science of rising interest in the expansionist eighteenth century.

Because of its style, date and socioscientific content, the dealer who had the picture believed it properly belonged in Williamsburg. When Hood saw it he agreed, although the museum could not afford the high, albeit legitimate, asking price. Tax considerations enabled Colonial Williamsburg to get the whole package. Hood met one of the dealer's clients, an industrialist who'd made a killing that year and faced an astonishingly high tax bill. By donating to Colonial Williamsburg the price of the independently appraised prints, maps and portrait, the businessman was entitled to reduce his obligation to the IRS. The same stroke enabled Colonial Williamsburg to buy the objects, while the dealer earned a tidy commission for his trouble. Everybody benefited.

A longer quest began some years ago when Hood received a letter from a Virginia gentleman who wished to sell a portrait of an English peer known to be a friend of William Byrd II. The painting had hung at Westover plantation whence it had come to another family's seat through one of those many marriages that made most members of Virginia's gentry cousins of some degree. The Westover connection piqued Hood's curiosity, but the painting didn't sound as though it was worth a special trip. He arranged to view the portrait the next time he happened to be in Richmond and indeed it turned out to be an "undistinguished portrait of an undistinguished knight." But hanging on the same wall was Charles Willson Peale's portrait of Benjamin Harrison which almost curled Hood's graying hair. Here was an American master's vision of an eminent Virginian, delegate to the First Continental Congress, Speaker of the General Assembly and more.

Visiting Williamsburg in 1774 and 1775 during his most productive decade, Peale is known to have painted a full-length oil of Peyton Randolph in full Masonic regalia. But, alas, that titanic likeness also is known to have been destroyed in a fire at the Library of Congress a century ago. This Harrison portrait had been "lost" to the art world; its whereabouts unknown—although one obscure catalogue had ironically and inaccurately listed it among the Restoration's holdings, where it certainly deserved to be. Nonetheless, no one here had laid eyes on the signed and dated canvas before Hood. Though its surface was dimmed by the dust of two centuries, he recognized it as "a masterpiece of colonial portraiture" that "summarizes perfectly the characteristics of the Virginia gentry."

Covering his excitement—and perhaps stalling for time to collect his wits—Hood learned that his host was descended from the colonial Benjamin Harrison through his namesake, the twenty-third president, and through William Henry Harrison, the ninth. But that was neither here nor there since, after all, W. Gordon Harrison Jr. was offering for sale a picture of an unrelated Englishman. For that he wanted $20,000, or substantially more than Hood thought it would be worth to Colonial Williamsburg. Because he knew the Peale might fetch ten times as much at auction, he felt an obligation to learn more about both

Charles Willson Peale personified the aristocracy of eighteenth-century Virginia in this portrait of Benjamin Harrison of Brandon, a member of the House of Delegates, which replaced the House of Burgesses after Independence, and of the first Council of the Commonwealth of Virginia. (This Benjamin Harrison was a cousin of Benjamin Harrison of Berkeley, a signer of the Declaration of Independence and father of the U. S. president of the same name.) Called a "great" Virginia portrait by cognoscenti, it combines a sense of the inner man with his clear likeness and graceful accoutrements in a picture of undisturbed elegance.

pictures for the following reasons:

All kinds of people come to own precious antiques, and Hood believes the moral museum deals with different sorts in different ways. There are idle inheritors who sell off family treasures to support lavish life-styles; and there are those whose only passion in life is buying and selling *objets d'art*. Still others assume whatever they inherited is common stuff, while there are dealers who work the tea-party circuit like sharks. Spotting a great antique in a spinster's parlor, such a buyer befriends the lady by offering an inflated price for a scrapbook of Currier & Ives magazine prints. The grateful and naive owner later parts with a masterpiece for a song when the new "friend" offers to "take it off her hands." Still stunned at seeing Benjamin Harrison's lost portrait, Hood wondered whether the descendant had been set up by an unscrupulous buyer who offered a high price for the lesser picture as bait. He needn't have worried.

While Mr. Harrison had not made a profession of trading in heirlooms, neither was he a babe in the woods. He knew the Peale to be a masterpiece, and he hadn't planned to sell it. But he'd been offered the handsome price for Byrd's friend by an august institution with very special interests; the painting suited their collection in the same way that the portrait of Mary Sabina suited Colonial Williamsburg's. It was plainly worth more to that institution than to Williamsburg. (This raises the matter of vagaries in art pricing. The "fair market value" of any precious object depends on such variables as economic conditions and even the circumstances of its sale or purchase. For example, furniture prices can rise or fall with the value of the dollar. A library of rare books to be liquidated by a debt-ridden estate brings a fraction of the price the same books would cost someone creating the collection from scratch.) Satisfied that the Peale wasn't going to vanish overnight, Hood asked Mr. Harrison to let him know if he ever wanted to find a permanent home for it.

In due time, the inheritor and his far-flung family decided to sell the portrait and a series of negotiations began. It proved relatively easy to agree on a price and terms, but the talks ripened just as Colonial Williamsburg entered "one of its poor periods" and the matter was tabled. Reopening the discussion a couple of years later, the principals agreed on a schedule of several annual payments in deference to the tax code—only to have the timetable scotched by their lawyers. Finally when the acquisitions budget was flush again, Hood reopened the negotiations yet again—casually as an apparent afterthought in a letter about another matter. New terms were proposed and Hood finally got the prize Peale for upwards of a quarter-million dollars nine years after first laying eyes on it.

Other of Hood's acquisitions resulted from the wandering hunt, often with Wallace Gusler, an antiquarian polymath who has served Williamsburg as gunsmith, furniture curator and conservator. (They sound like an unlikely team: Gusler a Virginia mountainman and native genius who with barely a high-school diploma practically wrote the book on antique gunsmiths and literally wrote the one on eastern Virginia's colonial furniture; Hood, an elegant Briton who attended Shakespeare's grammar school, then Oxford and the Courtauld Institute as a protégé of Sir Anthony Blunt, the royal art advisor who was later unmasked as a master spy.)

On one of their expeditions the two found themselves following a lead on an "Irish" table of special interest. The hunt was in rural Virginia where xenophobic folk were wont to give the accented Englishman bum steers when he asked directions to the farmsteads of wid-

This anonymous portrait of Mary Sabina was painted in Cartagena in 1740, the same year that Governor Gooch led an ill-starred expedition to the South American port. It is notable for its coincidental link to Virginia history, for its charming naivete of style, and for the information in its cartouche, which reflects intellectual concerns of the time.

owed neighbors. But Gusler spoke their language and, on this trip, convinced a postmaster of his bona fides and of the fact that a local lady was expecting them.

The museum men followed a winding road through the woods as it went from macadam to dirt, then narrowed to nothing but a track across a cornfield. Following it farther, they came to a Federal-era farmhouse that "looked as if it had been cleaved with a cake knife" then half of it moved elsewhere. A flock of chickens scratched in the yard and roosted in the carcasses of cars. Many windows in the house were boarded up and Hood suspected the place was uninhabited save for a tribe of cats coming and going through cellar holes. Then a woman clad in khaki overalls accosted them from the ruin and ushered them down a hallway blocked by a wheelbarrow and broken stove.

The collectors knew at a glance that the table wasn't Irish. It was a genuine Virginia antique, the work of one of the cabinetmakers whose oeuvre Gusler had painstakingly studied for his treatise, *Furniture of Williamsburg and Eastern Virginia, 1710–1790,* which helped revolutionize appreciation of southern furniture. He went to examine it closely while Hood made conversation with their hostess who proved as kindly as her wardrobe and domicile were rustic. He stepped over to look at a picture on the mantel when she cried out "Stop, Mr. Hood" and the Englishman jumped back wondering "what code of Virginia honor I'd transgressed." She apologized profusely: "That hearth is unsound. Two cats fell through last week."

Saved from bodily harm, Hood was then surprised that Gusler embarked on a conversational tangent about guns and the woman said, yes she had an old long rifle which she retrieved from its hiding place along with an engraved powder horn. Both were treasures in the collectors' eyes, artfully made utilitarian antiques from Virginia. After conferring in the yard among the chickens, the collectors offered the impoverished inheritor generous prices for the table and powder horn. The gentlewoman accepted but wouldn't even discuss a price for the prized rifle. "That's not for sale," she said, shooing a goat off the rickety porch, "That was my Daddy's. Things are going to have to get pretty bad before I part with that."

It is telling that the rumor the collectors chased down involved an "Irish" table which turned out to be as "Virginia" as salty ham. Time was when no quality eighteenth-century furniture was attributed to the South; the experts, most of them Northerners, insisted all the best work came from Europe, typically England, or anywhere north and east of Delaware. Studying ledgers, newspapers and other written records, Gusler realized that Williamsburg had a community of craftsmen in residence; further that people of taste like the Byrds and Jefferson bought entire room suites from them. Studying every stick in the Williamsburg collections, and tracking down Virginia pieces of ironclad provenance elsewhere, the self-taught antiquarian came to recognize the styles of individual shops, such as Anthony Hay's and Benjamin Bucktrout's. In some respects his analysis involved the more abstruse subtleties of traditional connoisseurship like line and style. Beyond that, Gusler learned to read regional and then local accents in types of woods and construction techniques. Recalling how he'd learned to recognize the work of different gunshops and then individual smiths in details like patch-box hinges, he looked for similar telltale signs in pieces of furniture. In time he found different makers' "signatures" in how they blocked a leg on a chest of drawers, morticed a secretary lid or carved a scallop shell on a chair. Thus when Hood unearthed some photographs of some "Scottish chairs," Gusler hurried out to Stewart

This unique mahogany chair, built for a Masonic lodge, rests once again in the city of its creation after a two-century absence. It was removed to a lodge in Edenton, North Carolina, in 1778 for safekeeping during the Revolution and remained there until 1983. One of the few pieces signed by a Williamsburg master, it was made by Benjamin Bucktrout, who worked with Anthony Hay. Monumental in the extreme, the chair was designed exclusively for ceremonial use. It features a bust of poet and diplomat Matthew Prior, a hero among Masons, and a veritable tool kit of fraternal heraldry.

Four Palace rooms, seen before and after their "reinterpretation" in 1981, are now decorated in keeping with Governor Botetourt's 1770 inventory. A bedchamber (below and right) gains a "bed round" carpet—a U-shaped rug surrounding the bed—and new, more vivid colors.

A "family dining room" (above) becomes the butler's pantry (right), domain of William Marshman, whose informative account books were discovered at Badminton, ancestral home of the bachelor governor's nephew and heir.

The formal dining room (left and below), *now set for dessert with sweetmeats in the pyramid centerpiece, also occasionally served as Botetourt's office. Thus, the 1770 map made by John Henry, Patrick's father, replaced the portrait of King James I that formerly graced the room.*

The ballroom (left and above) *gains blue wallpaper, the substantial reproduction Buzaglio stove, a harpsichord, massive state portraits of King George III and his queen as well as a settee and suite of chairs owned by Lord Dunmore, Virginia's last royal governor.*

Manor, an eighteenth-century house in Greenbriar County, West Virginia (once part of the Old Dominion), to take a look at them. The owner showed him to the attic where the chairs were stored, some of them broken, all of them uncomfortable, she said. He knew immediately that the suite, which included a settee, had been made in the Tidewater. Well, that confirmed the story she'd always heard: They came from the Palace in Williamsburg, according to family lore, given to one of her ancestors as a wedding present.

This all made sense to Gusler, but there was scant proof. Having steeped himself in Virginia's history, he knew that in about 1770 a trader named John Stewart had been one of the first to settle on the western frontier near Point Pleasant, scene of the 1774 battle that won Lord Dunmore's war against the Indians. In 1776 Stewart married Agatha Lewis Frogg for whom he built Stewart Manor. His bride, widow of a man killed at Point Pleasant, was the daughter of Thomas Lewis and kin to Col. Andrew Lewis, one of Dunmore's militia commanders. Gusler had an inspired hunch: that Andrew Lewis had served in Williamsburg after Dunmore fled and bought some of the governor's household goods that were auctioned off to help support the Revolution.

Hoping to add pieces to the puzzle, Gusler tracked down other members of the family in West Virginia who provided more than he could have asked for: two antique books with Lord Dunmore's bookplates *and* the signatures of Thomas Lewis and John Stewart. These proved that expensive articles once owned by Dunmore had passed from Lewis hands to Stewart in the distant mountains. Further, the family lore that the settee and chairs had come from the Palace supported Gusler's belief that the stately furniture was made in the Tidewater.

Needless to say, this furniture deserved to be in Williamsburg's museum, indeed restored to the reconstructed building whence family lore said it had come and where the physical evidence pointed. Colonial Williamsburg bought the furniture with the idea of placing it all in the Palace. But it was too rough and not nearly grand enough; it clashed with the gracious pieces that suited everyone's ideas of what should be there—notions in large part supported by what everyone was accustomed to. Yet that is where it was ultimately placed, much to the chagrin of some older Williamsburg hands and fans. The chairs and settee found their place in the ballroom after the reinterpretation of the Palace in 1981. That act, viewed as bordering on treason in some circles, demonstrates a substantial change in Williamsburg's course and priorities over the years, perhaps even a maturing in terms of the Historic Area and its contents.

When the Palace was first furnished, it contained grand pieces and won instant acclaim. The Restoration people who worked on it were justifiably proud of their accomplishment. They'd read the room-by-room inventory of furnishings compiled by the executors of bachelor Governor Botetourt's estate. They'd studied other source material as well and, as one participant remembers, decided to equip the edifice as it *might* have appeared when it was occupied by a "typical" governor and family man of the Georgian period. This scheme, though hypothetical, was undeniably pleasing. And because of Williamsburg's immense popularity and influence, the Palace came to serve as a model of Georgian grace and elegance. Hood and his curatorial generation, however, decided that it was inaccurate. Further, they took to heart the old ambition that Williamsburg should be restored as it actually had been—so far as research could discover—not as some would like to see it.

"Museum pieces" come to light in the dimmest places. In the attic of a manor built on Virginia's old frontier, curator Wallace Gusler examines chair fragments. He suspected they once belonged to Lord Dunmore— the owner's family lore said as much—and were then bought at auction after the royal governor fled on the eve of the Revolution.

Considerable knowledge had been compiled since the Palace opened in 1934, even since its decor had evolved under John Graham's stewardship. Hood took it upon himself to perform additional research. He located the ledgers and account books of Botetourt's butler in England, and concluded that the room opening off the front passage had been the butler's office, not the dining room. In an English country house he found an array of arms cunningly hung in a manner that sounded like the display an eighteenth-century Palace visitor had described, and concluded that Botetourt intended the entrance hall to reflect his presumed power rather than to make callers comfortable. (In fact, a governor's most potent weapon was political skill in balancing the interests of crown, councillors and burgesses. Things fell apart when an administrator like Lord Dunmore tried to rule by executive whim and threats of force.) Studying palettes of eighteenth-century prints, fabrics and ceramics, Hood concluded that the colonists favored far brighter colors than previously assumed.

His "reinterpretation" brought a whole new look to the once familiar mansion. A bedchamber sported purple hangings and trim with lime green bamboo chairs in the Chinese style. The entrance hall fairly bowled over the visitor with its arsenal of muskets, pistols and sabers suggesting that the royal governor was not a man to be trifled with. And the old dining room became a steward's drab lair. This may have been the crowning blow; even one Williamsburg executive who admits "I know better" misses the chamber that "*seemed* the perfect Georgian room." A hue and cry went up; old friends of the "old Palace" launched letter campaigns against this "desecration." Anti-revisionists even complained that the old decor had, after half a century, become a historical "document" in and of itself. Some aesthetes seriously offered this perplexing and unanswerable argument: Fifty years of scholarship may have advanced knowledge of the eighteenth century, yet the inaccurately furnished old Palace deserved to remain untouched because of its importance to the twentieth-century history of preservation! Saddest, perhaps, a colleague recalls that John Graham "went to his grave a bitter man" because his work—brilliant for its time and of lasting importance in many respects—had been superceded in this particular instance. The tragedy there was in the thought that Williamsburg could ever be perfectly finished and immutable.

Graham Hood's view prevailed, because Colonial Williamsburg had come to take itself and its purpose more and more seriously over the decades. It would profit from new knowledge and new talents (while never failing to credit contributions that were state-of-the-art in their day). Its curators would come to believe as an article of faith that they would do the best they could, but that almost inevitably their work would be amended by successors building on new information. They would try to present buildings as they actually were in the chosen period—so far as this could be determined and, always aware of the aim of breathing new life into these historic surroundings, they would increasingly show rooms in a way suggesting that they are inhabited. (The dining room at the Palace, for example, is shown at a chosen moment between courses as if the governor and his guests had just stepped outside for a second.) While Colonial Williamsburg might display the spectacular fruits of the old Grand Acquisitors splendidly in the Wallace Gallery or the Folk Art Center, it would increasingly make the Historic Area more faithful to its actual past. The collections would exist to serve history and historical study—thus to reveal the past to living people and to posterity just as Colonial Williamsburg's founders had so fervently hoped they would.

Gusler proved his theory when he found other descendants of the man who'd carried the furniture west. They owned books with the ancestor's signature and Dunmore's personal bookplate. This chain of evidence contributed to the Palace's new look, for the chairs and matching settee were returned to the ballroom.

Living
Williamsburg

Behind a fen of threads, the
weaver bends to her loom
(opposite) in a Wythe House
dependency. At the Anthony
Hay Shop four unfinished chair-
backs (left) await a cabinetmaker who, like artisans of
yore, borrows patterns from an
eighteenth-century catalogue.
Throughout this reborn town,
antique trades and occupations
thrive again.

Used to make boards from whole logs, the pit saw is once again powered by muscle and main. The sawyer standing above the sawpit shares the work with a pitman who labors below. Housewrights in the old Carpenter's Yard sawed all the lumber needed for the new Anderson forges, which were recently rebuilt on their original sites.

As Dr. Goodwin unabashedly explained, he knew Williamsburg to be inhabited by benevolent spirits of the past. (On an autumn evening when the moon brightens Scotland Path and crickets sing along the Palace wall, one finds oneself gladly listening for the voices he heard.) Yet this place has come to be animated with living spirits day by day: craftspeople plying myriad trades, street actors playing people known to have walked these colonial streets, interpreters in period dress explaining erstwhile ways. Not only a collection of buildings and objects, this is a community of people whose skills constitute a vital resource in another sort of collection if you will, one of constant activity.

They break flax here and dip candles, raise barns and pour pewter. They fill the kitchens at Benjamin Powell House and the Palace with the scents of stews and soups and meat pies baking in a Dutch oven set on beds of live coals with more embers blanketing their tight lids. (This works as well as any gas oven or microwave, if at a different pace; as one cook says, "heat is heat" whatever the source.) They tend day-long hardwood fires by the Magazine, turning sides of pigs fit to feed an army. One day soon the cookery mistress means to test how much heat it takes to penetrate a lark within a pigeon within a pullet within a duck within a pheasant within a goose within a turkey within a crust made from a bushel of flour in the shape of the fabled roc, perhaps, a receipt she found in Hannah Glasses's 1747 *Art of Cookery*. Using a basket spit indoors before the hobgrate of the Palace kitchen she also plans to test another of Glasses's recipes—this one for cooking tender pork. *Art of Cookery* neglects to say how long it will take; only that a suckling pig is done "when the eyes pop out."

Skilled drivers rein matched teams of horses and a brace of gray mules hitched to coaches, carriages and wagons as they ply the streets carrying visitors or goods. One teamster steers his oxen by voice alone, as they slowly haul the pale blue cart filled with hay and children around Market Square. In summer the days begin with the sound of martial tunes as the Fife and Drum Corps appears on Botetourt Street, then wheels around the corner onto Duke of Gloucester toward the Magazine, where militiamen raise the colors to the boom of cannon and chatter of musketfire. In the Mary Stith Shop a viola da gamba brightens the air by day; in the Palace ballroom, Handel and Vivaldi rule the night in concert again, while the Apollo Room trembles to the beat of a dozen couples dancing reels and cotillions. The sounds, sights and smells of old abide here because people of our time practice antique occupations. The benefits and fascination of these human activities are legion.

Artisans span the centuries as they produce an array of goods from shoes to silver sauceboats, from forged andirons to melon-backed lutes made of a dozen matched spruce slivers. All year long the shepherdess tends her sheep, then shears them in the spring. The weaving mistress and her bevy wash homegrown wool, then sort and card it, spin and weave it into shawls and such. Raw iron becomes rifles with eighteenth-century bores. Modern Williamsburgers make cornmeal and the linen sacks to hold it. They make wagons and harness for the horses, furniture for the guesthouses, candlesticks of brass or pewter, marrow spoons of bronze, mote spoons of pierced sterling, powdered periwigs of human hair, and enough other wares—the necessities of old or curiosities of now—to fill a brig bound for Bristol. Many of these things are made for sale, others for use around the colonial town. The black-

Cooking fires smudge the morning light (above) and Market Square becomes a brief encampment when historical regiments come to muster, bringing canvas tents, featherbeds, camp cots and other antique gear (right).

All at the Colonial Fair: A tri-corned sheriff auctions goods near the Magazine (above) and interpreters (below) beat out Afro-American rhythms like their ancestors. In late colonial times more than half of Williamsburg's residents were black.

275

smith wrought all the nails, hinges, door latches, leg irons and window bars for the reconstructed Public Hospital. The silversmith has copied the sterling escutcheon from Lord Botetourt's casket to someday grace the coffin of a visitor who paid for it with the "ready money" of our time, a plastic card.

The purpose of the so-called crafts here is neither modern utility nor artsy creativity. Rather the goal in each of the twenty exhibition shops is to replicate a profession practiced in the eighteenth-century town, to produce a line of goods using eighteenth-century materials, tools and techniques—even conventions of training and employment. If there's a major difference between then and now, it lies in output. Colonial artisans worked as fast and efficiently as possible. Their successors today are required to explain their work as they perform it; in some shops as much energy goes into discussion as production.

Blacksmith Peter Ross insists "We don't practice crafts" as in a summer camper's usage. "We work a trade." The day-in-day-out challenge for him is not to make the most exquisite spitjack, a clockwork device used to turn the governor's goose before his reconstructed kitchen's open fire. The task is to make a spitjack as close as possible to the one that graced the original kitchen. This requires a range of resources: coal, coke and bar iron, of course, and the blacksmith's considerable skills at handling hammer, tongs, texts and surmise. The work also calls for books, drawings and engravings along with intimate knowledge of the old manuals that guided the original Williamsburg smiths. Finally it takes antique examples, artifacts that serve as more than just visible models. An antique example not only tells the latter-day craftsman what shape to seek; its scars and scratches inform the experienced modern artisan how some long-dead predecessor used his tools and did the work turn by turn, blow by blow, stroke by stroke. Since no one can show him how to make a spitjack, the new smith must puzzle it out, tempering his own experience with clues found in the antique piece.

Here and now, as long ago, the man who runs the shop is called its "master," though the term has a slightly new meaning. Colonial Williamsburg's master craftsmen are indeed masters of their trade, as well as administrators of small operations within the organization. But in the colony, the title was not conferred by a guild to designate a special level of skill; young America was too short of skilled hands to observe all the Old World's pernickety rules of guilds and such. While he might be as accomplished as silversmith James Craig or cabinetmaker Anthony Hay, the "master" in Virginia was simply the person who owned the place—the widow who inherited a business after fever took her spouse, or a journeyman fresh off the boat who had the cash, skill and freedom to hang out a shingle. (Most newcomers lacked the money or the liberty.) In any case, if he'd fulfilled an apprenticeship in England, or here for that matter, he was called a journeyman from the French word *jour* for "day" since he was paid by his day's work. To reach skilled status—then as now—man or boy entered a lengthy apprenticeship, which today may last as long as ten years and in colonial times usually took seven. Thus the process of training, like the artisans' method, mirrors the colonial model.

The very length of an apprenticeship and the repetition it involves teaches lessons about the binding connections between tools and techniques, materials, methods, purposes and traditions. There are lessons in physics to be learned, lessons in the complexities of seemingly simple things, lessons in the purposes of patience. A most striking lesson trans-

In the gunsmith's shop, an apprentice patiently draws the huge corkscrew "rifling machine" (above left) several hundred times to cut the grooves that make a bullet spin in a handwrought barrel. Deft hands carve the stock from curly maple (above right) and fit the flintlock in place (below). Working slowly—and explaining colonial techniques to visitors while they work (as do all craftsmen here)—Colonial Williamsburg's gunsmiths turn out only a few weapons each year for patient collectors who buy them at premium prices.

lates into the rule that just as lost skills can be rediscovered, so too the modern master may reinvent lost tools. Witness an example from the gunshop:

The metal parts of old guns are fastened with screws. To fit one flush into a breech plate requires cutting some metal away from the plate itself to form a chamfer, a hole with slanting sides to seat the screw head, which has to fit snugly—and thus have a matching slope. It is certain that colonial gunsmiths had drills to bore holes, but some years ago Colonial Williamsburg's gunsmiths chamfered the screw heads any way they could because there didn't seem to be an old tool for the job. Yet old guns had chamfered screws. Thus an apprentice gunsmith, Gary Brumfield, thought about the problem, and experimented until he contrived a widget that worked. Months later a curator brought over a print of a tool he'd never seen before and asked what it might be. Brumfield recognized the mysterious device that had stumped the experts; he'd just made one remarkably like it after all. It proved to be an antique chamfer-cutter that confirmed the modern gunsmith's new invention. The lesson here: If a task must be newly done today at Williamsburg and the craftsman knows his stuff vis-à-vis old techniques, technology and materials, he might just reinvent a lost tool.

The reader might now ask: If chamfer-cutters were so useful, and therefore common, why haven't they turned up by the bushel? The answer: because they wore out and were thrown away or more likely were recycled into something else. As it happens, the least useful tools of any trade often last the longest to reach us in rummage sales and antiques bazaars. The more common tool, or a craftsman's favorite, got used up or worn down. The face of a plane that fit the carpenter's hand just-so shaved endless boards, lost its true shape, was planed itself each passing year until too little of the good rock maple remained. When the farrier's file broke off too short to dress horses' hooves, the man ground it down to serve as a knife. The bronze matchlock bent beyond repair was tossed into a crucible and melted down to become part of several doorknobs. It didn't survive intact. Neither does a backbreaking technique that's overtaken by technology.

The most stunning example of recovering a lost antique at Williamsburg involves not a single object but an entire method. Again it happened in the gunshop under the first master, Wallace Gusler. One of the first goals he set for himself and his crew was to build an eighteenth-century Virginia rifle from scratch, including lock, stock and barrel. But nineteenth-century advances obviated the laborious business of making barrels by hand and the old methods had been forgotten. Combing the countryside, Gusler and Brumfield talked to every old-timer they could find. None had made barrels on a forge but some had seen it done and others remembered hearing how, or so they said. Many of the stories proved specious, but the young gunsmiths gleaned and culled enough "oral history" and documentary evidence to have a go at it.

After much trial and error they learned to start with a hammered skelp, a long flat piece of iron. Working after hours at the Deane Forge, they practiced hammering skelps into long troughs. Heating the iron in a soft coal fire, the trick was to curl the skelp lengthwise around a cold iron rod and weld the edges together into a rough tube. Heating the skelp again in orange coals each time it cooled, they hammered out the tube, withdrawing the rod as they progressed. Once they'd beaten a skelp into a four-foot tube, it was relatively easy to bore out the rough hole left by the rod to a chosen diameter. For this they used a long bit and the sort of gunsmith's bench that had survived. Another antique wooden tool resem-

In the foundry behind the James Geddy House, a founder pours molten metal into cast-iron molds. The foundry makes silver candlesticks, harness brasses, bronze gun mounts and other such truck.

bling a huge patent corkscrew then scored the rifling grooves inside the barrel. The outside was then smoothed into an octagonal cylinder by hours of filing.

Handwelding iron is no mean trick; making a weld four feet long is a master's feat in any age. It took several years, but Gusler and his staff made a barrel in a manner at least approximating the eighteenth-century way. Was that precisely how they did it then? No one can say for sure, but the experts believe it must be close because Gusler's new barrels show the same weld patterns as the originals and because other ways he tried didn't work. Thus a lost aspect of colonial technology was evidently reborn at Colonial Williamsburg.

Other colonial skills had not quite died elsewhere before rebirth in the renascent town. Read you now of roundlet, terce, puncheon and tun, of firkin, kilderkin and butt. Each is an almost perfect object: a made-in-heaven marriage of material and design, of white oak, utility and workmanship united daily in the Taliaferro-Cole Shop. Each is a barrel, a container of exacting complexity. Once common to the point of baseness—the cardboard boxes and plastic bags of their day—these containers were perforce handmade by many men. (A cooper was among the first group to land at Jamestown; his craft was as important to their economy as the smith's.) But when Colonial Williamsburg thought to revive coopering they had to look an ocean away to find a cooper.

Master cooper George Petten- gell, who served his apprentice- ship in London, shapes a stave for an oaken bucket, one of the dozen or so vessels made in this cooper age.

George Pettengell's training and experience mirror those of colonial apprentices in many ways. The son and grandson of coopers, he entered a five-year apprenticeship at Whit- bread's, the London brewery, in 1950. There had been no question of his occupation. He'd reached fifteen, the "leaving age" from school, and it was time to go to work, a word syn- onymous with coopering in the family lexicon. (Nor was there much question about him staying on in the late 1960s; Whitbread's was one of the last holdouts, but the time had come to abandon wooden barrels for metal ones.) He came over to show Colonial Williamsburg how to set up a shop, then with his wife and brother he stayed. Thus Williamsburg's crafts program was doubly blessed. It got a living man with a dying skill, and in him a master who'd experienced the long labor of apprenticing.

Pettengell's boyhood wage had been cheap, about enough to pay carfare, and was somewhat analogous to the "meat, drink, cloths, washing and lodging" that Georgian boys received as live-in learners on both sides of the Atlantic. The pittance was considered fair, given the laboring tradition that would raise eyebrows today. For starters, a boy wasn't deemed worth very much because he had no skills. For another, he was paid largely in the coin of knowledge, the specie of a marketable trade. From the master's viewpoint—even in London circa 1950—an apprentice program wasn't a source of cheap labor so much as a provider of future skilled help. What the employer saved in cash was offset in part by the cost of providing training, of pouring his experience into the vessel of the apprentice's potential.

Hardly a generation ago, the rights and responsibilities were spelled out in a binding contract similar to those signed in eighteenth-century Williamsburg. Pettengell's compact with Whitbread's reads: "The Apprentice of his own free will and with the consent of the Guardian, hereby binds himself to serve the Employer as his Apprentice in the trade of COOPERING." The employer agreed that he "will during the said term to the best of his power, skill and knowledge instruct the Apprentice…in everything related to said trade as practiced by him." In return, "The Apprentice shall truly and faithfully…serve the Employer as his Apprentice *and his secrets keep.*"

Wielding a broadax, a journeyman cooper tapers a stave while cutting its edge at a constant angle (left). Another journeyman's drawknife rounds a stave's "back" (right) so that hoops will fit it snugly. The most common containers in colonial times, barrels were so important that coopers came with the little fleet that founded Jamestown.

Placed on their square ends edge-to-edge, two dozen staves naturally form a circle since each edge has been cut at the same angle. Here the cooper hammers temporary hoops over the staves to force them together so tightly that they compress slightly. Because each nearly identical stave tapers at both ends, the emerging barrel will bulge in the middle.

Now girded with permanent metal hoops, the barrel gets wetted down by one cooper while another lights a fire of shavings. Next they'll place the unfinished barrel over the blaze to temper the still-flexible staves. When they cool the staves become rigid, permanently curved members of a single unit.

The work was hard and repetitive, too fast for reason as Pettengell consciously weighed a thousand decisions while he learned each step of barrel-making: how to wield the broadax; to shave each stave then round its front and back; to gauge by eye each stave's slightly different width and weight; to distribute intrinsically unequal members around the girth of a barrel to assure uniform strength; to make container after container virtually identical. When he tried to reason out a step or choice, his master told him shortly "Don't think about it, do as I tell you. It'll work out."

Therein lay a secret of apprenticing: Thou need not reinvent the wheel, or in this case the barrel, but instead depend on the experience of uncounted generations. The apprentice learned not only from his own master, but from the work of coopers since time immemorial. Their ways worked; the learner was encouraged—nay ordered—to simply copy them. If in the process he happened to sort out why and how they worked, so much the better.

Learning by rote was a lifesaver for Pettengell—as it is for artisans plying any of the crafts hereabouts—who found after a time that he could perform the endlessly repeated tasks without thinking about each one. "And when you stop trying to think about it, that's when you get out of prison." The trained hand and eye do the work; the brain is freed to think about other things, like "the book I read last night" or the cricket game after work on Market Square. To think only about barrels while producing an endless train of them would make the man a slave, in modern or eighteenth-century Williamsburg. "Of course part of the mind keeps ticking on about the barrel in question," Pettengell says. That's another process "that keeps the cooper sane." For the challenge remains to make a barrel that works, which means constantly being unconsciously alert to the variations in pieces of wood, differences in weight, thickness and density that must be evenly distributed around the circle of staves.

Still and all, a barrel remains a miracle of contained stress, a feat of deftly judged tolerances. Because a barrel is a container, its shape and strength must oppose internal forces that press *outward*: the weight of ale or pressure of tightly packed Virginia bright. Hoops, the circular bands of riveted iron or split saplings, do most of this work, of course. Then the staves themselves must keep the circumference from collapsing in upon itself. The base miracle here lies in the irrevocably geometric properties of the circle and its parts. The geometry turns out to be as simple as pie in that a pie's wedge-shaped pieces cannot be squeezed closer together without being broken. But bear in mind that the cooper uses no measuring tools, only the eye as he turns three dozen flat slabs into the tapered, rounded and bent staves that make a barrel.

One ambiguity of a barrel lies in the fact that it is often used as a wheel, witness the thousand-pound hogsheads which were rolled—often for miles—down rough roads to a wharf for shipment to England. Their shape made them far easier to handle than anything with corners. Roundness also makes a barrel stronger than a box—equally strong all the way around its girth—since the straight sides of a box are relatively weaker in the middle. Stronger and more maneuverable, a tun can be moved by one man who tips it on edge, nudges it into motion, then lets its momentum do the work. Because they're used this way, a barrel must resist *inward* forces. An empty cask also must keep itself from collapsing inward—no mean trick for a few dozen wood slats bound side by side without benefit of glue, nails or pegs.

In making a barrel the eye and hand must accommodate an extraordinary range of

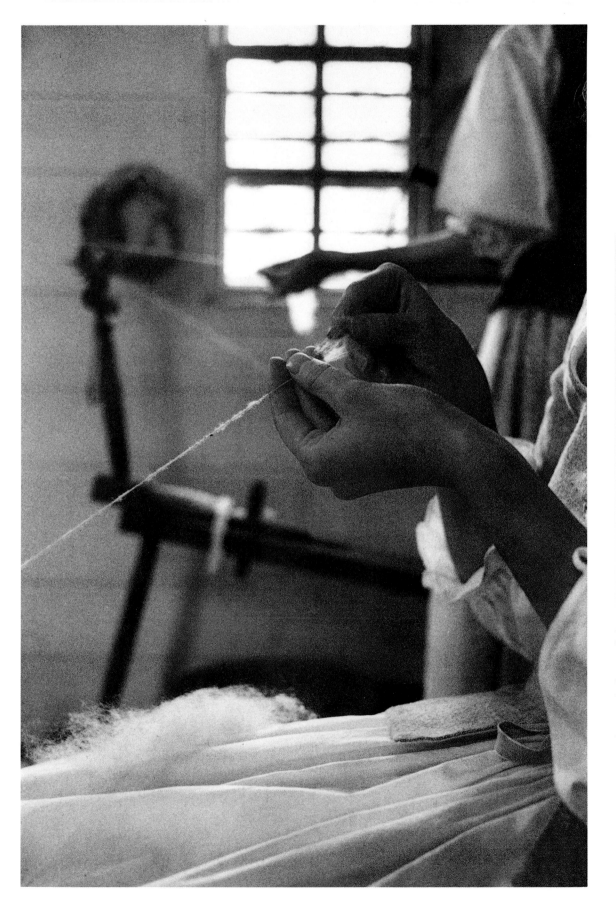

Like many colonial women, a modern Virginian spins yarn (above). Her foot drives a treadle, which turns the wheel, which spins a small vertical bobbin. All the while her fingers parcel out a few fibers from tufts of wool (left), adding to the twisting thread as it winds onto the horizontal reel.

Beating out a long tradition in the Golden Ball, master silversmith James Curtis (above right) puts the finishing touches on a sterling bowl. Using the polished end of an iron stake as an anvil, he gently taps twice around with a light planishing hammer. Nearly mirror bright, the minutely dented surface needs no abrasive buffing. Engraver's tools (above) hang beside a finished tankard and the sort of fish server that Curtis once made to gain his promotion to master's rank. The clock and some sterling objects in the wall cabinets (below right) are signed by this shop's first proprietor, James Craig, who arrived in 1765 and worked here for thirty years.

Woodworkers of diverse purposes share the tile-roofed Anthony Hay Shop on Nicholson Street. The cabinetmaking shop (above), boasting its man-powered "great wheel" lathe, produces furniture often modeled on colonial cabinetmaker Anthony Hay's celebrated examples, which men like Thomas Jefferson and George Wythe bought. Smaller work comes from the Hay shop's west end (below), where musical instrument makers specialize in the objects of Orpheus popular in the eighteenth century: violins, guitars, lutes, mandolins, viola da gambas, viola d'amores and the like.

An artisan dry-bends a violin's sides in sinuous yet exacting curves around a copper bending iron, a small stove that contains a spirit lamp.

variables: the wood's flexibility, its condition and propensity to expand or shrink, the necessity of compressing the staves yet not applying more force than they can bear. Cut a barrel's thirty-odd staves one-thirty-sixth of an inch too wide, and they'll never form the desired circle; cut them that fraction too narrow and the barrel will be too small.

Mind you, the capacity of these vessels could not vary with the cooper's whim or ineptitude; volumes and terminology were mandated by law. A "barrel" of beer contained 36 gallons, one of ale 32. A "barrel" of gunpowder came to hold 100 pounds; by Queen Anne's decree a "barrel" of soap weighed 256 pounds. As for firkin, kilderkin, roundlet, puncheon and terce, each had absolute specifications and uses. (Lest it seem there was absolutely no margin for error, the cooper had compensating tricks. If a vessel-in-the-making appeared too large, he could cut the groove for the head a little farther in. If he saw a barrel would hold too little, he could shave a little more from the inside of the staves. But again, day in and day out, the measurements were—and are—gauged by the cooper's eye.)

In sum, the lowly barrel and the cooper who made it exemplify the canny talent of preindustrial artisans and the superb utility of eighteenth-century craft. To visit the Taliaferro-Cole Shop today is to encounter a sort of rustic sophistication that rivals in sheer practicality our modern machines and methods.

This subtlety of senses is not unique to the cooperage. In the west end of the Anthony Hay Shop, for example, the musical instrument makers tune the wood of a violin by ear. First a curly maple board is split and its matched halves glued together edge to edge, the better to equally distribute strength through the instrument's back. Then the single piece is carved with tiny planes; the inner and outer curves are cut from the wood (not bent). Both curly maple back and spruce front are physically tuned—that is, carved with an ear to their natural resonances. This shop's master cuts a fiddle back so that a gentle thump produces the pitch of C#, the front so that it sounds a D. Were they tuned to the same note, the instrument would vibrate more when a string sounds that note (or any of its acoustical relatives). By tuning the wood, the maker builds a fiddle that resonates equally at every pitch.

At the heart of town silversmith James Curtis, master of the Golden Ball, can be found plying his trade. A full-fledged product of the apprentice tradition here, he is also something of a groundbreaker, being the first black to become a Williamsburg craftsman in an undomestic trade. Raised around the Tidewater, Curtis finished high school and took work where he could find it—in a pawnshop where he learned the value of silver with a sterling stamp. He married a Williamsburg girl and planned to strike out for California when his new mother-in-law asked them to stay around town a little longer. So Jimmy took a stopgap job in the Historic Area. One thing led to another; he had a way with people and was offered an apprenticeship in the Printing Office, though setting type soon paled for him. He switched to the old silversmith shop in the Geddy House.

Curtis enjoyed working silver: the near alchemy of raising a dull metal disk into a graceful bowl simply by beating upon it very carefully with different hammers that force the metal into different shapes. In those days it was accepted practice for craftsmen to work on private projects at night. One Christmas the apprentice started making a pair of porringers for his wife who'd just delivered their second daughter. Working on his own time, he was well pleased with the little vessels when the master happened to see them. Next thing he knew, the journeyman who supervised his work announced "We don't make porringers like this." With that, the apprentice had to put them under the "guillotine" which chopped them into bits of scrap. It was Christmas Eve and the normally amiable Curtis would remember years later that he almost hit the man who made him do it.

Returning to work after New Year's, he was assigned to make one porringer after another until they passed muster and he could raise them in his sleep. By then he knew his first efforts were not up to snuff. He also realized the extreme demands of the apprentice tradition, which he now believes made him the better craftsman.

In time he graduated to journeyman; the object he made to mark that giant step was a gravy boat which a visitor admired in the making and asked to buy. When he was promoted to master, he made a more difficult piece, and the same visitor bought that too. Another time, a steady and affluent customer, a doctor who would watch Curtis work for days at a stretch, bought out all the silver on display, at a cost of approximately two master craftsmen's wages for a year.

One reason Curtis excelled in the colonial town had little to do with his craftsmanship per se, but with his gift for gab. He could winningly explain his work and thus provide the interpretation that's a part of every visitor's experience. A moonlighter in the old days, he was waiting tables at a select Colonial Williamsburg dinner when one of the guests asked Carl Humelsine how the candelabra were made and the president introduced the off-duty craftsman. Jimmy delivered a brief ad hoc lecture, and when the applause died down, the guest declared he deserved a raise so he could stop waiting tables. In time he got the raise and more: promotion to master, and a certain special status. When dignitaries tour the town, their carriages typically stop at the Golden Ball to hear the old pawnbroker's especially illuminating talk about almost forgotten skills. The honored guests retire and he picks up his work again to raise a sterling cup upon a polished stake or planish a bowl, gently hammering its surface almost mirror bright with blows so light it seems they might not break a

A wagon wheel's integrity depends on physics and geometry. First the wheelwright gets an iron tire forged too small to fit the wooden felloes that make up the rim itself. Placed in a hot fire *(above), the tire expands so it can be slipped onto the spoked wheel. Then doused with water (below left), it quickly shrinks. A little hammering (below right) finishes the job of fitting the iron ring, which securely binds wooden parts into a single unit—much in the way hoops bind a barrel's staves.

In the Printing Office, a wooden case holds type (above) to be set by hand into new editions of colonial broadsides and such. After placing letters one by one in a composing stick and locking the lines within an iron frame, which then lies on a flat-bed press, the printer applies ink with wool-filled, covered balls (below). Then the printing can begin—one sheet at a time.

Colonial readers bought books in a basic state—in separate "signatures" of four to sixteen loose pages, which they then had bound and decorated to suit their taste. First the bookbinder stitches signatures together on a sewing frame using linen threads to bind the paper to cords of hemp. In the finished product these cords appear as distinctive raised ridges across the spine. After the "boards" have been glued on front and back, the book is covered with thin leather and dyed.

looking glass. Twice around he precisely works the entire surface of the piece in a spiral of overlapping taps leaving marks that likewise overlap so that there are hardly any marks at all. The tempo is *andante*, the tone no louder than a fairy's drum as he beats out the timpani of the Golden Ball.

Other notably antique musical sounds abound in several quarters here. Twice a week at least, Bruton's nave becomes a sacred concert hall with visiting choirs and solo performers. Playing an antique harpsichord or the modern organ rebuilt in memory of Vernon Geddy, musicians are encouraged to perform music of the eighteenth century. Bruton, a living church first and a visitors' attraction second, proudly is a hub of Williamsburg restored. Its dedicated choir presents period music during Sunday services and for special events, while four professionals in the group also perform as the Williamsburg Madrigal Singers, providing secular song around the town.

In the 1930s, Colonial Williamsburg launched a concert series that may now be the oldest of any American museum's. The Palace ballroom offered a unique opportunity that has been artfully fulfilled: to present what's now called chamber music in the kind of intimate surroundings for which it was written long before the symphony orchestra evolved. This was an art for aristocracy, a genre composed and performed by court musicians in salons for princely patrons. The instruments were typically smaller then; tuned lower than today, they thus possessed a softer sound. The violins and violas had shorter necks and were held differently than now. All these varied aspects of eighteenth-century music are respected here as modern musicians present an antique repertoire on instruments of the colonial era in the style that held sway then.

In addition to resident performers, there have been notable guests, recalls James S. Darling, Bruton's organist and choirmaster as well as Colonial Williamsburg's consultant in musical matters for decades. For one, there was the classical woodwind recital by as skilled an oboist as America then knew, a virtuoso by the name of Mitch Miller, who found broader fame virtually inventing the sing-along. Ralph Kirkpatrick, then the premier American harpsichordist, was another unforgettable performer. But when he sat down to practice, so the story goes, he startled the staff by requesting that someone go out and shoot a crow at once. His sensitive ear told him that some plectrums used to pluck the ancient instrument's strings were broken; he needed certain quills to replace them.

The quality of Williamsburg's music has a surprising apogee—the shrill sound of martial airs performed by a Fife and Drum Corps whose clarity and precision are rare indeed. Much of the credit must go to the boys themselves, many of whom start marching and piping at the age of eight. The inspiration and the starch, however, come from John Moon, as knowledgeable a drummer of eighteenth-century rolls as one is likely to find on this side of the water. A Canadian by birth, Moon was raised a Scot and joined the army as a drummer boy at the age of fourteen. When he finally mustered out, he was a member of the royal household and drum major of the Queen's band at Windsor Castle. In mufti he was a serious scholar of military airs and instruments, and a performing timpanist at Covent Garden as well. Thus when he finally left the Scots Guards, this child of martial music found in Colonial Williamsburg a place to purposefully carry on the tradition—one complex of skills among many others that, were it not for Williamsburg, might have vanished from these shores to our inestimable loss.

Decorating leather bindings requires sure hands, brass stamps and gold leaf applied with egg white. As it rolls, the heated stamp cooks the egg white, making the gold adhere only where the stamp has pressed.

Epilogue: Sojourn in an Antique Place

An ancient town reborn
has rhythms all its own: the
muted roll of martial drums
(opposite), the symphonies of
Christmas colors (left), the
remembered laughter of distant
friends. Williamsburg renewed
remains a capital place: a city
of the past, living in the present,
inspiring the future perhaps.

*Even winter brings
its own adornments to
the timeless scene.*

*A*lmost three hundred years after its founding—more than four lifetimes ago—Williamsburg blends yore with now:

On a winter night the town looks deserted. A pale moon rises behind the Capitol to shine down the frosted empty street. At our end of town almost every house is dark, and even the taverns are closed. Listen to the only sound: my footsteps. Anthony Hay's shop is empty, like the Printing Office, and Peyton Randolph's long white clapboard home. Then across the Green the mist grows bright and the Courthouse of 1770 rises like an ark, its fogged windows ablaze. Inside seven men sit on the dais before an audience of peers discussing the rights of men and law—a panel debate for public television.

By winter's day artisans ply their trades before blazing hearths and forges, though few visitors feel the welcome warmth in this slow season. The only person in modern dress may be a convention delegate skipping a session at the Conference Center, until the Antiques Forum brings a flurry of collectors. Then spring steals in with crocuses; the Garden Symposium brings another eager throng by lambing time. The redbud gives way to blizzards of dogwood blooms and the ghostly mantle of shadblow trees.

The days grow bright with birds and endlessly loud with song—cardinals, goldfinches, buntings bluer than any sky, and quick-tailed mockingbirds quite capable of singing all night long from treetop or chimney pot to claim a place and lure a mate. Pigeons roost in niches between offset chimneys and eighteenth-century walls. Flights of Canada geese follow the rivers north and mallards settle down in the Inn's ponds, finding spots to brood among the water plants. Two mute swans circle the tiny swamp near Carter's Grove, hissing to defend their young while herons and egrets dot the marshes white. Starlings nest in putlog holes and sparrows in bird bottles. Starlings and sparrows? They played no part in any ancient cycle here! However natural and familiar these speckled birds may seem, they were not in these trees when Nicholson paled the town or Colonel Washington took his first command. A century ago some New Yorker stocked Central Park with all the birds Shakespeare called by name; every species perished save two that adapted with a vengeance throughout America. As English immigrants displaced Powhatan's people, so these pests pushed native birds aside. Man was not the only European invader to seize a Tidewater domain.

Honeybees, another immigrant breed, haunt the gardens near the Raleigh by the Ides of April. Their sound dies down over the length of days, then they come again to make our basswood tree a symphony of humming. To stand beneath its little-blossomed limbs is to be surrounded by a gentle din. Quieter are the flights of native hummingbirds sipping the nectar of trumpet vines suspended in midair. Catesby painted them for his volume on natural history and saw them drink so deep they were caught within the crimson blooms.

As summer settles in, people too add myriad sounds. The town awakes soon after dawn as cleaning crews make their sweeps. Hear the slap-slap of runner's feet, the shopgirls in long dresses greeting each other, the shepherdess driving her flock from sheepfold to lea. Once schools let out the martial boys return of a sudden each morning with fifes and drums to pace off along what some irreverently call "D.O.G. Street" or "The Duke." They march to the rolling thunder of snares and the bright airs of "Roast Beef" and "The King of Denmark."

The city's nights gleam with many-splendored lights (clockwise from above left): "soldiers" and other visitors gather round a campfire; fireworks explode above a tent pitched for the Colonial Fair encampment; a cresset makes a beacon for a Fife and Drum Corps unit.

The lights bring music to the town as well. Each Capitol window shines (above left) for the Grand Illumination on the festive night that opens every modern Christmas season, and throngs of visitors go caroling. The interior of Bruton Church gleams for Evensong (above right). A chamber orchestra performs by candlelight in the Palace ballroom (below), their antique instruments playing works heard when royal governors hosted musicales.

Visitors gather along the way and minutes later the militia flies the colors to the cannon's clamor. When morning has officially begun some lads disperse to spend the day employed around the town in antique garb, just playing solo airs and brightening the scene with music.

The Golden Ball and milliner's shop next door open at nine o'clock to throngs of families, school groups, white-haired couples holding hands, women in shorts, men in mottoed caps. They chatter, of course, and the words drift in through windows that edge the street. The sounds must resemble Public Times (lacking pigs and geese perhaps) with only the diction changed, the din made livelier by a lad in knee breeches playing his piccolo on the steps of Brick House Tavern, and the clop-clop of horse-drawn carriages.

In June the cherries appear, both sweet and sour, brightening the trees behind the Unicorn's Horn like clusters of Christmas treats. They first emerge as little green knobs that harden and grow, then full-sized turn buff yellow in a day. The yellow seems to brighten, then tomorrow it's red—but only for another day or two. As quickly as it ripens the fruit begins to rot and squirrels make a feast. Beyond Wythe's garden the flax begins to bloom, its tiny blossoms opening wide at dawn, fringing this ethereal grass with palest blue that fades toward noon as the little flowers fold and close.

The cotton in the field near the old brick kilns raises broad dark green leaves, another crop for the weavers to think about once they've reaped the flax and shorn the sheep. In July the fireworks, of course, draw hordes to gaze at rockets glaring red and white and blue for one brief night. Crepe myrtles color the edge of Market Square and almost every yard with every hue of red. Robertson's Windmill's white canvas sails spin in the wind to grind new grain. Wetherburn's apricots come in rock-hard with velvet skins, and round plump yellow plums in the little orchard opposite the Church beg to be picked, and are. As evenings fall you must blink to make certain of the century; then a streetlight proves the date.

But the years blur again with the Colonial Fair, when Market Square becomes a festival and companies of militia from throughout the erstwhile colonies camp upon this green. A few hundred strong—plus complements of families—they muster, march, practice the ancient manual at arms, and display their shooting skills to cloud the autumn air with the rancid smoke of black powder like the stuff that Dunmore stole. Their women cook on open fires, their babies crawl happily about in linen shifts.

Inevitably, in a place as busy as this the old town's denizens encounter uninvited guests along with expected company. On one occasion, a group failed to observe the discreet sign "Private Residence" because they spoke no English. A local lad left the door unlatched and his mother looked up from housework only to find a score of Japanese tourists photographing her reconstructed hall and parlor. "This is my house!" she exclaimed. They lowered their cameras, made steeples with their fingers and bowed graciously. "This is my kitchen," she explained as the ladies from the East ran their fingers over the porcelain, wondering at the ancient ways of the mysterious West. After they toured the entire downstairs, murmuring musically, they all bowed again, expressed their great pleasure at having been so honored and went on their way to lunch.

At a much earlier hour, Carl Humelsine fetched the Sunday papers and hatched a myth bound to mushroom through the years. As the story's told, he fixed a breakfast tray, complete with a rose in a bud vase, and carried it up to his awakening wife. Relishing their sunny Sunday peace upstairs they suddenly noticed a family of four at the bedroom door.

Humelsine did not get here by being slow of foot or tongue. "May I show you this historic house?" he asked bounding out of bed again. "This is the master bedroom, as you can see. And this handsome staircase is original, dating from the eighteenth century." The foursome nodded and gawked as they followed him downstairs, the smallest son testing the balustrade with a drumstick to find it less resonant than a picket fence. "The passage would have seen many a minuet two centuries ago," the instant guide continued. "But as you know, Blackbeard's pirates went to the gallows from the Gaol just down the hill to your right...." He opened the door and the boy led his family out into the sunshine, quickened by the prospect of a hanging. The pajamaed president closed the door behind them without another word. This time he locked it.

(Years later Humelsine amends the myth a trifle. It didn't happen in Coke-Garrett House where the president now lives, but in Norton-Cole, which indeed has an original stair. There was no flowered breakfast tray, just the Sunday *Times*. And it wasn't a family of four, but a whole busload of folks who lost their way. And, in truth, he showed them all around the house, for his motto was "Always make a visitor feel welcome.")

Perennial residents have fonder tales of Christmastimes when every Historic Area tenant decorates their doorways on Grand Illumination morning. Some visitors come every year to see the garlands before the colors fade or before the birds peck the wreathes (and, if the weather's warm, get falling-down drunk on fermented fruit). For thirteen years the mistress of one house was attended in her decorating tasks by a Scottish terrier who predictably got older and older. Hanging an apple wreath before the passersby one year, she was addressed by a middle-aged lady whom she thought a stranger. The visitor asked "Where's Flora?" and offered condolences upon hearing the dog had died. The news saddened her, a member of Williamsburg's family one day each year.

The doorway decorating is part of an annual competition in which cash and ribbon prizes are awarded for the most pleasing decorations that reflect eighteenth-century style and taste. Beyond that, there's just one rule: Only materials *available* to colonial Virginians may be used, not that they would decorate this way or waste a precious pineapple on a door. Thus the houses bear garlands of apples, rings of lemons and oranges, clusters of sickle pears. There are pinecones, sprigs of boxwood and fir, sprays of bayberry, ropes of cedar, burst cotton bolls flashing silver linings, rosettes of flowering kale, rainbows of pomegranates, persimmons, kumquats. Some doors boast escutcheons of crab carapaces, oyster shells and wreaths of guinea feathers.

These decorations represent part of a brilliant and necessary compromise for modern Williamsburg, which gives up its insistence on accuracy for the season. Our eighteenth-century cousins did not much celebrate the Yuletide; the first Christmas tree was trimmed in 1842 by a professor at the College, a refugee who brought the custom with him from Germany and bedecked the parlor at St. George Tucker's house. Heaps of ribboned gifts came even later. Philip Fithian, who tutored Robert Carter's children, recorded that he gave the house boy "half a bit" at Christmas. So much for presents. On the day of the Nativity, George Washington "went to church and home for dinner." So much for special feasts. Less lofty people made a habit of firing guns in noisy witness of the holy birth, according to some antique accounts. But today folk of all faiths (or none) expect to practice contemporary customs.

With Christmas, special decorations appear all around the town, indoors and out. Each doorway in the Historic Area bears a wreath at least, like this one (above), decorated with apples, pineapples and magnolia leaves. The Wythe House table is set for an eighteenth-century feast (above right). The entrance hall at Carter's Grove (below right) sports a fir hung with toys in the late-nineteenth-century tradition.

A boxwood wreath with pomegranates (left) hides King George's monogram atop the front gate at the Governor's Palace. Oak leaves, pomegranates, lady apples, pears and chinaberries bedeck one shuttered door (top); oystershells and pine cones add texture to another (above).

The holiday season is one of the busiest times of year here and Colonial Williamsburg encourages people to feel at home. Rather than stick to the stoicism of colonial Christmas traditions, the establishment brightens the calendar with extra attractions, many of them the kinds of entertainments that colonists favored on special days at any time of year such as coronations, royal birthdays or welcomes for new governors. For decades modern visitors marched in torchlit parades, until these became too popular for safety along the rough dim cobblestones. There are feasts and games, outdoor fairs, concerts in Capitol and Palace, the ways lit with flaming cressets and a "Grand Illumination" in which a white candle (albeit electric) burns in every window. These are "vignettes of colonial activity from other festive times of year," says senior executive Peter A. G. Brown, for many years the self-styled overseer of "wreath-making and elf work."

Of course Bruton Parish Church is a focal point. In living memory, one Christmas Eve service by candlelight was enough for all. But just the local parishioners now number twice the church's capacity; it takes five services Christmas Eve and four on Christmas to accommodate the throngs. A longtime rector feels Bruton satisfies a special need during the season. The flock embraces people who want or need to be away from home for Christmas: couples whose children have left the nest, the recently bereaved, broken families and whole ones wanting a resort holiday. All are welcome and Bruton is bedecked for the occasion with garlands, its bright brass gleaming like gold in the candlelight. The choirmaster chooses music of the period: "Adeste Fideles" transcribed in 1740–43, Handel's *Messiah* and such. The texts are older, from King James' Bible, the version published in 1611, the year after "starving time" was done and Virginia seemed likely to survive: "And in the sixth month the angel Gabriel was sent from God unto a city in Galilee named Nazareth to a virgin espoused to a man whose name was Joseph, of the house of David. And the virgin's name was Mary...." The gentle words resound; it might be Christmas of any year.

For half of December the Inn is full and every tavern table booked. Around the town bonfires of four-foot logs laid cabin style brighten each night and provide the light for caroling, the singing of songs that colonists did not know. There are plays, all sorts of evening goings-on like dances at the Raleigh and at-homes at Mrs. Powell's. Then by New Year's Day the visitors go home, and the village seems to sleep.

Those privileged to live or linger here find their lives enriched. The first word my little son ever said without prompting was "moon" as he pointed from my arms to the yellow orb rising behind the Magazine's pointed roof. His second word was "boom" at the sound of cannon. For town tots there's nothing strange about kind ladies in farthingales and men in buckled shoes and Sampson's ox cart; nor about scrambling in the perfect playground of Bruton's churchyard with its iconed obstacles of hoary tombs. In the Golden Ball they hold the hammers that a smith gently wields to turn flat metal into sterling bowls; and watch with awe as an apprentice pumps the bellows to turn the coal fire's flames pale green; and clap their hands to see the journeyman pour liquid silver to make a solid sterling ingot in an instant. Yes, the present tense applies; these tasks are plied in an endless chain of time as if then and tomorrow are all todays.

Overleaf: *Another season, another year, the calm abides in Colonial Williamsburg.*

Deft-fingered women taught my wife to stitch sylvan scenes in silken yarns and brighten our home away from here with stenciled cloths and handiworks that reflect more patient arts than most folks practice now. Bruton's music master let me join the vested choir in procession down the ancient aisle of well-worn ledger stones that bear names of those who lived and listened here centuries ago. Music's meaning rings more clearly in a place like this, as if the walls that Nicholson raised and Goodwin restored somehow resonate more truly for their very age. Yet music is art of the moment; you cannot touch its sheen nor hang its motifs upon a parlor wall. It echoes and it's gone—until like voices raise its strains again, as we so often sing tunes of the Founding Fathers' time, and read their names on pews and know this place will last beyond our time.

Like those who come here for just a few brief days, like friends who spend their lives' work at manifold tasks in this antique town, we have been changed—by the gentle pace; by the evening strolls to the Capitol and back with older neighbors who match their pace to our toddling boy's; by the shade of live oaks and shades of folk like Peter Pelham and Christiana Campbell. We've dined by candlelight in the room where addled Lucy Paradise used to sup; we've debated the little issues like "Should the pillory be moved?" and the greater ones such as "Was the war that started here a Revolution—did it make things really change?" We've walked where Patrick Henry strode, and sat beneath the oak adored by Rockefeller, and wondered that a country parson was possessed to resurrect a town that was—and never was and ever more shall be—in memory of a nation's lost and legend birth.

In sum I am perplexed and glad that Williamsburg abides.

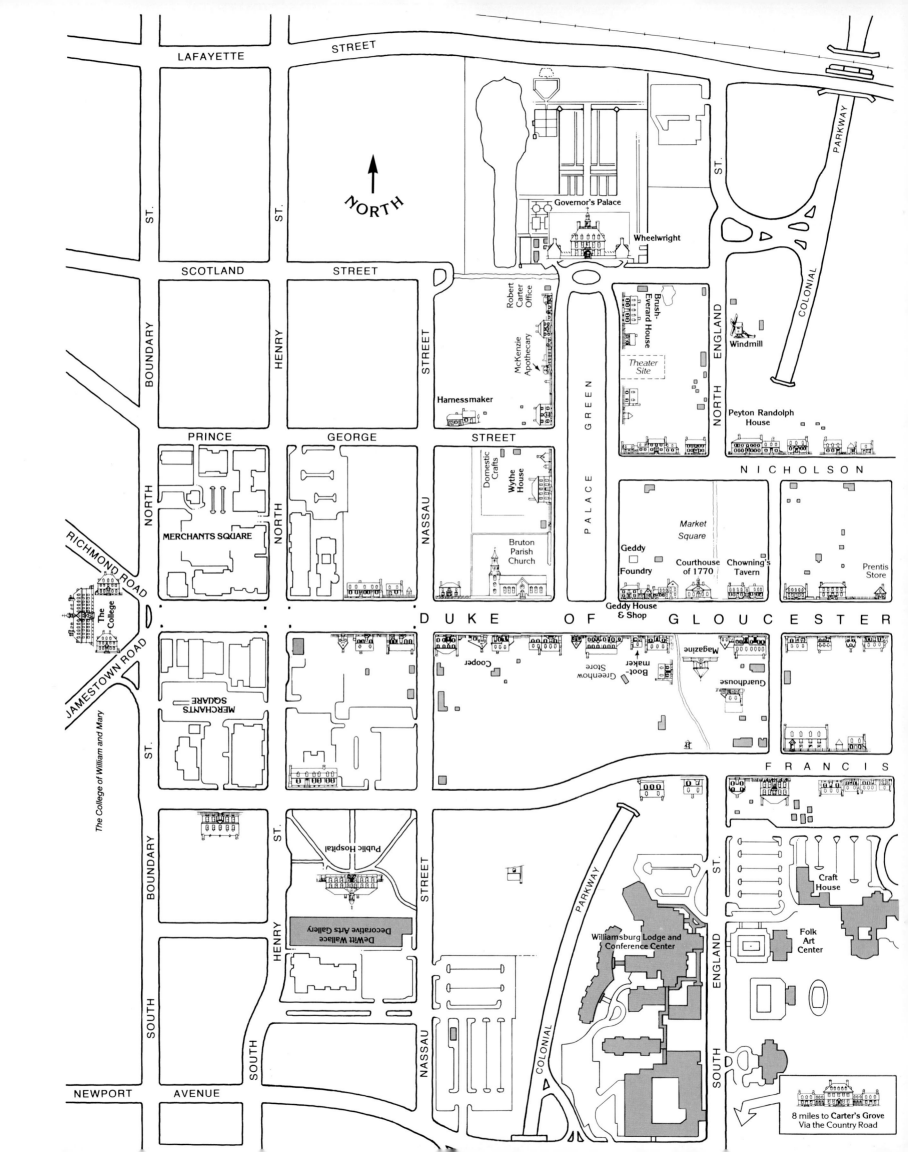

NORTH

LAFAYETTE STREET

SCOTLAND STREET

BOUNDARY ST.

HENRY ST.

NASSAU STREET

Governor's Palace

Wheelwright

Robert Carter Office

McKenzie Apothecary

Harnessmaker

Brush-Everard House

Theater Site

Windmill

Peyton Randolph House

PALACE GREEN

NORTH ENGLAND ST.

COLONIAL PARKWAY

NICHOLSON

PRINCE GEORGE STREET

MERCHANTS SQUARE

Domestic Crafts

Wythe House

Bruton Parish Church

Market Square

Geddy Foundry

Courthouse of 1770

Chowning's Tavern

Prentis Store

RICHMOND ROAD

The College

DUKE OF GLOUCESTER

Geddy House & Shop

The College of William and Mary

JAMESTOWN ROAD

MERCHANTS SQUARE

Cooper

Greenhow Store

Boot-maker

Magazine

Guardhouse

FRANCIS

BOUNDARY ST.

SOUTH ST.

HENRY ST.

Public Hospital

DeWitt Wallace Decorative Arts Gallery

NASSAU STREET

COLONIAL PARKWAY

Williamsburg Lodge and Conference Center

SOUTH ENGLAND ST.

Craft House

Folk Art Center

NEWPORT AVENUE

SOUTH

8 miles to **Carter's Grove** Via the Country Road

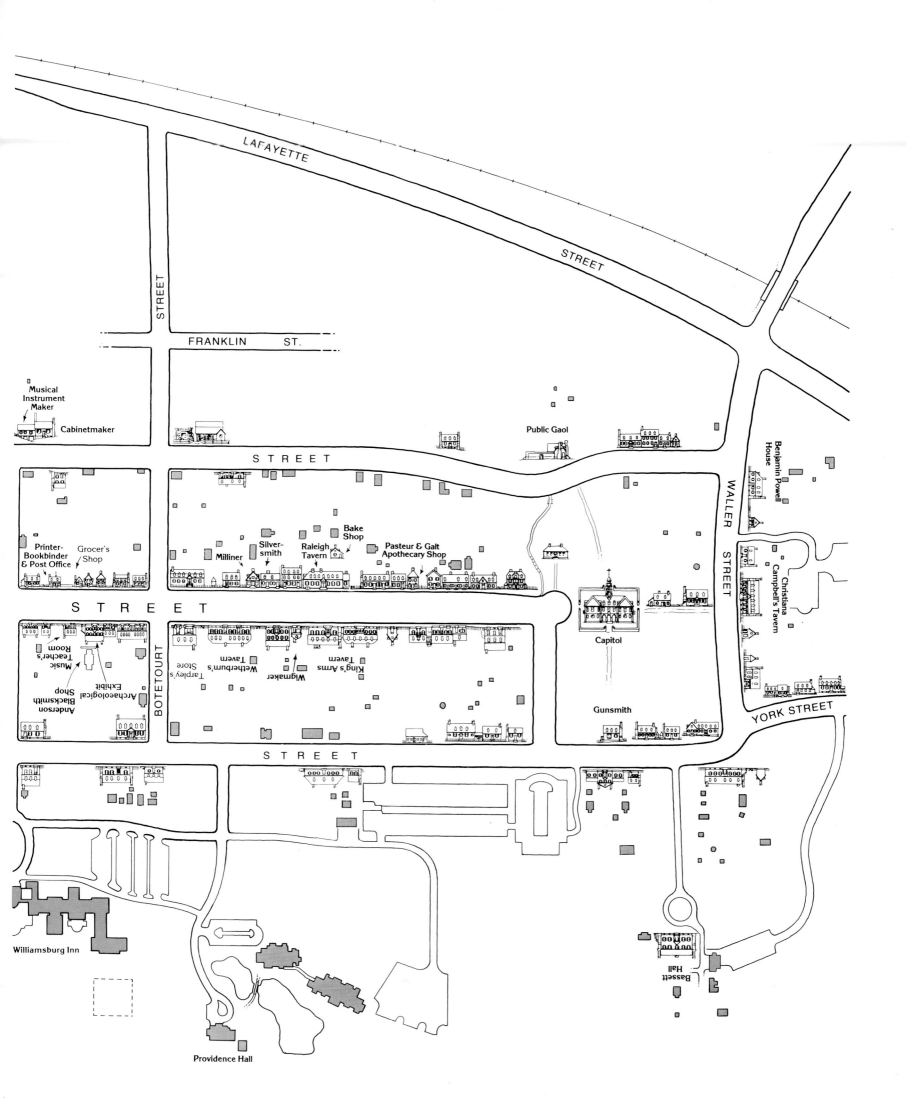

LAFAYETTE STREET

STREET

FRANKLIN ST.

STREET

Musical Instrument Maker
Cabinetmaker

Public Gaol

Benjamin Powell House

WALLER STREET

Printer-Bookbinder & Post Office
Grocer's Shop

Milliner
Silver-smith
Raleigh Tavern
Bake Shop
Pasteur & Galt Apothecary Shop

Christiana Campbell's Tavern

STREET

Music Teacher's Room

Anderson Blacksmith Shop
Archaeological Exhibit

BOTETOURT STREET

Tarpley's Store
Wetherburn's Tavern
Wigmaker
King's Arms Tavern

Capitol

Gunsmith

YORK STREET

STREET

Williamsburg Inn

Bassett Hall

Providence Hall

Acknowledgments

Finally, I have the pleasure of thanking the many people—most of them citizens and workers at Williamsburg—whose energy, work and thought contributed to this book.

Vice-president Richard A. Schreiber, who championed the idea of cooperating with an outsider, suggested I live in the town and arranged for me to rent the Unicorn's Horn. My first host and frequent facilitator, Dick maintained a shrewd and friendly interest in the project. I thank him for his counsel and for the countless courtesies that he and his wife, Lynn, extended. Colonial Williamsburg's other officers from President Charles R. Longsworth down cooperated unstintingly. Senior vice-president Robert C. Birney, chief curator Graham Hood, resident architect Nicholas A. Pappas, Historic Area programs and operations executive Dennis A. O'Toole and research director Cary Carson opened their doors—and their departments—whenever I knocked. Former chairman and president emeritus Carlisle H. Humelsine generously shared his deep knowledge, rich recollections and unique experience.

My special tutors in the mysteries of historical re-creation, preservation and administration were ceramics curator John Austin, martial musician John C. Moon, historian Patricia A. Gibbs, picture archivist Patricia Maccubbin, senior executives Roger F. H. Leclere and Peter A. G. Brown, publications boss Joseph Rountree. Others who most generously shared their knowledge include furniture expert Wallace Gusler, tools curator Jay Gaynor, fund-raiser Forrest Williamson, metals curator John D. Davis, historian Linda Rowe, cooper George Pettengell, historical architect Travis McDonald, hotelier James C. Miles, silversmith Jimmy Curtis, wheelwright Dan Stebbins, blacksmith Peter Ross, Lodge factotum Peggy Greene. Retired vice-president of architecture A. Edwin Kendrew's canny recollections of the Restoration's early years added greatly to my view of the recent past.

Other Colonial Williamsburg employees who helped in memorable ways, large and small, include media manager Denise Adams, secretary Sally Barnes, editor Wayne Barrett, textiles curator Linda Baumgarten, vice-president Norman Beatty, metals founder Dan Berg and his wife, librarian Susan Berg, archivist Bland Blackford, cooking mistress Rosemary Brandau, publicist Susan Bruno, gunsmith Gary Brumfield, reproductions creator Gail Burger, upholsterer Gene Burleson, archival sleuth Pat Butler, bookstore manager Delois Campas, architectural historian Edward Chappell, horticulturist Gordon Chappell, journeyman silversmith George Cloyed, Wallace Gallery director Wendy Cooper, marketing master Hugh DeSamper, leather-crafter Irvin Diehl, wizard secretary Fredericka Dooley, archaeological field boss Andrew Edwards, executive D. Stephen Elliott, folk dramatist Rex Ellis, designer Diana Freedman, facilities and property management director William Gardiner, second-generation board member Vernon Geddy Jr., trades historian Harold Gill, retired executive Donald Gonzales, associate ceramics curator Leslie Grigsby, library director Pearce Grove, engineer Will Gwilliam, drama director John Hamant, Inn manager Bruce Hearn, wigmaker Joyce Hedgepeth, Lodge manager James Hisle, furniture curator Ronald Hurst, special collections curator John Ingram, apprentice silversmith Preston Jones, architectural librarian Mary Keeling, historian Kevin Kelly, master of many trades Lew LeCompte, our neighbors Tom and Louise Limerick, buildings historian Carl Lounsbury, Folk Art Center curator Barbara Luck, horticulturist Richard Mahone, filmmaker Richard McCluney, secretary Margaret Miller, special events troubleshooter Trudy Moyles, secretary Dianne Murray, archaeologist Ivor Noël Hume, landscape architect Donald Parker, master printer Willie Parker, mistress of protocol Kathleen Pickering, prints and maps curator Margaret Pritchard, secretary Sonnie Rose, vice-president Beatrix Rumford, Motor House manager James Ryan, secretary Patricia Schell, executive secretary Joyce Seaman, secretary Emily Seats, crafts program director Earl Soles, director of museum services Edward Spencer and his wife, secretary to the president Emily Spencer, domestic arts mistress Mary Stebbins, calligrapher Richard Stinely, vice-president F. Roger Thaler, carpenter Roy Underhill, landlady Peg Waite, architectural historian Mark Wenger, weaving mistress Marilyn Wetton, fife and drum director William White, secretary Mary Jean Wilson, actress Mary Wiseman, illustrator Vernon Wooten, travel marketing veteran George Wright, historian Shomer Zwelling.

Staff historians provided useful advice and read the text for accuracy in matters of "historical fact." (Obviously any remaining errors are mine.) John Hemphill II and Lou Powers brought the standards of their discipline to bear and I thank them for their candid comments and friendly help ante-factum.

People outside Colonial Williamsburg's official pale added substantial lore, especially two members of the Goodwin family, who showed great generosity of spirit: Rutherfoord's widow, Mary Randolph Mordecai Goodwin, and his thoughtful brother, Howard Goodwin. Bruton Parish was also a source of wonder, in the form of three persons: now retired rector, the Reverend Cotesworth Pinkney Lewis; former curate, the Right Reverend John T. Bentley; music director James S. Darling, who let me sing in his famous choir. Life tenant Dr. Janet Kimbrough and life resident Judge Robert T. Armistead provided valuable insights from special vantage points.

At the College of William and Mary, president Thomas A. Graves Jr., librarian Clifford Currie and manuscripts and rare books curator Margaret Cook opened their facilities. Scholar Thad Tate gave sound historical guidance. At the State Department, White House curator Clement Conger and deputy chief of protocol Timothy Towell provided expertise.

Members of the cofounder's family graciously shared their views: Mrs. John D. Rockefeller 3rd, Laurance Rockefeller and longtime board member Abby O'Neill. Rockefeller Archive Center director Joseph Ernst provided useful documents.

I am also pleased to thank Abrams editor Sheila Franklin Lieber for her unwavering attention and thoughtful commitment, art director Samuel N. Antupit for his inspired design and good-humored patience and photographer Langdon Clay for his superb pictures. Without these three, the book simply would not be what it is. And it would never have gotten to the printer without the tireless layout work of Doris Leath.

In quintessentially personal terms, this assignment took on extra meaning when my wife, son and I settled in the Historic Area for an unforgettable year. Our lives were especially brightened by Peter and Jean Brown; Elizabeth Blagojevich and her late husband, Miodrag; Mary Panza and her family; Don Ackley, his wife, Melissa, and daughter, Elizabeth. We found ourselves welcomed into a remarkable community rich in common purpose and uncommon caring. At the risk of invidious omission, my wife, Mary, joins me in expressing warm gratitude to the special friends of our sojourn: John and Scottie Austin, Marley and Katie Brown, Cary and Barbara Carson, Nick Pappas, Al and Tessa Louer, Charles and Barbara Driscoll, Joe and Sue Rountree and especially Denny and Trudy O'Toole.

Photograph Credits

The author and publisher wish to thank the following museums, libraries, institutions and individuals for permitting the reproduction of works of art (or photographs) in their possession and for supplying the necessary photographs. All other photographs are by Langdon Clay.

Abby Aldrich Rockefeller Folk Art Center, Williamsburg, Va.: 109 (above), 132–33, 234, 250 (both), 251; Nathan Benn / National Geographic *Traveler*, Washington, D.C.: 78–79; Nathan Benn / Woodfin Camp, Inc., Washington, D.C.: 286 (above right), 298 (above left and below), 299 (below); Trustees of the British Museum, London: 20; Burgerbibliothek, Bern, Switzerland: 44, 45; Colonial Williamsburg Foundation, Williamsburg, Va.: 12–13, 21, 22, 25 (above and below right), 26, 27, 28, 29 (above), 34, 47, 54, 55, 65, 75, 100, 107 (top), 113 (top), 116, 117, 120, 122, 124, 129, 130, 134 (both), 136, 137, 143 (above left), 144 (both), 145, 152–53, 154, 156, 157, 158 (both), 162 (all), 164, 168, 176, 177 (both), 180, 184 (top, above right and below right), 185, 186 (both), 188 (right), 189 (above), 191, 195, 196, 199 (top), 200 (above right and below right), 201, 202 (both), 205 (both), 206 (above and above right), 207 (above left and above), 208, 215, 221 (all), 224, 225 (above), 236, 237 (both), 240, 241 (all), 242, 243, 244, 245, 246 (all), 247 (both), 249, 260, 261, 262, 263, 264, 265, 266 (above left and below left), 267 (above right and below right), 268, 269, 279, 280, 296, 304; Thomas Coram Foundation for Children, London: 127; Mary Goodwin, Williamsburg, Va.: 141 (both), 209; Library of Congress, Washington, D.C.: 108; Maryland Historical Society, Baltimore: 84, 125; Massachusetts Historical Society, Boston (photograph courtesy the University of Virginia Alderman Library, Charlottesville): 200 (above); Muscarelle Museum of Art, College of William and Mary, Williamsburg, Va.: 40, 184 (above); National Galleries of Scotland, Edinburgh: 121; National Portrait Gallery, Smithsonian Institution, Washington, D.C.: 25 (below left); Rockefeller Archive Center, North Tarrytown, N.Y.: 155, 214; Swem Library, College of William and Mary, Williamsburg, Va.: 31 (above), 49 (above), 118; University of Virginia Alderman Library, Charlottesville: 109 (below); Henry Francis du Pont Winterthur Museum, Winterthur, Del.: 128.

Index

All numbers in this index refer to page numbers; those in *italic* type indicate illustrations. An asterisk* identifies original buildings.

314